YOUR CAREER IS OUR BUSINESS®

Roadmap to the
Senior Executive Service (SES)

How to Find SES Jobs, Determine Your Qualifications,
and Develop Your SES Application

CareerPro Global Publishing, Georgia

CAREERPRO GLOBAL, INC.
173 Pierce Avenue
Macon, GA 31204

Printed in the United States of America
Roadmap to the Senior Executive Service, 2nd Edition: How to Find SES Jobs, Determine Your Qualifications, and Develop Your SES Application

ISBN: 978-0-9823222-6-0

CareerPro Global's 21st-Century Career Series

Publication Team:

Interior Page Design/Layout: Patricia Duckers
Cover Design: Alesha Sevy-Kelley
Proofreading: Carla Lowe
Contributors: Stefanie Sealy, Jim Gourley, Michelle Czyz

Disclaimer: The information, tips, best practices, and resources in this book are based on several decades of experience in the career management industry, but individual experiences and results will vary, and depend solely on your efforts. While CareerPro Global gladly shares this information to assist you, we can in no way be held responsible for the results in your own job search. In addition, the sample resumes are adapted from and based on actual clients, but the names, dates, organizations, and many other details and specifics have been fictionalized to protect individual privacy. The information published in this book is accurate at the time of printing; however, over time, some of the information may change, and CareerPro Global is not responsible for any of these changes.

About the Authors

BARBARA ADAMS has led CareerPro Global, Inc. (CPG) for almost three decades, and has built CPG into one of the largest and fastest-growing career services organizations industry-wide, having served more than 60,000 clients to date. Barbara positioned CPG to raise the bar by developing an ISO 9001:2008-guided quality process (the first in the careers industry) through which all of CPG's processes were reviewed and measured for quality. CPG held full ISO 9001:2008 certification/registration from 2010 to 2017, and still maintains an internal quality control system based on those standards.

Barbara earned the Career Innovation Award for this implementation and focus on quality of workmanship, process, and people. Barbara has also co-authored several books in CareerPro's 21st-Century Career Series, including ***Roadmap to the Senior Executive Service, Roadmap to Job-Winning Military to Civilian Resumes, Roadmap to Becoming an Administrative Law Judge*** and ***Roadmap to Federal Jobs***. Barbara employs some of the best—if not *the* best—writers and career advisers in the industry, and provides ongoing training in support of hiring trends and protocol. CareerPro Global is one of the most trusted career management services in the industry.

LEE KELLEY is the senior member of CPG's writing team, and serves on the executive staff as Director of Training and Managing Editor for over a dozen other writers. He is also a veteran who spent 10 years in the U.S. Army, working his way from Private to Captain. He spent a year in Ramadi, Iraq (2005–2006) in support of Operation Iraqi Freedom, and his last position in the Army was Commanding Officer of a 275-person headquarters organization.

Since leaving the military, Lee has leveraged his writing and military background to work with more than 650 clients from the government, military, and private sectors. He holds three industry certifications: Master Federal Career Advisor/Trainer, Master Federal Resume Writer, and Master Military Resume Writer. Finally, Lee co-authored four books in CareerPro's 21st-Century Career Series, and won the "Best Military Transition Resume" Toast of the Resume Industry (TORI) Award in 2011.

About CareerPro Global, Inc.

In business since 1986, CPG offers world-class services in resume writing, career coaching, onsite career training, career publications, and webinar-based training. Our multi-credentialed Master Writers and Career Advisors are some of the best—if not the best—in the careers industry. Our team members specialize in corporate, military, and federal clients seeking to stand out in a competitive job market. They are published authors, journalists, editors, branding experts, Human Resources (HR) professionals, engineers, Information Technology (IT) professionals, educators, public-relations professionals, and veterans from both the enlisted and officer ranks. Our track record of setting industry standards has been attributed to our methodology, delivery, and commitment to excellence. Utilizing our expertise, thousands of clients across all fields and professional levels have succeeded in reaching their career goals.

Our Mission Statement: At CareerPro Global, we are committed to producing premier resume and career services products, providing service excellence, hiring talented professionals, and remaining abreast of global employment and hiring trends. We are also committed to continuous improvement of the quality management system.

Books, Articles, Publications, and Media: CareerPro Global and its team members have created/published 300+ online and print articles relating to career coaching, resume writing, job searching, interview skills, and salary negotiations, and has published the following titles:

- Roadmap to the Senior Executive Service – 2nd Edition
- Roadmap to Job-Winning Military to Civilian Resumes
- Roadmap to Becoming an Administrative Law Judge
- Roadmap to Federal Jobs

Quality Management System: CPG's culture has been built upon, and remains committed to, our core factors, which include: honesty, integrity, excellent customer service, and a passion for helping others achieve their career goals. We believe so strongly in these core factors that our company has raised the bar by developing a Quality Management System, where all our processes are reviewed for quality.

Longevity and Success: CPG combines three decades of industry writing experience with the most advanced technology in the industry, empowering us to produce job-winning resume presentations for our clients. We also pride ourselves in producing results and outstanding customer service. And it shows. We hold a 99.6% customer satisfaction ratio. These statistics are backed up by our monthly customer service survey and ongoing commitment to delivering quality products and services.

Research, Development, and Systems: CPG is extremely proactive in research and development. Investing in our own in-house Information Technology department has given us the capability to ensure secure transaction processing and data warehousing. CPG developed and utilizes one of the most robust system architectures in the industry, integrating and customizing portfolios of collaborative and communication services designed to connect people, information, processes, and systems, both within and beyond our firewall.

TRAINING, CERTIFICATION, AND INDUSTRY EXCELLENCE:
- Authored and administer: MFCA (Master Federal Career Advisor)
- Authored and administer: MFCA/T (Master Federal Career Advisor/Trainer)
- Authored and administer: MMRW (Master Military Resume Writer)
- Authored and administer MSEW (Master Senior Executive Writer)
- Authored and administer MFRW-T (Master Federal Resume Writer/Trainer)
- Launched new in-house SES SOPs for Senior Executive Service
- Authored and administer Master Federal Resume Writer (MFRW)
- Industry experts and mentors in military, federal, and civilian resumes
- Recognized as industry leaders and innovators
- Career conference presenters and speakers
- Webinar presenters on resume topics
- Innovation Award, Careers Industry
- Seven TORI (Toast of the Resume Industry) nominations
- Winner, Best Military Transition Resume (Toast of the Resume Industry)

HOLDERS OF THE FOLLOWING CERTIFICATIONS:
- Certified Professional Resume Writer (CPRW)
- Certified Advanced Resume Writer (CARW)
- Certified Expert Resume Writer (CERW)
- Certified Electronic Career Coach (CECC)
- Master Military Resume Writer (MMRW)
- Master Federal Resume Writer (MFRW)
- Master Federal Career Advisor – Trainer (MFCA-T)
- Certified Employment Interview Coach (CEIC)
- Master Senior Executive Writer (MSEW)

*This book is dedicated to all those government, military, and corporate leaders
who make it their high aim to serve in the Senior Executive Service
and help lead our government through the challenges
of the modern world and workplace.*

TABLE OF CONTENTS

SYMBOLS

You'll notice the following graphics throughout the book. Think of them as signposts along your roadmap, offering best practices and other useful information to guide your learning experience and career journey.

 **PRACTICAL EXERCISES**

 **DECISION TIME**

 **SAMPLES**

 **BEST PRACTICES**

 **CPG EXCLUSIVE**

 **TAKE NOTE**

INTRODUCTION

CONGRATULATIONS ON TAKING THE FIRST STEP IN YOUR JOURNEY TO THE SES!

We are honored that you chose us to help you on that path. CareerPro Global, Inc. (CPG) takes great pride in empowering our customers, and we have been providing career management services for civilian, military, and federal clients for the past 30 years. Leveraging all of our combined knowledge and best practices gained over the years, we have secured our place as the industry leader in assisting thousands of senior military officials, senior federal government employees, and private-sector executives to take the next step in their careers.

We pride ourselves on producing results and outstanding customer service. And it shows. More than 48% are repeat clients and referred by satisfied customers. Overall, CPG has boasted a 99.6% customer satisfaction rate since 1986. No other team has as much experience or success in helping clients develop SES application packages.

We are also the only company of our kind that formally trains our writers and has internal controls and quality control measures in place to ensure world-class customer service.

One SES application can encompass up to 15 or more pages, including a resume and narrative statements that present a candidate's top skills and accomplishments, with a strong emphasis on executive leadership skills and versatility.

We will give you a brief history and understanding of the SES process, and then guide you through developing and submitting your application materials by using our exclusive 5-Check Point process. Once you've completed each Check Point, the final section of the book (SES Application Samples and Templates) will illustrate what your completed documents might look like, and provide you with detailed examples of each element within an SES application.

Finally, we have included a CD that contains a wealth of resources, including templates for your resume, Executive Core Qualification (ECQ) statements, and Technical Qualification (TQ) statements. The CD also includes many samples and templates so you can easily reference and model completed applications.

The first step in completing your own SES application is to create a basic understanding of the SES, so let's get started!

Notes

Check Point 1

Understanding the Senior Executive Service

UNDERSTANDING THE SES

What is the SES?

There is a great deal of information available on the Office of Personnel Management's (OPM) website about how and why the Senior Executive Service (SES) was formed, but here's what you really need to know: The SES was created in 1979 as part of the Civil Service Reform Act of 1978 to streamline disparate hiring practices across 75 government agencies and to provide an added level of leadership above the GS-15 level.

Since then, the SES has grown, and oversight of the federal government's most critical functions and programs has grown with it. Today, SES members oversee almost all of the missions taking place within about 75 federal agencies. Their positions include Executive Branch supervisory, policy, and managerial positions classified as higher than General Schedule (GS)-15 or equivalent positions.

Behind only the President of the United States (POTUS) and Presidential appointees, SES members are among the highest-level leaders in our nation's government.

Serving within Executive Branch federal agencies, SES members lead the way in transforming Presidential policies into the missions and daily activities carried out by thousands of personnel employed by the federal government.

Even while Presidents and their appointees change and move on, SES members remain. They are the link between administrations and federal workers. The nature of their roles demands a commitment to public service and the democratic ideals of our Constitution.

It is no exaggeration to claim that those who make up the SES Corps are among the best leaders in our country, and persons deemed qualified enough to join these ranks can be certain that they, too, are considered "best of the best." Although more than one person has scoffed at this perhaps over-the-top description of the SES, it really is a level of leadership, management, and oversight reserved for the most elite, high-performing federal executives.

According to OPM, there are close to 9,000 SES positions across the federal government. As with much of the federal government, it is estimated that as much as 90% of current SES members will retire within the next 10 years, and that approximately 75% of all SES positions are located in Washington, D.C.; Maryland; and Virginia. As SES members depart and new positions are created, there will be increased demand for new leaders to join the ranks around the nation.

Learn more about how and why the SES was formed, OPM offers an in-depth history at https://www.opm.gov/policy-data-oversight/senior-executive-service/overview-history/#url=History.

In addition, this link provides answers to some of the most frequently asked questions: https://www.opm.gov/policy-data-oversight/senior-executive-service/faqs/.

What Types of SES Positions Are There?

Within the SES, there are two types of positions—Career Reserved and General. Career Reserved positions are those that can be filled only by career appointees. Most SES applicants fall in the category of General, and these positions can be filled through any of the four types of SES appointments described below:

Career Appointments. This is by far the most common type of SES appointment. Individuals hired under Career Appointments must be selected by the hiring agency as "Best Qualified" and then have their executive qualifications approved through OPM.

Non-Career Appointments. Positions filled under Non-Career Appointments must be approved by OPM on a case-by-case basis and are not intended to be long term. Once individuals in these positions leave, appointment authority reverts to OPM, meaning agencies have to once again obtain OPM's approval to fill the position with another Non-Career Appointment.

Limited-Term Appointments. As the name implies, positions filled under this type of appointment authority are temporary. Limited-Term Appointments cannot exceed three years and the terms are not renewable. Limited-Term Appointments are intended to fill SES positions that are not expected to be needed indefinitely, such as positions created to oversee special projects. At the end of the three years—or sooner if the need ends—the Limited-Term Appointment authority expires, so agencies cannot appoint another individual to the position.

Limited Emergency Appointments. Like Limited-Term Appointments, Limited Emergency Appointments are non-renewable. However, Limited Emergency Appointments have additional, stricter requirements. These appointments last for no more than 18 months and OPM's authorization for such appointments is granted only when an agency can demonstrate an urgent, unanticipated, and justifiable need for such a position.

Other SES Positions. While SES positions are primarily executive leadership roles, other categories for high-level positions do not fall within the purview of the SES. Since they don't fall within the SES, they will not be covered in detail. However, to gain a complete

understanding of high-level roles in the federal government, it is important to be familiar with these positions.

Scientific or Professional Personnel System (ST)

While previously discussed SES positions focus on executive leadership roles, there are also senior-level positions that are non-executive in nature. These are referred to as Scientific or Professional (ST) positions, and they include senior-level (above GS-15) positions involved in research and development (R&D) fields such as medicine, engineering, and biology.

ST positions are those primarily involved in using or performing experimentation, systematically testing theories or conducting studies, and documenting findings or developing end products. For example, a senior-level cancer researcher would fall under this categorization.

Because these positions emphasize scientific/professional skills over executive abilities, the criteria for working in these positions are different. Usually, ST members:

- hold advanced degrees in their fields;
- are recognized nationally and/or internationally for their expertise;
- have significant research experience;
- have authored works that are regularly cited and used within their fields;
- are regularly sought to serve as advisors for scientific and technological issues; and
- have received important honors and recognitions from the leading organizations in their fields.

How Much Can You Expect To Make in the SES?

Federal agencies have a certain degree of flexibility in terms of pay. Below is the 2020 SES pay scale, and the average pay is approximately $165K annually. You can find this and other related information by conducting an online search for "current SES pay scale" or browsing OPM's official website.

Salary Table No. 2020-ES
Rates of Basic Pay for Members of the Senior Executive Service (SES)

Effective January 2020

Structure of the SES Pay System	Minimum	Maximum
Agencies with a Certified SES Performance Appraisal System	$131,239	$197,300
Agencies without a Certified SES Performance Appraisal System	$131,239	$181,500

www.SESWriters.com

All ST positions are Competitive Service, and, like SES, agencies must have allocations for these positions. While ST members may also perform management or supervisory duties, these do not constitute the majority or focus of their roles.

In fact, ST members are restricted from having more than 25% of their duties fall within supervisory or management responsibilities. If these duties do exceed 25%, these ST members will typically meet the qualifications for classification as SES.

SENIOR-LEVEL POSITIONS (SL)

Prior to 1990, the federal employee pay grades included the grades 16, 17, and 18. However, the Federal Employees Pay Comparability Act of 1990 (FEPCA) eliminated these grade levels, capping General Schedule (GS) positions at 15 and creating the core of positions that comprise Senior-Level positions (SL).

As with ST, the SL category is for non-executive, high-level positions that would not qualify for SES. However, since these positions do not involve significant amounts of scientific research and development, they would not qualify for ST. Instead, SL positions require a great amount of field specialization, but they do not encompass supervisory or management roles as primary functions. A senior attorney is an example of the type of position that would fall under SL.

SL positions are always Competitive Service unless they are specifically "excepted" by regulations or statutes. Similar to ST, SL positions must be allocated by OPM, and members are limited to no more than 25% of their duties in management or supervision. Any amounts over that would likely qualify them for SES.

EXCEPTED SERVICE POSITIONS

OPM provides "Excepted Service" hiring authorities to fill special jobs or to fill any job in unusual or special

circumstances. These authorities enable agencies to hire when it is not feasible or simply impractical to use traditional competitive hiring procedures, and can streamline hiring.

Are You Ready for the SES?

You now know that the SES is an elite level of government leadership made up of former GS-15s, corporate executives, former military officers, and other high-level professionals. The federal government is seeking visionary men and women with well-honed executive leadership skills and qualifications that can continue to transform our government. Are you one of them?

Maybe you are a civil servant, and you've been at the GS-14 or GS-15 level for a while and your SES colleagues are nudging you to go for SES. Maybe you have been at that level for the past decade.

Maybe you are a military officer at the O-5 level or above, and you have held multiple command positions. Now you are ready to leave the military, but you'd like to continue to serve your country by working within the federal government.

Or, maybe you are a corporate leader or seasoned government contractor and feel that you could play an important role in the SES. All of these and other scenarios have played out numerous times, and you should certainly set high professional standards and goals, but we also want you to be realistic about whether you qualify.

Having the drive, ambition, passion, and vision is important, but it might not be enough, unless you can prove it on paper highlighting your experience and accomplishments. Even if you are the most motivated Army Colonel or GS-15 Contracting Specialist, you must be able to demonstrate in your application materials that you do indeed possess the experience, training, and background to thrive in the SES. Put another way:

The process might not be easy, but it can be, and has been, done, and you can do it, too!

Determining Your Eligibility

Many people transitioning to the federal government are often attracted to the high level of responsibility and compensation offered at the SES level. However, just because someone has run his/her own small business and held the title of CEO or CIO doesn't necessarily mean that he/she is automatically eligible for SES status.

Eligibility falls into one of three categories, as follows:

A certified career advisor can help you to decide if you are SES qualified. Here are seven questions you should ask yourself if you are considering applying for a federal SES position:

1. Do you share a broad perspective of government and a public service commitment that is grounded in the Constitution?
2. Are you interested in serving in the key positions within federal government just below the top Presidential appointees?
3. Would you like to serve as one of the major links between Presidential appointees and the rest of the federal workforce?
4. Are you qualified to lead and oversee complex program activities in one of approximately 75 federal agencies?
5. Do you have the personal and professional passion to serve as one of the top executives in federal government?
6. Are you a visionary leader and able to motivate personnel, build interagency partnerships, and communicate with diverse customers?
7. Do you possess solid management skills in order to produce optimum results for your customers with limited resources?

If you answered YES to most (or all) of these questions, and you have the senior-level experience to substantiate it, then OPM wants to hear from you! If not, then you might want to consider targeting GS-15 positions and spending a couple of years at that level, then using that experience to move toward SES more confidently.

Criterion A cases are based on demonstrated executive experience. Candidates must demonstrate that they have experience/competence in all five ECQs as part of their application for SES positions.

Criterion B cases are based on successful participation in an OPM-approved SES Candidate Development Program (CDP). Candidates who compete government-wide and successfully complete a CDP are eligible for non-competitive appointment to the SES. However, successful completion does not guarantee placement in the SES.

Criterion C cases are based on the candidates having special or unique qualities that indicate a likelihood of success in the SES. Candidates must demonstrate that they have the qualifications for the position and the potential to quickly acquire full competence in the five ECQs.

The package submitted for QRB approval must contain the agency's assessment of why the selectee uniquely qualifies for the position and an Individual Development Plan (IDP) that focuses on the specific ECQs that need to be enhanced.

Candidate Development Programs

If you are determined to gain employment in the SES, but don't yet have the necessary qualifications, you might be interested in a government-offered Candidate Development Program (CDP) designed to help give candidates a competitive edge for SES consideration.

Participating agencies that offer an SES CDP have collaborated with trainers to ensure candidates receive the most comprehensive training to prepare them for a challenging career at the SES level. The CDP class size typically consists of 20-50 eligible participants who are at the GS-14 or -15 level and have put in at least one year's time in that grade.

While the class size, application process, and topics vary according to the agency, typically, the program must be completed within 12-18 months of enrollment and concurrently with a candidate fulfilling his/her other job responsibilities.

The goal of a CDP is to:

- Prepare participants for SES certification by OPM
- Establish a pool of qualified candidates for SES positions
- Prepare future executives for collaborative leadership

Activities of the CDP include a combination of lectures, workshops, seminars, guest speakers, group meetings, and field trips, as well as:

- Leadership development experiences
- Personal skills and behavioral assessment
- Leadership training
- Capitol Hill exposure
- Developmental assignments
- Action learning projects
- Mentoring
- Team-building exercises

The program also features feedback-intensive and

mentoring components to further assist candidates in their developmental journey. Candidates who complete the program and obtain certification by an SES Qualifications Review Board (QRB) may be selected for an SES position anywhere in the federal government without further competition.

Is a Candidate Development Program Right for You?

Are you a GS-14 or GS-15 who feels that the SES could be in your future? Imagine expanding your normal career path and daily activities to participate in a 12-month program (sometimes longer) designed to enhance your leadership, scope of experience, and executive potential.

Although each person's experience will be a little different, during a CDP, you can expect to receive personal mentoring, an Individual Development Plan (IDP), specialized training, and a developmental or "stretch" assignment.

At the end of your CDP, you'll have an opportunity to develop your Executive Core Qualifications (ECQ) essays and submit them for OPM approval. Going through a CDP doesn't guarantee you an SES position, but it can certainly give you an advantage.

Plus, if you are selected for an SES position at some point, you may already have a certified set of ECQs. So, while all of your competition is still working to

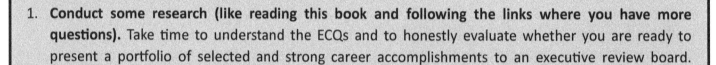

Five Tips for Becoming a Member of the SES

Some current or former SES members were asked to list the top tips a leader should follow to make that next step into the SES, and here are their top five:

1. **Conduct some research (like reading this book and following the links where you have more questions).** Take time to understand the ECQs and to honestly evaluate whether you are ready to present a portfolio of selected and strong career accomplishments to an executive review board.

2. **Let your leaders know you're interested.** Don't assume that your senior executives know you want to be SES just because you work so hard. It's a good idea to find a mentor you can speak to candidly about your goals and what it will take for you to achieve them. Ask them about how they became a member of the SES and the kinds of challenges they overcame.

3. **Take action! Leaders create their own paths.** To demonstrate the ECQs, you'll need a broad base of experience and training. You might want to join a professional association or volunteer for an interagency governing board or taskforce. Leadership development programs are a great idea, and there are many leadership books and articles out there to help you develop your strengths and identify your weaknesses.

4. **Set some goals to enhance your career and then follow through.** For example, you could write and submit an article or an op-ed for a professional journal, volunteer to speak at a conference, or suggest a new transformation initiative and volunteer to lead the effort.

5. **Move on when the time is right.** While it is possible to stay in one organization for most of your career, the SES Corps is increasingly seeking people with experience in multiple organizations and work environments when filling their senior positions. To land one of those positions, you may need to move out of your comfort zone.

get ECQ approval, you will simply need to show proof of your ECQ certification.

CDPs aren't always available, and they are coveted opportunities among many federal employees. Not surprisingly, they are also highly competitive. In terms of applying, the programs are advertised on USAJOBS just like any other position.

Make sure you read the entire vacancy announcement and submit exactly what they ask for—nothing more and nothing less.

Some CDP announcements call for a full set of ECQs just to apply, while others require you to submit what we've coined a "5-Page All-Inclusive Resume." This is simply a resume focusing on the past 10 years of your career that shows your executive potential.

Most importantly, these submissions require you to demonstrate your experience and potential in each ECQ category: Leading Change, Leading People, Results Driven, Business Acumen, and Building Coalitions.

So, if a CDP is something that interests you, it's a good idea to start thinking about (and actively seeking) career experience in each of these areas.

Check Point 1 Summary

You should now have a basic understanding of the history of the SES, the different types of SES appointments, and some helpful tips on how to determine whether you are ready and qualified. In the next Check Point, you'll gain a better understanding of the actual SES hiring process.

Check Point Notes

_____

_____

_____

_____

_____

_____

_____

_____

_____

_____

_____

_____

_____

_____

Check Point 2

Finding SES Jobs and Navigating the Hiring Process

FINDING SES JOBS AND NAVIGATING THE HIRING PROCESS

Patience and Persistence are Key

Once you decide to actively seek an SES position, you are embarking on what could be a highly challenging and rewarding process. Of course, some candidates land the first SES job for which they apply, but in most cases, it seems to take even the most qualified candidates a few tries. The process of recruiting, evaluating, and approving potential SES candidates before they are selected to fill a vacancy can be a lengthy one. It can take as little as a month, or two to six months or even more from the time the initial position announcement is posted to the time the position is actually filled.

Research and Identify Federal Occupation(s) or Agencies of Interest

Many professionals have a range of backgrounds and skills, and, in theory, could thrive in multiple jobs or business areas. But the first step is to familiarize yourself with the occupational areas in the federal government, and start to focus on where you could best serve and lead. The General Schedule (GS) series consists of 23 occupational families that are further divided into more than 400 white-collar occupations. The following are the core GS descriptions, and you can find more details online by searching for "OPM general schedule classification qualification."

GS-000: Miscellaneous

This group includes all classes of positions, the duties of which are to administer, supervise, or perform work that can't be included in other occupational groups.

0006 Correctional Institution Administration Series
0007 Correctional Officer Series
0017 Explosives Safety Series
0018 Safety and Occupational Health Management Series
0019 Safety Technician Series

0020 Community Planning Series
0023 Outdoor Recreation Planning Series
0025 Park Ranger Series
0028 Environmental Protection Specialist Series
0060 Chaplain Series
0062 Clothing Design Series
0072 Fingerprint Identification Series
0080 Security Administration Series
0081 Fire Protection and Prevention Series
0082 United States Marshals Series
0083 Police Series: Grade Evaluation Guide for Police and Security Guard Positions
0084 Nuclear Materials Courier Series
0085 Security Guard Series
0086 Security Clerical and Assistance Series
0090 Guide Series
0095 Foreign Law Specialist Series

GS-100: Social Science, Psychology, and Welfare Group

This group includes all classes of positions, the duties of which are to advise on, administer, supervise, or perform research or other professional and scientific work, subordinate technical work, or related clerical work in one or more of the social sciences: in psychology, in social work, in recreational activities, or in the administration of public welfare and insurance programs.

GS-200: Human Resources Management Group

This group includes all classes of positions, the duties of which are to advise on, administer, supervise, or perform work involved in the various phases of personnel management.

GS-300: General Administrative, Clerical, and Office Services Group

This group includes all classes of positions, the duties of which are to administer, supervise, or perform work involved in management analysis; stenography, typing, correspondence, and secretarial work; mail and file work; the operation of office appliances; the operation of communications equipment, use of codes and ciphers, and procurement of the most efficient communications services; the operation of microfilm equipment, peripheral equipment, duplicating equipment, mail-processing equipment, and copier/duplicating equipment; and other work of a general clerical and administrative nature.

GS-400: Natural Resources Management and Biological Sciences Group

This group includes all classes of positions, the duties of which are to advise on, administer, supervise, or perform research or other professional and scientific work or subordinate technical work in any of the fields of science concerned with living organisms, their distribution, characteristics, life processes, and adaptations and relations to the environment; the soil, its properties and distribution, and the living organisms growing in or on the soil; and the management, conservation, or utilization thereof for particular purposes or uses.

GS-500: Accounting and Budget Group

This group includes all classes of positions, the duties of which are to advise on, administer, supervise, or perform professional, technical, or related clerical work of an accounting, budget administration, related financial management, or similar nature.

GS-600: Medical, Hospital, Dental, and Public Health Group

This group includes all classes of positions, the duties of which are to advise on, administer, supervise, or perform research or other professional and scientific work, subordinate technical work, or related clerical work in the several branches of medicine, surgery, and dentistry or in related patient care services, such as dietetics, nursing, occupational therapy, physical therapy, pharmacy, and others.

GS-700: Veterinary Medical Science Group

This group includes all classes of positions, the duties of which are to advise and consult on, administer, manage, supervise, or perform research or other professional and scientific work in the various branches of veterinary medical science.

GS-800: Engineering and Architecture

This group includes all classes of positions, the duties of which are to advise on, administer, supervise, or perform professional, scientific, or technical work

concerned with engineering or architectural projects, facilities, structures, systems, processes, equipment, devices, materials, or methods. Positions in this group require knowledge of the science or art—or both—by which materials, natural resources, and power are made useful.

GS-900: Legal and Kindred Group

This group includes all classes of positions, the duties of which are to advise on, administer, supervise, or perform professional legal work in the preparation for trial and the trial and argument of cases; the presiding at formal hearings afforded by a commission, board, or other body having quasi-judicial powers, as part of its administrative procedure; the administration of law entrusted to an agency; the preparation or rendering of authoritative or advisory legal opinions or decisions to other federal agencies or to administrative officials of own agency; the preparation of various legal documents; and the performance of other work requiring training equivalent to that represented by graduation from a recognized law school and, in some instances, requiring admission to the bar; or quasi-legal work that requires knowledge of particular laws, or of regulations, precedents, or departmental practice based thereon, but that does not require such legal training or admission to the bar.

GS-1000: Information and Arts Group

This group includes positions that involve professional, artistic, technical, or clerical work in (1) the communication of information and ideas through verbal, visual, or pictorial means; (2) the collection, custody, presentation, display, and interpretation of art works, cultural objects, and other artifacts; or (3) a branch of fine or applied arts, such as industrial design, interior design, or musical composition. Positions in this group require writing, editing, and language ability; artistic skill and ability; knowledge of foreign languages; the ability to evaluate and interpret informational and cultural materials; the practical application of technical or aesthetic principles combined with manual skill; and dexterity and related clerical skills.

GS-1100: Business and Industry Group

This group includes all classes of positions, the duties of which are to advise on, administer, supervise, or perform work pertaining to and requiring a knowledge of business and trade practices, characteristics, and use of equipment, products, or property, or industrial production methods and processes, including the conduct of investigations and studies; the collection, analysis, and dissemination of information; the establishment and maintenance of contracts with industry and commerce; the provision of advisory services; the examination and appraisement of merchandise or property; and the administration of regulatory provisions and controls.

GS-1200: Copyright, Patent, and Trademark Group

This group includes all classes of positions, the duties of which are to advise on, administer, supervise, or perform professional scientific, technical, and legal work involved in the cataloging and registration of copyright, in the classification and issuance of patents, in the registration of trademarks, in the prosecution of applications for patents before the Patent Office, and in the giving of advice to government officials on patent matters.

GS-1300: Physical Science Group

This group includes all classes of positions, the duties of which are to advise on, administer, supervise, or perform research or other professional and scientific work or subordinate technical work in any of the fields of science concerned with matter, energy, physical space, time, nature of physical measurement, and fundamental structural particles, as well as the nature of the physical environment.

GS-1400: Library and Archives Group

This group includes all classes of positions, the duties of which are to advise on, administer, supervise, or perform professional and scientific work or subordinate technical work in the various phases of library archival science.

GS-1500: Mathematics and Statistics Group

This group includes all classes of positions, the duties of which are to advise on, administer, supervise, or perform research or other professional and scientific work or related clerical work in basic mathematical principles, methods, procedures, or relationships, including the development and application of mathematical methods for the investigation and solution of problems; the development and application of statistical theory in the selection, collection, classification, adjustment, analysis, and interpretation of data; the development and application of mathematical, statistical, and financial principles to programs or problems involving life and property risks; and any other professional and scientific or related clerical work requiring primarily and mainly the understanding and use of mathematical theories, methods, and operations.

GS-1600: Equipment, Facilities, and Services Group

This group includes positions, the duties of which are to advise on, manage, or provide instructions and information concerning the operation, maintenance, and use of equipment, shops, buildings, laundries, printing plants, power plants, cemeteries, or other government facilities, or other work involving

services provided predominantly by people in trades, crafts, or manual labor operations. Positions in this group require technical or managerial knowledge and ability in addition to a practical knowledge of trades, crafts, or manual labor operations.

GS-1700: Education Group

This group includes positions that involve administering, managing, supervising, performing, or supporting education or training work when the paramount requirement of the position is knowledge of, or skill in, education, training, or instruction processes.

GS-1800: Inspection, Investigation, Enforcement, and Compliance Group

This group includes all classes of positions, the duties of which are to advise on, administer, supervise, or perform investigation, inspection, or enforcement work primarily concerned with alleged or suspected offenses against the laws of the U.S., or such work primarily concerned with determining compliance with laws and regulations.

GS-1900: Quality Assurance (QA), Inspection, and Grading Group

This group includes all classes of positions, the duties of which are to advise on, supervise, or perform administrative or technical work primarily concerned with the QA or inspection of material, facilities, and processes, or with the grading of commodities under official standards.

GS-2000: Supply Group

This group includes positions that involve work concerned with finishing all types of supplies, equipment, material, property (except real estate), and certain services to components of the federal government, industrial, or other concerns under contract to the government, or receiving supplies from the federal government. Included are positions concerned with one or more aspects of supply activities from initial planning—including requirements analysis and determination—through acquisition, cataloging, storage, distribution, and utilization to ultimate issue for consumption or disposal. The work requires knowledge of one or more elements or parts of a supply system and/or supply methods, policies, or procedures.

GS-2100: Transportation Group

This group includes all classes of positions, the duties of which are to advise on, administer, supervise, or perform work that involves two or more specialized transportation functions or other transportation work not specifically included in other series of this group.

For current information on the GS series, visit www.opm.gov/policy-data-oversight/classification-qualifications/classifying-general-schedule-positions/occupationalhandbook.pdf

Take Note

GS-2200: Information Technology (IT) Group

This group includes all positions for the administrative work in IT. The primary subcategory is 2210, which covers IT management. Within IT management are 11 possible areas of responsibility (or combination of responsibilities).

Wage Grade Trades and Labor Job Families and Occupations

The Wage Grade (WG) group offers an additional 36 occupational families: WG-2500 through WG-9000. These are typically considered the blue-collar positions. You can find more information online by searching for "OPM WG classification standards."

SES Resume Writers

Search for Vacancies on USAJOBS.gov

Next, you want to focus even more and research agencies or programs you would like to join. You can research all the government's agencies easily online, or by using this link: www.usa.gov/federal-agencies. After reviewing an agency's history, mission, and other materials, you may come closer to a decision.

When you're ready, visit www.USAJOBS.gov, the federal government's official employment website.

All current SES positions and CDPs can be found at USAJOBS.gov (www.usajobs.gov), the federal government's official hiring site. You can also search for SES positions by city and state, but the majority of SES jobs (more than 75%) are located in and around Washington, D.C., the epicenter of our federal government.

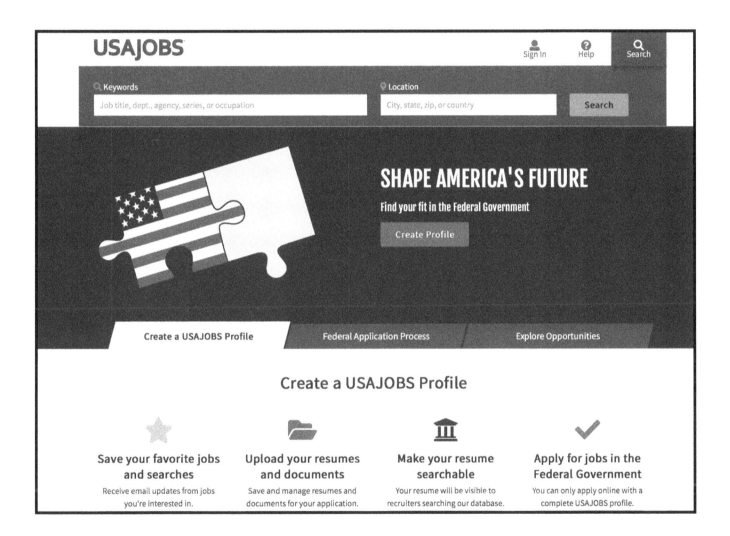

The USAJOBS.gov website has undergone many updates and changes over the years, and is now more functional and user-friendly than ever. For instance, in 2016 and 2017, the site launched several new features, including:

- The entire online application process was updated.
- The USAJOBS Help Center and "Contact Us" page has been revamped and now lists agency recruiting events and job fairs.
- They added a profile dashboard that lets you easily view the status of your applications and review saved job announcements and searches.
- They added new search technology to deliver faster and more relevant job search results.
- You now have the ability to search for jobs based on unique hiring paths. They added hiring path filters to the search feature to increase their visibility and help you find jobs based on your eligibility. You can see all the hiring paths on the USAJOBS.gov homepage, and learn more about eligibility here: https://www.usajobs.gov/Help/faq/application/eligibility/
- You can now search for positions based on country, state, and zip code, and filter search results based on a variety of criteria, such as pay, work schedule, security clearance level requirements, department, and appointment type.
- Job searches are now more intuitive because the basic and advanced search options have been combined into one search view, which will yield better and more relevant results. These new filter options basically replace the old "advanced search" feature.

The site also offers lots of helpful tutorials and information at www.usajobs.gov/Help/

At the end of the day, you simply want to use agency names, occupational series, or relevant keywords to begin your search and narrow down your options.

Create Saved Searches

Candidates seeking federal employment can take advantage of the search agent function on www.USAJOBS.gov. Applicants can establish searches by geographic location, grade, pay, job category, and/or agency. This way, you'll be the first to know when a suitable vacancy becomes available, and you can avoid the last-minute rush to put together a federal resume application package.

The website has many useful instructions at www.usajobs.gov/Help/how-to/search/save/. Here are the steps provided to create a saved search and to sign up for email notifications:

1. Sign into your USAJOBS account. If you don't have an account, you need to create one. Only signed-in users can save their searches.

2. Start a job search by entering a keyword or location in the search box and click "Search." You can also choose the Advanced Search option to narrow your results.

3. Click "Save This Search" on the search results page located on the left side of the page under the search filters.

4. Enter additional search criteria if you want; the more information you add, the more specific your results will be.

5. Name your search—this will help you manage your saved searches.

6. Choose how often you want to receive an email notification with all jobs that match your search. We recommend daily notifications if you're looking for very specific positions, since some announcements can open and close within a week. If you select daily, you'll receive one email per day only if new jobs have been posted that match your criteria in the last 24 hours.

7. Click "Save Search" or "Save and View Results." By clicking the latter, you can see if the saved search returns the results you want. If not, you can edit the saved search.

Read and Interpret Vacancy Announcements

SES positions are most often filled through a merit-based, open competitive process, but in some instances, they may be filled through non-competitive means. In addition, there are certain requirements that must be met:

- The vacancy announcements advertising the positions must be available to all potential candidates, including those without prior federal work experience. This requirement is met primarily through OPM posting the vacancy announcement on its job website, USAJOBS.gov, but the announcements may also be posted elsewhere (such as on agencies' own websites).

- The vacancy announcements must be open for at least two weeks to allow interested candidates time to prepare and submit their applications.

- All candidates submitting applications must include their responses to the five Executive Core Qualifications (ECQs) detailing the candidate's leadership abilities and achievements (unless the hiring agency chooses to modify this process).

- Veterans' Preference eligibility does not apply to SES positions, as it is prohibited by statute USC 2108(3).

- Because SES positions under open competition are available to individuals without prior federal work experience, these positions are not subject to the time-in-grade requirements found with most federal positions.

Positions being filled through the non-competitive process are usually open to candidates who have completed an SES Candidate Development Program (CDP) certified by OPM.

These individuals may be placed in SES positions without competition. Non-competitive positions may also be filled by reassigning or transferring current SES members.

A vacancy announcement (also known as a job posting) contains all of the information you should need to decide whether you qualify for the position and then to develop your application materials.

Federal agencies have quite a bit of latitude in how they present job announcements and often have specific requirements that are not constant across all job announcements. For example, one may ask for full ECQ narratives, while another may only want the ECQs summarized in a short resume presentation.

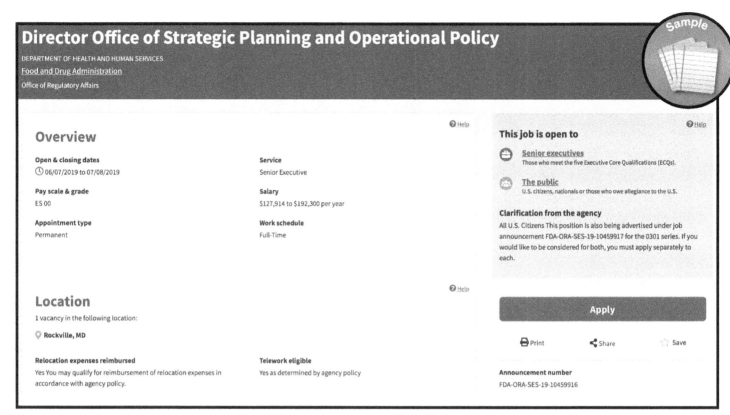

Director Office of Strategic Planning and Operational Policy

DEPARTMENT OF HEALTH AND HUMAN SERVICES
Food and Drug Administration
Office of Regulatory Affairs

Overview

Open & closing dates
🕐 06/07/2019 to 07/08/2019

Pay scale & grade
ES 00

Appointment type
Permanent

Service
Senior Executive

Salary
$127,914 to $192,300 per year

Work schedule
Full-Time

Location

1 vacancy in the following location:

📍 Rockville, MD

Relocation expenses reimbursed
Yes You may qualify for reimbursement of relocation expenses in accordance with agency policy.

Telework eligible
Yes as determined by agency policy

This job is open to

Senior executives
Those who meet the five Executive Core Qualifications (ECQs).

The public
U.S. citizens, nationals or those who owe allegiance to the U.S.

Clarification from the agency
All U.S. Citizens This position is also being advertised under job announcement FDA-ORA-SES-19-10459917 for the 0301 series. If you would like to be considered for both, you must apply separately to each.

Apply

🖶 Print   ◁ Share   ☆ Save

Announcement number
FDA-ORA-SES-19-10459916

Here are the major elements of a typical SES vacancy announcement:

1. **Vacancy Announcement Number:** The identification number issued to each vacancy announcement. It is critical to reference this number wherever it is required on all the materials submitted.

2. **Opening Date:** The date the vacancy announcement was opened.

3. **Closing Date:** The final date that applications may be submitted for consideration for an available position.

4. **Position:** The vacancy title.

5. **Series and Grade:** The pay plan, occupational series, and grade of the position.

6. **Promotion Potential:** Indication of whether the position being filled has the potential for promotion and description of the full performance level.

7. **Salary:** Salary range.

8. **Duty Location:** The geographic location of where the position is to be filled or where the position is located.

9. **Who May Apply:** Description of who is eligible to apply for the available position, such as "Federal Civil Service Employees" or "Public."

10. **Major Duties:** The duties and responsibilities of the available position.

11. **Qualifications Required:** Basic knowledge, skills, and abilities required for applicants to qualify for the position, such as similar experience or a related educational background.

12. **How You Will Be Evaluated:** This section describes how applicants will be evaluated for the position—whether they will be ranked on their knowledge, skills, and abilities or on other characteristics required to perform the duties of the position.

13. **How to Apply:** This section describes all of the materials required to complete the application. When applying, applicants must answer all of the questions contained in the vacancy announcement. They must also submit a resume. When a vacancy announcement states that documentation is required, candidates must follow the announcement's instructions to submit required documents. Failure to submit required documentation may result in disqualification.

a. It is extremely important to read the vacancy announcement in its entirety to make sure all requirements are met.

b. Applications with questions or requiring clarification should contact the HR representative listed on the vacancy announcement prior to the closing date. The HR representative can provide guidance and assistance, as needed.

c. Applicants should avoid applying for a position on the day the vacancy announcement closes. Almost all vacancies close at 11:59 p.m. EST. In the event a candidate encounters technical difficulties and has waited until the last day, he/she may not be able to complete the application process.

Five Tips for Navigating an SES Vacancy

Let's face it—pulling up a Senior Executive Service vacancy on your monitor can be a bit overwhelming. A resume, five Executive Core Qualifications, and how many Technical Qualifications? Gulp!

One of the best things you can do to reduce this overwhelming feeling is to break the application materials down into bite-sized chunks, and then reverse-engineer your time so that you have a plan for getting it all done well before the job closes.

These five tips will also help:

1. **Read the entire vacancy from top to bottom.** It's important to take a few minutes and do this, with a keen attention to detail. Write down any questions you might have.

2. **Take a close look at the duties and qualifications section.** Think of the information in these areas as questions, and ask yourself, "Will I be able to show in my resume that I possess some, most, or even all of these skills, experiences, and education?" If the answer to all those "questions" is no, that could be a red flag.

3. **Take a look at any Technical Qualifications.** Ask yourself if you will be able to provide strong narrative responses that show you have relevant and recent experience in the technical areas they want to see. Again, if the answer is no, it could be a red flag that this job isn't the best fit.

4. **Carefully read the "How to Apply" and "Required Documents" section.** This is critical, as each agency may have slightly different instructions. Sometimes you can email in your resume, other times you can upload your own resume to your USAJOBS account, and still other times, you will be required to actually use the USAJOBS resume builder. Similarly, sometimes there are length restrictions or other formatting requirements.

5. **Read the vacancy again to make sure you didn't miss anything.** At least scan the whole vacancy again, and then email the agency contact with any questions about qualifications, timelines, or how to format your documents in terms of length, font size, etc.

By following these five simple tips, you can minimize the chances of missing critical information, or of spending your time applying for something that clearly isn't a good match based on your skills, education, and experience.

The SES Application Process

The SES application process is highly competitive and can be quite daunting and intimidating for some applicants. The vacancy announcements, which are posted on USAJOBS.gov, require a resume, and normally 10 to 20 or more pages or executive and technical essays. However, the process can be successfully negotiated by presenting your most valuable contributions and potential assets to the hiring organization through robust, descriptive, and compelling language.

First, you need a resume that clearly demonstrates your progressive leadership and potential over the past 10 years. Avoid using a laundry list of your basic job duties, and instead try to show executive scope, impact, and results.

Since at least 2014, the standard for SES resumes is a five-page format with size 12 font and one-inch margins all around. However, you should check each vacancy announcement for specific application instructions, and ask the HR contact if you need clarification.

The agency has the option of including TQs (they usually do), which drill down into some of the specific "technical" areas you will be expected to oversee in the position.

Again, it's best to use the CCAR (Challenge-Context-Action-Result) format and stick to size 12 font with one-inch margins. Each TQ is a different, but it usually works great to provide a brief "introductory" response/paragraph to the question, followed by one to two specific examples in the CCAR format.

While agencies have some latitude internally, the SES application process is generally as follows:

1. Application is received and reviewed by lower-level human resources (HR) specialists to ensure all materials asked for in the vacancy

announcement are included with the application and that all instructions were followed. Those who make this "cut" will then be passed to mid-level HR specialists who will check the application for "minimum qualifications."

2. Those applications making it past the first two screenings may be referred to the hiring agency's Executive Review Board (ERB) to review all applications. This is the point where the Technical Qualification (TQs) become critical. Failure to meet any one of the mandatory TQ/ECQ standards will eliminate a candidate from further consideration.

3. A screening panel composed of a diverse mix of senior executives will evaluate candidates. The panel members will individually review each of the applications in terms of the qualifications criteria contained in the announcement. The panel will reach a consensus decision as to the "Best Qualified," "Qualified," or "Not Qualified" candidates. Each application will be given a score between 70 and 100 and only those applicants who score in the top 10% based upon the entire application are considered viable candidates.

4. The panel will interview the top 10% of the "Best Qualified" candidates based upon consistently applied criteria. The panel will then

make a recommendation of those who should be referred to the selecting official, in priority order. If there is any debate, discussion, or disagreement about who the selected candidate will be, the scores of each of the candidates' TQs will be used to "break the tie." Final selection of a candidate is contingent upon the selecting authority.

5. After the interviews, several names will be referred to the Selecting Official, then sent to the hiring agency, and then to OPM for vetting. Some agencies will then have their high-level HR (or in some cases, hired consultants) thoroughly review your ECQs and put you through a "mock review board" to give feedback and input before sending to OPM for certification.

6. Finally, a job offer is made, and the selected candidate's ECQs are sent up to OPM for certification (or not) by a Qualifications Review Board (QRB).

The Qualifications Review Board

Federal law requires that all new SES appointees undergo an extensive executive qualifications review by an independent board prior to appointment. These reviews are based on criteria established by OPM, and the board that conducts the review is the Qualifications Review Board (QRB).

The QRB consists of three volunteer members, and at least two of them must be SES career appointees.

This format allows current SES members to help in selecting new appointees and to play a key role in shaping the future of the SES.

The board does not rate or rank candidates' qualifications against other candidates. Neither does the board qualify a candidate for a specific job. Instead, the board evaluates each application individually and determines whether the candidate's experience meets the requirements established in the ECQs set forth by OPM.

The QRB judges each candidate's application in terms of overall quality, scope, and depth as they relate to the five ECQs. The reviews are "anonymous and objective" since you will never personally meet the board members, or get to know who they are, or have the opportunity to ask them any questions. If OPM does not consider the applicant to be SES material (i.e. based upon breadth and scope of answers to ECQs), the applicant is rejected, and the agency is notified. The applicant is then given a limited timeframe (usually 60 days) to correct deficiencies and then resubmit either selected essays or the whole set.

If OPM considered the ECQs to demonstrate executive core qualifications, they will be certified by OPM and the applicant will never have to generate another set of ECQs again.

QRB Review Types

The QRB conducts three types of reviews that evaluate potential candidates based on specific criteria that are most applicable to them. The three QRB Criteria are:

Criterion A: By far the most common, Criterion A evaluates candidates' executive experience to determine whether they demonstrate the required levels of experience detailed in the five ECQs. Candidates who do not specifically fall into Criterion B or C are evaluated in this Criterion. For example, candidates with no prior federal work experience who are seeking career appointments are likely to fall into Criterion A.

Criterion B: Candidates in Criterion B are those who have successfully completed an OPM-approved SES Candidate Development Program (SES CDP). These candidates are eligible for non-competitive appointments to the SES, but their completion of an SES CDP does not in itself guarantee these candidates will be appointed to the SES.

Criterion C: Criterion C is reserved for those candidates holding special or unique qualities indicating a high likelihood of success in the SES. Unlike Criterion A candidates, who must demonstrate their qualifications according to the five ECQs, Criterion C candidates must demonstrate they are qualified for the position and have the ability to quickly acquire required competency in the five ECQs. For Criterion C candidates to qualify for QRB approval, hiring agencies must include in the application packages their own assessments of why the candidates are uniquely qualified and Individual Development Plans (IDPs) detailing how they will ensure candidates acquire any ECQs skills and experience they currently lack.

Why ECQs Get Rejected

The ECQs identified by OPM are considered essential qualities and abilities that SES candidates must possess in order to be successful. As such, they are taken very seriously in considering a candidate for SES appointment. Poorly crafted ECQs can derail even the best-qualified candidates.

Because SES members hold such high-level, influential leadership positions, the QRBs are exacting in their evaluations. Moreover, while candidates may well have the required leadership background and experience, many do not pass the QRBs.

Over the years, we have seen candidates who wrote their own ECQs fail the QRB for a variety of reasons. For example, their narrative ECQ statements:

1. Do not describe the personal action they took to achieve the results;

2. Do not focus enough on leadership skills;

3. Seem more managerial/project management-oriented than executive in nature;

4. Lack quantifiable results;

5. Lack evidence of the core competencies, such as leveraging diversity, creativity, vision, and/or strategic thinking;

6. Contain too much philosophical or vague language;

7. Are not presented in OPM's preferred format, CCAR (Challenge-Context-Action-Result); and

8. Spend more than one robust paragraph on challenge/context. The boards want to see a clear and concise challenge/context paragraph that tell them your job title, role, the date of the example, and the problems/challenges you faced. Further, they want you to spend the majority of the space on the page to highlight your specific actions and results.

The QRB members will be representative of any of the more than 200 government agencies. They will not necessarily be familiar with your background or specialty area, so it's important to state your accomplishments in clear, non-technical language that any executive can understand.

Even the best-qualified candidates are not likely to pass the QRBs if their ECQs are not well presented and told through the "lens" of the competencies.

Over the years, we have assisted thousands of people with applying for SES positions. Many of them have turned to us for help when they are disqualified and the QRB calls for a rewrite. In these cases, the QRB provides feedback as to why they rejected the ECQs.

The following excerpts will demonstrate how stringent and specific the QRBs tend to be:

"... did not present evidence of, or demonstrate, executive leadership in the write-up.

Accomplishments appeared to be routine staff work. There appeared to be no substantial challenges as well as no significant results that had impact on the organization."

"The QRB noted that the candidate's ECQ statement was weak and lacked scope and depth, and did not delve into experiences that demonstrate executive leadership. Overall, the QRB noted that it was difficult to determine if the candidate possesses the leadership and executive-level qualifications. Board noted that accomplishments appeared more on a manager's level versus executive. Not enough evidence of executive leadership. Candidate did not appear to have the broad-spectrum focus; rather, a narrow and limited focus on the smaller tasks and projects accomplished. Appeared more process-oriented versus outcome-oriented. What difference did the candidate make?"

SES Application Trends

We have seen a number of changes in SES application requirements in the past few years. In response to these changes, we have developed new products to meet our customers' needs. Federal agencies will probably develop more changes to the application and hiring process. The following are a few new SES application package requirements that we now develop and that you might very well come across in your job search.

FIVE-PAGE SES RESUME & SEPARATE ECQS/TQS
This includes a five-page SES resume, up to ten pages of ECQ documentation, and anywhere from two to ten pages of TQ documentation (approximately one to two pages per TQ).

THREE OR FOUR-PAGE SES RESUME WITH EXECUTIVE COMPETENCIES
This involves a four-page SES resume with cover letter; alternatively, you may omit the optional cover letter and extend the resume to five pages. Traditional ECQs are replaced with the selecting agency's choice of five executive competencies, such as Strategic Vision, Resilience, Leadership, Coalition Building, or Human Capital Management. The hiring agency may choose to select other competencies relevant to its goals. Finally, on rare occasions, we have seen agencies give candidates up to four pages for their SES resumes, and require one or two examples per ECQ integrated into this comprehensive document with limited space.

OTHER UNIQUE APPLICATIONS
Certain agencies within the intelligence community use a different approach to select their senior executives. Not only do they require resumes, TQs and ECQs, but they might also require candidates to respond to Senior Intelligence Officer Core Qualifications.

Likewise, the Federal Aviation Administration (FAA) has its own set of "Dimensions" that its senior leaders must respond to, and that closely mirror the ECQs. Additionally, the Intelligence Community requires its candidates to address the "Intelligence Community (IC) Senior Officer Core Qualifications." You can learn more about these in Check Point 4.

Further, the Department of the Air Force has a unique set of parameters for their senior executive positions. Candidates must of course provide resumes, TQs and ECQs, but they often require "Desirable Qualifications" as well. They also limit the resume to four pages (with each job summarized into one paragraph), and the entire application package is limited to a certain number of pages. All the details will be included in specific vacancy announcements under the "How to Apply" and "Required Documents" sections.

USAJOBS SES RESUME WITH ONLINE ECQ/TQ POSTING

In these cases, applicants are required to use the USAJOBS resume builder and then enter their ECQ narrative statements online. These usually contain a character limitation of 4,000 to 8,000 characters per ECQ and TQ.

THE FIVE-PAGE ALL-INCLUSIVE RESUME

Some vacancy announcements do away with full ECQ and TQ narratives and require the applicant to address them within the body of the resume. SES job applicants tend to appreciate this because it shortens the amount of information they have to submit. CareerPro Global has adapted to this change, and developed the Five-Page All-Inclusive Resume.

Summarizing ECQs in your resume is completely different from writing full narratives. However, it can be done, and there are examples of how to do so in Appendix A and on the CD in the back of the book. Not every job announcement will be exactly the same, but here is an example of what to look for:

To meet the minimum qualification requirements

for this position, you must submit a resume, which provides evidence of how you possess the five Executive Core Qualifications (ECQs) and the Technical Qualifications (TQs) listed in this announcement.

We recommend that your resume emphasize your level of responsibilities, the scope and complexity of programs managed, and your program accomplishments, including the results of your actions. The application package cannot exceed a total of five pages. Any information submitted in excess of five pages WILL NOT be considered.

Check Point 2 Summary

As you can see by now, your entire package will undergo significant scrutiny. First, there will be an initial review of all documents to assess whether you are "SES material" and if you've followed the application instructions in the job announcement.

Next, the hiring authority will take a close look at your resume and any TQs. After all, the hiring authority—not OPM—is the agency that wrote the TQs. The hiring agency will also review the ECQs during its assessment. "Best Qualified" candidates are invariably those whose resumes, with supportive and definitive ECQ statements, clearly present the candidates' leadership skills and achievements.

As an SES application makes its way through the hiring process, it may have been reviewed multiple times, and the application package has to be strong enough to withstand the scrutiny of multiple evaluators.

Check Point Notes

Check Point 3

Developing an Effective SES Resume

DEVELOPING AN EFFECTIVE SES RESUME

What Makes a Strong SES Resume?

Years ago, SES resumes could be ten or more pages, but the accepted standard has become a five-page maximum length. As you learned in Check Point 2, the rare exceptions include vacancy announcements that specify fewer pages or require SES applicants to use the USAJOBS resume builder. But just as the SES itself represents a higher level of excellence in government and leadership, so should your SES resume portray a higher level of achievement and ability.

Federal agencies may receive dozens of SES application packages, but typically, only a few of the top applicants will be interviewed. As such, the SES federal resume must highlight executive traits and provide strong examples of a candidate's executive leadership and professional accomplishments and contributions.

Compared to a resume that is developed to target the private sector, a federal SES resume also contains substantially more information, such as full addresses of previous employers; supervisor names and contact information; a detailed listing of education and training; and all honors/awards, publications, and volunteer service demonstrating leadership and involvement.

Human Rresources specialists cannot infer anything; simply claiming years of experience is not enough information to demonstrate qualifications. The resume must fully explain your work experience, identifying for whom you have worked, for how long, and your specific role/contributions.

Sections of an SES Resume

Contact Information: Physical mailing address, telephone numbers (sometimes they specifically ask for day and evening numbers), and primary email address

Vacancy Announcement Information: Vacancy announcement number, job title

Other Information: Citizenship, current federal position and dates, security clearance, and Social Security Number (only if requested, which is rare)

Executive/Professional Summary: This is the first part of the resume to which a reviewer will be drawn

Work History/Job Descriptions/Accomplishments

List jobs in reverse-chronological order, beginning with the present position and going back 10 years. While we do recommend describing in detail only your most recent experience (10 years), there is sometimes value in including experience farther back in your career.

Perhaps you were employed by a well-known, prestigious company, and it can benefit you to document the full scope of your cross-industry experience, much of which occurred in your early career. Perhaps you still have contact with valuable networks from 15 or 20 years back.

In any case, it will be apparent to the reader that your executive career did not suddenly materialize in the last 10 years, so a brief summary of your early experience would be appropriate. Of course, this does not mean you must give equal page weight to your early career, or your resume will expand to an unmanageable size, and your chances of having the resume read in its entirety will decrease.

In your Job Description, include the following elements:

- Brief summary of your current employer's organization, purpose, and mission and what type of services it provides from how many divisions (nationally or internationally). Describe the organization's customer base and, if possible, detail the number of people the agency/division employs and its impact on its market.

- Professional accountabilities: A four- to five-line paragraph summarizing your major job duties—position purpose, number of direct reports, dollar amounts of budgets managed, and areas of management authority.

- Keyword-enriched, detailed "breakout" description of your position.

Consider/List:

- Your function in dealing with other divisions or agencies;

- Responsibility/Accountability for annual operating/capital budget (formulation, defense, execution, etc.);

- The number of employees you manage/supervise and their levels/titles;

- Any contracting/acquisition responsibility, naming the largest contract you have developed, negotiated, and/or managed;

- Responsibilities in program performance planning, management, and evaluation (e.g., getting a

project from "red" or "yellow" to "green" or some other scorecard system).

Position Achievements:

List your position accomplishments concisely, providing explicit details and results or the organizational impact they had.

Numbers and facts are very important here, as they will make your achievements more credible. You should be direct and specific in your career achievements so the reader can see exactly what you're capable of and what you have to offer.

Don't be afraid to pat yourself on the back; remember, your SES resume is a marketing and sales presentation of what you bring to the table.
Some other things to consider include:

- Your contribution to cutting costs and/or increasing productivity/efficiency in any way (include details);

- Any working group you've established or led, its purpose, and what it accomplished;

- Any major-scale projects/programs you've directed (establishing objectives, developing milestones, assigning responsibilities, holding people accountable, making tough decisions to avoid project delays, and completing the project on time and within budget, despite obstacles) that positively affected your organization, either by improving business practices or by saving money/increasing profit;

- Any problems you've solved that increased productivity or resulted in other benefits;

- Ideas you turned into reality that had positive financial or operational impact on the organization.

Education:

- Name of degree-granting institutions, listing first the most recent degree earned;

- Degree received and major/concentration/emphasis;

- Graduation date or projected graduation date, or the dates of attendance if no degree was completed;

- Any minors, specialization, or focus areas;

- Overseas academic experiences;

- Courses relevant to the positions for which you are applying;

- Honors and GPA are optional, although recommended if they are a strong selling point (be sure to indicate GPA as based on a 4.0 scale— e.g., 3.6/4.0), and a number of hours;

High school experience is not typically listed; however, there are exceptions, like if you attended an extremely noteworthy high school or academy, or you were awarded a full academic scholarship.

Documents You Will Need to Gather

A federal SES resume is a complex document. It is a good idea to gather and organize the following materials before you start developing your resume:

1. Performance evaluations for past 10 years
2. Job descriptions for past 10 years
3. Record of accomplishments (both your individual professional and related organizational achievements)
4. Record of professional training (include dates)
5. Any professional certifications or licenses (include certifying organization and dates of validity)
6. Education: college, degree/major, date of degree, number of semester or quarter hours, GPA, any honors
7. Awards, with accompanying write-ups, if applicable
8. Professional organizations
9. Community service
10. Publications

Five-Step SES Resume Development Process

Step 1. Use a Job or Sample Vacancy Announcement to Identify Keywords/Headlines/Core Competencies

Step 2. Set Up Your Resume Using the Headline Format

Step 3. Write Your Professional/Executive Summary

Step 4. Write the Duties and Accomplishments for Each Position

Step 5. Edit Your Resume

Step 1. Use a Job or Sample Vacancy Announcement to Identify Keywords/ Headlines/ Core Competencies

In order to stand out and optimize your resume, any keywords or recurring phrases in the vacancy announcement should be extracted and utilized by connecting your experiences to those core performance expectations. Further, you want to use keywords throughout the resume, but especially in the work history and professional summary.

In most cases, keywords are nouns. What types of nouns are sought? Nouns that relate to the skills and experience the employer is looking for in a candidate are the ones to shoot for.

More specifically, keywords and core competencies can be precise "hard" skills—job-specific/profession-specific/industry-specific skills, technological terms, and descriptions of technical expertise (including hardware and software in which the client is proficient), job titles, certifications, names of products and services, industry buzzwords and jargon, types of degrees, names of colleges, company names, terms that tend to impress, such as "Fortune 500," and even area codes for narrowing down searches geographically.

Where Do You Find Keywords?

Keywords are intentionally placed in all vacancy job announcements. You can find keywords in job vacancy announcements under three sections: Job Summary, Major Duties, and Qualifications (specialized experience and how you will be evaluated).

Keywords are *always* listed in order of importance; if someting is listed twice, *pay careful attention* to those words.

You might also find keywords in:
- Job-description books
- OPM Classification Standards
- OPM Qualification Standards
- Websites of professional associations in your field to look and listen for current buzzwords
- Government publications, such as the "Occupational Outlook Handbook," at libraries or online
- Website of the employer you are targeting; look for keywords describing the organization's culture and values; note the mission statement and look for ways to quote it in your resume
- Web search engines, such as Google and Yahoo, to search for job descriptions

Associate Administrator for Research and Program Development

DEPARTMENT OF TRANSPORTATION
National Highway Traffic Safety Administration

Overview   Locations   Duties   Requirements   Required Documents   Benefits   How to apply

❓ Help

Overview

Open & closing dates
🕐 04/24/2019 to 05/24/2019

Pay scale & grade
ES 00

Appointment type
Permanent - Career

Service
Senior Executive

Salary
$127,914 to $192,300 per year

Work schedule
Full-Time - Permanent

❓ Help

This job is open to

The public
U.S. citizens, nationals or those who owe allegiance to the U.S.

Senior executives
Those who meet the five Executive Core Qualifications (ECQs).

Clarification from the agency
Open to all U.S. Citizens

Responsibilities

NHTSA is dedicated to achieving the highest standards of excellence in motor vehicle and highway safety. The agency strives to exceed the expectations of the American traveling public through its core values of Integrity, Service and Leadership.

The **Associate Administrator for Research and Program Development** is responsible for the development of behavioral safety programs of the Administration including applied research, program conception and design, demonstration, evaluation, technical assistance and national leadership to guide organizations, states and local communities as they plan, develop, implement, and evaluate traffic safety programs to reduce traffic crashes and their resulting deaths, injuries and property damage/economic costs.

• Leads a team of more than 60 people with diverse professional experience in highway safety, behavioral and public health sciences, research, public safety and law enforcement. Determines organizational, human resources and budgetary parameters necessary to support the office.

• Plans and directs the development and dissemination of research and of transportation safety programs related to functions such as impaired driving; occupant protection; traffic law enforcement; pedestrian, bicycle, and motorcycle safety; emergency medical services; behavioral research, as well as other special programs that may be assigned.

• Partners with a variety of internal and external stakeholders including researchers and academics, emergency response professionals, safety advocates, international, federal, state and local officials to develop and implement transportation safety programs, and leads collaborative planning activities with public and private sector stakeholders.

• Oversees a program that monitors and evaluates activities of the NHTSA regional offices, in collaboration with the offices for Regional Operations and Program Delivery and Communications and Consumer Information, to ensure that the agency is optimizing its effectiveness in supporting states and local communities in planning, developing, and implementing comprehensive transportation injury prevention and control programs.

Above, you will find an excerpt from a Regional Administrator vacancy announcement. Note the highlighted words and phrases.

Step 2. Set Up Your Resume Using the Headline Format

In this step, you simply want to create the overall framework for your resume. We'll finish building it in the next steps, but first you need to create a blueprint. Remember the keywords you identified in the previous step? Now it's time to drill those down

into two to five relevant headlines for each job. Later, you will add in your duties for each position, and organize them under these headlines. You might use different headlines for different jobs, depending on the position.

But your goal is always to organize your duties within relevant headlines, and to create parallels between your work experience and the duties/qualification of the job for which you're applying.

Federal Human Resources professionals have welcomed CPG's Headline Format-Style Resume for years, and our federal applications have earned thousands of job candidate interviews leading to job offers. These bold headline statements represent relevant core competencies and skills. They draw attention and make HR representatives want to read more about the experience to determine whether the headlines utilized are on the mark.

Think of the federal resume as an advertisement to sell yourself. When writing a federal resume, you'll want to keep it original and let it express everything original about you. However, you want to express that uniqueness in the language of the vacancy announcement.

Put yourself in the shoes of the HR Hiring Manager. What will he or she look for in your resume? What specific keywords are in the announcement?

What keywords best exemplify your strengths and experience?

Step 3. Write Your Professional/ Executive Summary

There is definitely an art to writing a compelling and effective professional summary. With its placement at the top of the first page, it lands in prime real

---

How Your Resume Might Look at the Completion of This Step:

04/2015–Present, Program Manager, Department of Veterans Affairs, Crait, MD; Federal Grade: GS-XXXX-14; Salary: $130,000 USD Per Year; Hours/Week: 40; Supervisor: Amylyn Holdo, Telephone: 555-555-5555; OK to Contact: Yes

Executive Leadership & Program Management:

Organizational Change:

Leadership Development & Mentoring:

Strategic Planning & Policy Development:

Selected Accomplishments and Key Results:
- XXX
- XXX

Take Note: We don't recommend arbitrarily placing keywords in your resume just to try to "trick" a system. Keep in mind that a human being is going to review the resume, so you want to present relevant, impactful duties and accomplishments. If you don't have the required skills and experience, then no amount of keywords is going to land you an SES job.

estate on the document—the first item noticed and read by decision makers.

As such, you don't want to include just a few sentences of philosophy, unsupported, vague claims ("able to leap tall buildings in a single bound"), soft skills, or rote job descriptions.

Instead, you want it to grab the reader's attention, be concise, include some specific accomplishments, and set a positive tone for the rest of the resume. Try to hone in on what makes you truly special while contributing to the core principles of the company—making and/or saving money, improving customer satisfaction, improving efficiency, etc.

To be effective, the Summary of Qualifications (a.k.a. Career Highlights, Profile, Executive Summary, etc.) should include:

- **A "Branding" Statement:** A statement displaying your experience and highest level of qualifications. Be specific (for example, "Twenty-seven years of progressive experience in office administration and executive support. Entrusted to lead diverse groups of more than 250 federal and contractor employees, while overseeing $44M in budgets and resources annually").

- **Record of Improvement/Accomplishment:** Whenever describing accomplishments, be precise. If possible, quantify results. For example, if you felt it was one of your most relevant/impactful accomplishments, you could include, "While serving as Regional Administrator, reorganized order-processing procedures to reduce time required by 30%."

- Specific skills and training applicable to the job objective

- Areas of specialized proficiency (include Security Clearances)

Religious and political affiliations, country club memberships, and non-relevant hobbies have no place on a federal resume.

Accomplishments for Each Position

By now, you should have gathered all the information you'll need to write your **duties and accomplishments** for each position you will include on your resume.

As for your "duties," while you don't want to simply copy/paste your position description into your resume, it is important to show the reader "a day in the life."

Through two to five headline-style paragraphs, the reader should be able to understand your major duties/scope of responsibility. Obviously you won't have room to include everything you do, so you should focus on the most important and relevant activities.

By paraphrasing your job objectives and including specific budget amounts, people managed, programs you oversaw, (e.g., "Planned and managed a budget of $10M" or "Supervised a staff of 16 while providing oversight and direction to 450+"), you can clearly inform readers of the standards to which you were held.

Next, it's time to work on your specific career accomplishments. Resumes are no longer built around rote job descriptions; anyone can up job descriptions. Further, resumes are frequently weakened by a lack of key achievements. Achievements differ from duties—achievements are your notable accomplishments in your employment; duties are your functions.

TIPS TO WRITE STRONG ACCOMPLISHMENTS

Be specific. Accomplishments are not generic. Accomplishments are the specific achievements that YOU did, and improvements YOU made.

As yourself the right questions. Think of a duty, initiative, challenge, or problem you overcame. And then ask things like, "Okay, so what happened? What short- and long-term results happened due to my actions? What did I improve or change? What statistics, metrics, or other specific evidence can I share to tell a 'story' and demonstrate my experience and potential?"

Focus on outcome. You'd be amazed by how many people forget to mention this critical aspect of experience. When discussing outcome, be sure to discuss the whats, the hows, and the breadth and scope of your experiences:

- What occurred. Did you improve the workplace? Perhaps you refined technology tools, created programs, or organized procedures. Regardless, let the agency know what occurred. Use brief examples to best illustrate your point whenever possible.

- How much and how many. Did you start new projects? How many? Did you save the office money? Time? How much? Don't forget percentages, numbers, and degrees that apply.

Showcase your role. Did you work on your own? As part of a team? In a supervisory capacity? For example, the following response ignores the candidate's role(s):

Helped organize conferences. Among responsibilities were sending invitations, calling potential guests, and preparing conference materials.

The **Challenge-Context-Action-Result (CCAR)** approach can help you write strong accomplishments and tell mini "career stories."

Challenge/Context: Describe the position you were in and the challenge(s) or conditions you had to overcome.

Action: Describe your action(s) in detail, but be as concise as possible.

Result: Describe the results of what you accomplished. Be specific when writing accomplishments. Don't leave it up to others to presume your contribution. If you feel you exceeded expectations with the accomplishment, say so, and explain how.

A stronger way of phrasing would be:

Played a key role in coordinating and facilitating an executive-level conference with representation from more than 16 program offices. As a result, group developed and approved more than six critical policy updates in support of customer and strategic goals.

Value your experience. Many experiences illuminate your significance as a candidate. For example, you might have published relevant articles or gained valuable experience through:

Leadership positions. Were you president of a sorority or fraternity? Did you lead a team either as part of a classroom experience or a volunteer group? If they are relevant to the position you're targeting, you may want to mention these positions and the outcome of your efforts.

Extracurricular activities. Perhaps you volunteered or belonged to a club that enabled you to hone your business acumen and executive skill sets. Let the agency know specific details, including initiatives, dates, and how that experience applies to the field.

Internships, training assignments, and special details. Never underestimate the importance of hands-on education such as Candidate Development Programs (CDPs), acting SES roles, or other "stretch" assignments.

Make it relevant. Make the connection between what you did and why that mattered to the organization's mission. Highlight how the organization benefited from what you contributed by describing the tangible benefits, such as cost savings, to the organization or a solution that enabled employees to perform better.

Highlight specific instances in which your behavior made a positive difference. Overcoming challenges is an important part of overall performance. Challenges may be technical or interpersonal. They

Use the worksheet on page 251 or on the CD to help capture your top accomplishments and results.

Practical Exercise

also may involve succeeding, despite limited resources or difficult circumstances.

Be action-oriented. Begin each sentence with an action verb (e.g., architected, drove, grew, designed, developed, directed, etc.).

Sample Headline Format-Style Resume

Below is one job to demonstrate how you can strategically use keywords to create headlines within the employment section of your resume. Note how the "headline" section of each job is followed by a brief description that captures the key duties/scope of responsibility within the headline and avoids restating job descriptions. Just as importantly, notice that all jobs include at least a couple of specific accomplishments.

JONATHAN A. DOE
123 Alphabet Drive Alexandria, VA 22002 U.S. Citizen
Home Phone: 123-456-7890; Work Phone: 123-456-7890; john.a.doe@careerprocenter.net
Highest Grade Level and Dates: GS-0340-15, 8/2014–Present
VACANCY IDENTIFICATION NUMBER: xxxxxx
JOB TITLE AND GRADE: Director, Forest Management Staff

PROFESSIONAL SUMMARY

Senior executive with the U.S. Department of Agriculture (USDA) Forest Service with more than 21 years of service, many of them in high-impact positions of leadership, including policy formulation, program development, and coordination and evaluation of major segments of resource management programs. Professional knowledge of forestry principles, laws, acts, executive orders, and regulations. Expert in principles and practices of public land stewardship and developing/ implementing strategic plans (i.e., legislative proposals, national resource positions, and resource-related issues).

WORK EXPERIENCE

USDA FOREST SERVICE
Regional Forester, GS-340-15/7
USDA Forest Service
1720 Peachtree Road NW
Atlanta, GA 30309

2000–Present
08/2014–Present
Hours/week: 40-60
Salary: $129,000
Supervisor: Lee Kelley
Telephone: 435-272-4618
OK to Contact: Yes

LEADERSHIP/MANAGEMENT: Supervise and manage multicultural organization administering programs of work, including workforce, budget, equipment, facilities, and other resources. Provide direct technical and administrative supervision to staff comprising 17 professional, 10 technical, and 6 clerical employees of the Southern Region/Region 8, spanning 13 states from Virginia through Texas and including 189 million acres of state and private forested lands characterized by complex variations in geologic, climatic, biologic, and hydrologic conditions and political subdivisions.

ADMINISTRATION/HUMAN RESOURCES (HR): Plan, direct, and delegate work, setting and adjusting long-term priorities and schedules. Interview and select subordinate supervisors and employees. Approve within-grade increases, overtime, and travel. Hear and resolve complaints and grievances from non-supervisory personnel. Further the goals of Equal Employment Opportunity (EEO) by adhering to non-discriminatory employment practices. Create a work environment that respects, appreciates, and accepts employee contributions and per-

spectives. Ensure creative learning work environment that provides measurable, quality service to public and customers.

FOREST MANAGEMENT: Develop and implement interventions to affect the forest ecosystems, including both conservation and economic activities, such as extraction of timber, planting and replanting of various species, cutting roads and pathways through forests, and techniques for preventing or making outbreaks of fire. Direct application of research results to obtain a modern and effective approach to protection, management, and utilization of forest, state, and private resources.

POLICIES/OBJECTIVES/STANDARDS: Recommend and formulate nationally significant policies to administer National Forest System, State and Private Forestry, and Forest and Range Research programs. Formulate internal operation policy and advice and lead complex issues regarding the Southern Region management. Set standards for work; conduct performance appraisals; and ensure equity of work, performance standards, and ratings.

PROJECT/PROGRAM MANAGEMENT: Develop and implement new and unique programs; make recommendations and carry out decisions region-wide. Direct inspection and review activities to maintain surveillance over program progress and ascertain conformity with policies and program objectives. Evaluate extent to which Region 8 programs are meeting national and regional cultural, socioeconomic, and security requirements for assigned resources, state and private services. Initiate organizational realignments to improve program execution.

RESOURCE MANAGEMENT: Direct major programs of $6M in resources, preparing budget proposals to initiate, direct, or redirect projects and programs. Supervise, direct, develop, coordinate, implement, and evaluate short- and long-term programs. Communicate and coordinate Southern Region's budget programs among 14 national forests, 13 states, and Puerto Rico, the Regional Office, the Washington Office, National Finance Center, USDA Office of the Inspector General, and Government Accountability Office (GAO).

AGENCY REPRESENTATION: Regularly designated agency point of contact (POC); interact with high-ranking military and civilian managers, supervisors, and technical staff, agency headquarters (HQ) administrative support, and personnel from other federal agencies. Conduct formal briefings for public-interest groups. Conduct interviews with journalists representing city or county newspapers, radio, and television. Respond to inquiries of Congressional committee and subcommittee staff assistants. Interact with contracting officials and high-level technical staff of large industrial firms. Work with local officers of regional or national trade associations, public action groups, or professional organizations and/or state and local government managers doing business with the agency.

TEAMS/COMMITTEES: Represent Regional Forester in meetings, conferences, and negotiations with other federal and state agencies and with non-governmental organizations and partners. Authorized to commit the agency to a course of action on controversial administrative and/or resource matters. Forest Service Executive Staff member tasked with formulating and executing national Forest Management policies, involving consideration and recommendation of nationally significant policies under which the Nation Forest System, State and Private Forestry, and Forest and Range Research programs are administered. Regional Office Management Team member tasked with formulating, promulgating, and effecting policies and programs of regional scope and significance for the management of administrative or resource programs.

CUSTOMER SERVICE: Define the "primary" customers served and negotiate expectations with customers regarding services provided. Solicit feedback on performance and suggestions for improvements in service.

SIGNIFICANT ACCOMPLISHMENTS:

- Mediated dispute in 2016 between National Forests and an off-road vehicle group resulting from recent Environmental Assessment decision to cease construction of off-road vehicle trails. Persuaded Forest Supervisor to withdraw Environmental Assessment decision to avoid potentially costly appeal and litigation. Additionally, involved off-road vehicle user group in development of the Travel Management Plan, identification of possible locations for future trails, and discussions on cost-sharing of trail construction and maintenance.

- Initiated and entered into a successful contract stewardship with National Wild Turkey Federation on a multiple-year basis to eradicate noxious weeds from the national forest.

- In Fiscal Year (FY) 2017, kept several forests at preliminary budget numbers in order to keep commitments of timber volume to industry, despite shortfalls in preliminary budget allocations; reviewed budget for possible increases in allocations that could be used in the preparation and sale of timber volume.

- Briefed Deputy Chief for the National Forest System on the criteria used to allocate initial FY 2015 budget to the nine regions in the Forest Service, which had affected Region 8's ability to fund other regions, allowing them to maintain program level objectives; collaborated with Washington Office Program Area Directors to transfer funding from another account related to vegetation management work, thus reducing the impact of the Congressional language on affected regions.

Director, Forest Management, GS-460-15
USDA Forest Service, Region 1
1720 Peachtree Road
Atlanta, GA 30309

4/2008–08/2014
Hours/week: 40-60
Salary: $109,204
Supervisor: Lawrence Dominguez
Telephone: 123-456-7890
OK to Contact: Yes

LEADERSHIP/MANAGEMENT: Performed a wide variety and complexity of scientific, technical, economic, and management problems associated with the 12.7 million (M) acres of national forest land in Southeast U.S. administered by 14 national forests, Savannah River Natural Resource Management, and Research Institute and the Land Between the Lakes (LBL) National Recreation Area. Directed forest product disposal, by sale or other means, of more than 750M board feet of timber annually via more than 4,000 timber sale contracts and permits with an aggregate value in excess of $100M. Provided leadership, direction, policy formulation, administration, and supervision of the Total Forest Management programs of the Southern Region.

ADMINISTRATION/HUMAN RESOURCES (HR): Directly supervised operational activities of 15-member staff of professional, technical, and clerical support employees, including (1) Deputy Director, GS-14, (9) GS-460-13, (1) 05-1101-11, (1) GS-1101-09, (1) GS-1101-07, (1) GS-0334-12, (1) GS-0334-09, (1) GS-0303-04/05, (2) GS-460-12, one forest employee and another state employee under agreement with University of Tennessee at Knoxville serving the genetics resources mission, (1) GS-0460-13 Logging Engineer, and (1) GS-0462-11 Forestry Technician. Interviewed candidates for positions and made selections for grades GS-13 and below. Recommended awards or bonuses for non-supervisory personnel and change in position classifications. Developed and implemented regional recruitment program for new professional foresters and/or forestry technicians. Directed Regional Forest Management training program, including advanced certification training, formal continuing education programs, and in-house U.S. Forest Service training and/or workshops.

FOREST MANAGEMENT: Managed Forest Management program with an annual budget exceeding $71M, including all phases of forest product sale design and preparation, valuation, forest product sale operations and contract administration, logging engineering, genetic resources conservation, forest inventory, planning and appeals, trust-fund management, and program oversight. Directed program's completion of 42,000 acres of reforestation and 38,000 acres of forestland improvement work annually. Directed genetic resource conservation to meet Forest Plan goals and objectives.

POLICIES/OBJECTIVES/STANDARDS: Participated in the formulation, establishment, and monitoring of regional policies and programs. Interpreted broad national policies and other guidelines in the development and implementation of the Regional Forest Management programs. Led the development and implementation of policy, standards, and guidelines for the appropriate use of Knutson-Vandenberg (K-V), Salvage Sale (SS) Reforestation, Brush Disposal (BD), and Pipeline Restoration (PR) trust funds. Conducted and/or directed program management and activity reviews on forests and states for compliance with program standards, policies, and objectives. Conducted and/or directed technical and administrative review to determine conformance with established programs, policies, and cooperative agreements.

PROJECT/PROGRAM MANAGEMENT: Developed balanced Forest Management program with short- and long-range plans, objectives, and budget proposals that met the needs of National Forests, state forestry agencies, and other federal and public agencies and recommended allocation of funds into resource-management programs. Directed genetic resource-management and forest product sale programs, including management of trust funds, and Pilot initiatives.

PROJECT/PROGRAM ASSESSMENT/EVALUATION: Assessed the relevance, effectiveness, funding, and staffing for programs and projects. Made authoritative recommendations on the need for new staff projects, the redirection of existing projects, and the curtailment of those no longer relevant. Evaluated the effectiveness of staff activities with respect to Forest Service-wide and nationally legislated programs, and initiated organizational realignments necessary to more effectively execute programs consistent with budget and ceiling constraints. Determined if contract work performed met standards of adequacy necessary for payment.

ANALYTICAL METHODOLOGY: Improved region-wide Forest Management productivity, promoting the transfer of technology, reducing cost, wherever possible, and improving the quality of Forest Management services and products. Maintained work environments that promoted the rapid exchange and implementation of appropriate technology. Provided regional leadership and technical direction in the formulation of plans for testing and implementing advanced and non-standard logging systems.

RESOURCE MANAGEMENT: Developed and formulated annual and long-term budget requests. Emphasized cost efficiency in the forest products program, including analysis of no-bid timber sales as well as using All Resource Accounting processes to identify methods of improving cost efficiency of individual programs. Implemented and updated cost-efficiency action plans. Reduced opportunities for waste and fraud and worked with Regional Special Agent-in-Charge to implement the Region 8 Timber Theft Prevention Plan. Analyzed Regional and Forest budgets for cost-effectiveness, program tradeoffs, and alternative funding methods.

AGENCY REPRESENTATION: Coordinated all Forest Management activities with other RO Staff Units, l4 National Forests, Southern Research Station (SRS), Savannah River Institute (SRI), and the LBL National Recreation Area. Represented Regional Forester in meetings, conferences, and negotiations with officials in the Washington Office, state officials, and managers of forest industries, military officials, and managers of federal agencies. Maintained contact to exchange and seek information and to keep abreast of current policies and programs. Served as regional spokesperson to communications media on questions relating to impact of legislation, changes in administration policies and practices, and other similar actions. Reviewed and recommended response to the Washington Office on legislative proposals.

TEAMS/COMMITTEES: Coordinated Forest Management activities with other directors, Research, Washington Office, and external agencies to ensure an integrated approach to supporting Natural Resources Agenda and Forest Plan implementation. Worked with directors or their representatives to develop integrated approaches to address issues and to aid resolution of complex, precedent-setting problems.

ACCOMPLISHMENTS:

- Key player in the successful planning, transition implementation, and management of Natural Resource Information System (NRIS) corporate database.

- Chaired for three years the newly created Budget Steering Team, established to improve budget-allocation process to the forests as well as the preparation of the out-year budget to improve region's competition for agency funds; in three years, reduced the total amount of funds allocated to the Regional Office by $3M and thus increased funds allocated to the forests for necessary resource-management work.

- Chaired the first Healthy Forest Initiative/Healthy Forest Restoration Act (HFI/HFRA) Integration Team, a newly created Regional Office committee tasked with establishing a framework to prepare five-year integrated vegetation management plan; Region achieved the assigned targets and outcomes consistently as a result of team's development and implementation of process of integrating vegetation-management programs of work on the national forests.

- Directed development of presale/tree measurement version of Stewardship Contract, a new tool approved by Congress that permitted agencies to trade goods for services.

- Served for three years as Regional Office Representative to the Northern Administrative Zone Board, to reduce the overall cost of conducting human resources (HR), the duplication of effort, and the acquisition/procurement functions. Oversaw recruitment and hiring process and reduced costs by $400K.

EDUCATION

Bachelor of Science in Forest Resources, University of Montana, Missoula, MT, June 1992

PROFESSIONAL TRAINING

Harvard, Kennedy School of Government Executive Programs, 2018; USDA Computer Security Awareness, 2018; USDA Privacy Basics, 2017; No Fear Act, 2016; Alternative Dispute Resolution, 2016; FS: 1700 Reasonable Accommodations, 2013; FEI: Leadership for a Democratic Society, 2012; Incident Command for Executives, 2010

AWARDS

Certificate of Merit and Cash Awards, 2011, 2013, 2015, 2017

Step 5. Edit Your Resume

In this final step, it's time to step back a bit and do some quality control. As with any piece of writing, we recommend getting someone else to review, provide feedback, and even offer editorial suggestions.

You might ask a co-worker, mentor, professional writer, or the English major in the family to take a look. The goal is to have a resume that is error-free, grammatically correct, and written in an active voice, whenever possible. You should also use Microsoft (MS) Word's spelling and grammar check functions.

Writing a Five-Page All-Inclusive Resume

As we have learned, sometimes SES positions require only a five-page resume. More and more often, you will also be required to demonstrate possession of the Executive Core Qualifications (ECQs), and sometimes Technical Qualifications (TQs), within the body of the resume.

CPG has developed the Five-Page All-Inclusive Resume in response to this requirement. Developing a five-page all-inclusive resume is not very different from developing a traditional federal resume.

You will still include the same information, but you will have less space in which to do it. You need to be even more concise and condense your career to the most vital accomplishments so that you can fit it all in five pages. There are numerous ways in which you

can accomplish this, but we recommend using one of the two following methods:

One method is to include a short summary of each of the five ECQs on the first page of your resume, as you'll see in the first five-page resume sample at the end of this book. You have the option of listing the name of the ECQ you are addressing (e.g., Leading Change), but let's be clear: The new Office of Personnel Management (OPM) 2010 SES Guide addresses this issue directly, stating: "It is not necessary or even advisable to annotate the resume with ECQ titles." Moreover, the example actually included in the OPM 2010 guide (p. 29-32) does not reflect this method.

While some of our clients have landed SES jobs after including the ECQ headings on their resume, we still strongly recommend that you always follow the exact rules in the job announcement and those laid out by OPM regarding SES applications.

Another method is to include accomplishments within the employment history portion of the resume; however, using subtlety in this way will increase the chance that the person reviewing your resume will overlook your accomplishments.

You may want to leave out the ECQ titles and simply highlight, bold, or capitalize keywords within your ECQ summaries that clearly demonstrate that particular ECQ. We have provided several samples in the Appendix and on the CD included with this book.

Here are some tips and examples to demonstrate what you should—and should not—do in your own resume.

Write your resume in the assumed first-person point of view, without using personal pronouns such as "I," "me," or "my."

I managed a team of 20 people in organizing and tracking a major warehouse operation.

 Directed a multifunctional team of 20 federal and contractor personnel in organizing, tracking, and improving a 24/7 warehouse of critical inventory valued at $50M+.

(This uses action-based verbs and adjectives, but don't overuse them!)

 Detail-oriented, drive, versatile, results-focused, and dedicated leader with 20 years of experience.

(This uses too many action-oriented adjectives in a row without any specific action verbs that clarify actual tasks.)

 Skilled Strategic Planner with 20+ years of broadening experience in developing, gaining support for, implementing, and improving comprehensive strategies for Fortune 500 companies.

(This uses relevant action verbs descriptive of the applicant's tasks.)

Avoid vague language.

Example of vague language: Worked with supervisor to send equipment to other units in Iraq and the U.S.

Example of specific language: Planned logistical movement of 350 different tools, systems, and related equipment across international boundaries to support the Global War on Terrorism; more than $10M worth of inventory shipped with 100% accountability.

In general, choose active voice over passive voice when describing duties and accomplishments.

Example of passive voice with first-person POV (avoid): As part of my responsibilities, hardware and software were developed and a help desk was operated.

Example of active voice with assumed first-person POV, without personal pronouns (use): Oversaw a 24/7 help desk that provided expert technical support and customer service to more than 20 globally dispersed stakeholder agencies, troubleshooting and solving a broad range of Information Technology (IT) problems to support continuity of operations.

Use Plain English
Describe skills and experience in universally accepted terms common to your occupation and profession that could be readily understood in both the public and private sectors. Minimize the use of acronyms. If you must use them, spell them out at least once and explain what they represent, what processes or systems they describe, and how you have used the knowledge, skills, or abilities associated with them.

Keep Paragraphs Short
To make your resume easier to read to the human and electronic eye, add a blank line after every 10 lines or so. It's fine to include more than one paragraph for each experience; just keep the paragraphs short.

Don't Be Fancy
Don't use fancy tools such as graphics, italics, underline, shadows, and reverses (white letters on black background) or signs and symbols (% # * =), and don't type your information in all capital letters.

Don't Be Vague
Emphasize nouns and verbs and provide concrete statements of your accomplishments in the correct tense for past or present positions.

Using Acronyms

When you use acronyms (such as IT, TQM, QDR, COTR, SOW, and so forth), you must type out the full designation/title for the initial usage—e.g., Total Quality Management (TQM).

This will make it easier for the Human Resources (HR) Manager or hiring authority at whom your resume is aimed. OPM also advises against using too many acronyms within an application. The reader, often an HR staffer, may not be familiar with the specifics of the applicant's job or industry.

> **Take Note**
>
> We cannot stress attention to detail enough. Read the vacancy announcement and the "How to Apply" tab closely before applying. Each job announcement can be a little different (and some can be unique). You want to submit exactly what the announcement asks for, in exactly the way it asks—no more and no less.

How to Write Your SES Application Cover Letter

SES hiring agencies will rarely request a cover letter as part of an SES application. In fact, watch very carefully for vacancy announcements that specifically instruct you not to send a cover letter. However, there are occasions for which a vacancy announcement will request a "letter of interest" or "letter of intent."

These two documents are very closely related and almost interchangeable. This document will serve as the hiring manager's first impression of you, so make it memorable. Introduce yourself in a professional manner, with a brief summary of your main accomplishments and qualifications and strong interest in candidacy for the position.

Although it is perfectly acceptable to formulate a basic template for your cover letter for use on numerous applications, be sure to target each organization specifically with some research. Go to the agency's homepage and read about its mission and purpose, reiterate its purpose, and demonstrate the similarity between your own goals and aspirations and those of the agency.

Remember, your application is a marketing presentation and you are the product, so generate interest in yourself by making the cover letter short, interesting, and engaging. Make the reader want to learn more about you by presenting a few tidbits of information, such as degrees from notable educational institutions, similar experience with other organizations, and a brief summary of your top three accomplishments that directly relate to the position for which you are applying.

A few additional tips:

Examine the vacancy announcement to find the Point of Contact (POC) for the position to which you are applying and address the letter specifically to that person. Do not open the letter with the too generic and widely overused "To Whom it May Concern," or even "Dear Hiring Manager."

Part of the purpose of the cover letter or letter of interest is to help the Human Resources (HR) or Hiring Manager narrow down the pool of applicants by asking you to include certain elements such as geographic location preferences, salary history, or military experience. Ensure you have addressed everything requested in the vacancy announcement.

If the agency wants to know about your education, include it. If it wants to know what geographical locations you're willing to accept, let the agency know. If it wants your salary history for the last 10 years, list it. Remember, being able to follow instructions is a top priority in working for the government.

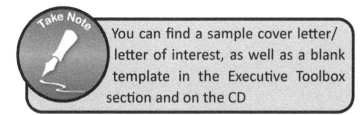
Your closing paragraph should reiterate how well you would fit in with the organization. You should be assertive here: Ask for action to be taken in the form of an interview or consultation.

Check Point 3 Summary

By now, you should be well on your way to developing a detailed and compelling SES resume. As we've discussed, it's extremely important to include all required information and to focus on your accomplishments, rather than just general or vague job descriptions that could apply to anyone working in the same position.

Your accomplishments should be strong, specific, and quantifiable and demonstrate skills that are relevant to the position for which you are applying. It is equally important to submit exactly the information the vacancy announcement calls for, and in exactly the right format (page length, font size, margins, etc.)

The only way to do this is by reading the job announcement closely and contacting the HR representative on the announcement to clarify any questions. Now that you have learned what you need to know to write your own SES resume, let's move on to your ECQs and TQs.

Check Point Notes

Check Point 4

Writing Your ECQs and TQs

WRITING YOUR ECQs AND TQs

Graduate-level Writing Assignment, Anyone?

Now it's time for another reality check. Executive Core Qualifications (ECQs) are not easy to write. They must be written at an executive level, they must be formatted in the way that the Office of Personnel Management (OPM) requires, and the topics must also be executive and impactful in scope. For many SES applicants, the problem isn't that they can't think of an example; the problem is that they have so many examples that they can't seem to express just one or two for each ECQ!

Moreover, no matter how hard a Qualifications Review Board (QRB) might try to be objective about every set of ECQs it reads, let's face it—QRB members are still human beings, and there may be any number of unknown factors and variables affecting them when they read your ECQs.

Ultimately, there is no way to be completely sure what a given QRB will think and decide on a given day, and there is no mathematical formula or guarantee for "getting ECQs right." Perhaps it's not surprising to know that some poorly written ECQs have made it past QRBs and some fantastic ones have been rejected.

Similarly, some less-qualified applicants have passed because they presented their experience and addressed the competencies so well, while other immensely qualified leaders have not passed because they ignored the competencies and other best practices.

All you can do is present your strongest career accomplishments in the various ECQs, follow the rules of submitting ECQs, and make it as easy as possible for the reader to find clear and strong evidence of all the competencies.

Within the ECQs are 28 competencies or skills seen

As you learned in our review of the SES hiring process, there are multiple parts of your application, and they are all important. But the ECQs are at the very heart of an SES application package. ECQs are a set of qualifications developed by OPM to represent the leadership knowledge and abilities deemed essential to SES success. The five ECQs are: Leading Change, Leading People, Results Driven, Business Acumen, and Building Coalitions.

as collectively demonstrating a particular ECQ. There are also six fundamental competencies and these are attributes that serve as the foundation for each of the ECQs. Below you will find explanations of each ECQ and the associated competencies.

Think of your ECQs as a "portfolio" that highlights some of your most impactful career accomplishments. They are putting time limits (past five to seven years, and definitely not older than ten), page limits, and even margin limits on you. In other words, they don't want you to use broad, overarching language and try to talk about everything you've done. They want to see a collection of selected stories/accomplishments, and then they can assume/infer that you can apply the skill sets you've gained in other, higher-level roles.

ECQ 1: Leading Change

Leading Change is the ability to engender strategic change, both inside and outside of an organization, so that it can achieve its organizational goals. Accomplishing this requires establishing and implementing an organizational vision, even within shifting environments. Leading Change is composed of six skills:

Creativity and Innovation

Creative, innovative leaders are those able to think "outside the box" by questioning conventional ways of doing business, developing new insights, and designing or implementing cutting-edge processes.

External Awareness

External awareness is the ability to understand and stay abreast of policies and trends that may affect the organization or the views of its stakeholders. These trends and policies can be local, national, or international. The effective change leader is equally aware of how internal organizational trends and policies can have external effects.

Flexibility

Flexibility is essential to Leading Change since, by its nature, change can be fluid, requiring shifts in approaches. For change leaders, flexibility is the ability to remain open and adaptive to potential changes, new information, or unanticipated obstacles.

Resilience

No matter how difficult situations may become, change leaders are able to recover quickly, respond effectively, and remain persistent and optimistic.

Strategic Thinking

Strategic thinking is the ability to formulate and implement priorities and plans that capitalize on opportunities while also managing potential risks and remaining consistent with an organization's long-term interests.

Vision

While strategic thinking seeks to remain consistent with organizational interests, vision is the ability to build and shape those interests. Visionary change leaders serve as the catalysts for organizational change, building shared, long-term views and consensus, and translating those into actions.

> **Writing a Leading Change Narrative**
> First, think about situations in which your efforts brought about strategic change to meet an organizational goal.

Here are some examples of topics you might use for your Leading Change ECQ:

- Developing a new vision for an organization in disorder or garnering support for another's vision under difficult circumstances, overcoming resistance, and obtaining buy-in;

- Starting up a new organization; garnering support, resources, and manpower from scratch;

- Designing/implementing new, streamlined work procedures or processes to improve operations, cost reductions, and overall performance;

- Introducing automated programs, tools, and technologies to optimize business performance;

- Leading a merger, acquisition, joint venture, and business-building initiative.

Once you select an appropriate topic, try starting with an external vision of the program, describing how it was perceived by outsiders or government entities or if you had to deal with and overcome any internal or external resistance.

What were some of the key national and international policies as well as economic, political, and social trends affecting the organization? (external awareness)

Now that you've set up the problem or situation you needed to change, including all of the obstacles in your path, it's time to describe your actions and results. Write about how you took a strategic view (strategic thinking) of the situation, and established an organizational vision (vision) and change management plan.

Next, describe exactly what you did to overcome resistance, gain support for the vision/plan, and lead a transformation. You also want to show how you remained positive and proactive, even when there were bumps in the road. Did you maintain focus and intensity, even in the face of adversity, pressure, and pushback? (flexibility/resilience)

Finally, you want to show how something you did, or a plan or method you used, was new to the organization. How did you think "outside the box" to manage and drive positive change? (creativity/innovation)

Since you need to tell your story in the Challenge-Context-Action-Result (CCAR) format, and you've addressed all the competencies above, it's time to capture the results. What changed as a result of your efforts? Did the culture around a specific issue or program change?

Hint: The problem or change that you explained in the challenge/context section should be addressed in the results section. Also, it's nice to include any formal or informal recognition you or your team received for these efforts.

ECQ 2: Leading People

The ability to lead people is an essential skill for any leader in any organization or setting. For the SES, OPM defines this ECQ specifically as also encompassing abilities to foster others' development within an

inclusive workplace. Here, Leading People is more than simply managing or directing their actions and the skill set that makes up this ECQ is indicative of that difference. There are four key competencies involved in this ECQ:

Conflict Management
Conflict management refers not only to resolving conflicts constructively but also to the ability to balance the encouragement of creativity and differing opinions against the potential for counterproductive confrontations.

Leveraging Diversity
Leveraging diversity is considered one of the most important skills within the Leading People ECQ. It is the ability to effectively foster within an organization a level of inclusiveness that values and leverages diversity and individual differences to achieve organizational goals and missions.

As noted previously, a failure to demonstrate this skill effectively is one of the top reasons candidates do not pass the QRB.

Developing Others
Some of the most effective leaders are those who actively develop the skills and abilities of those in their organization. The ability to develop others includes providing regular feedback and

opportunities for development through formal and/or informal means.

Team Building
The leader who excels at team building is one who promotes a sense of pride, trust, and commitment in an organization's members and who motivates them to accomplish the organization's mission. Effective team building leads to all members having a sense of ownership in the organization's success.

Writing a Leading People Narrative
Imagine a senior military officer who is retiring after 20 years of distinguished service and trying to enter the SES.

Now, imagine that he/she is writing his/her Leading People narrative. This individual is clearly a strong leader, and had led organizations of more than 1,000 people and provided executive oversight to 12 different organization comprised of more than 100,000 people stationed around the world.

Now, let's say this individual provides a great description of all this leadership, but focuses purely on leadership philosophy and the complex missions the organization had to accomplish.

Shouldn't those folks in the QRB still be able to tell what a great leader this person is? Maybe, but maybe not. Even though this individual is clearly a seasoned leader with worldwide experience in a variety of field and office environments, the ECQ likely won't pass muster and the board will deny it.

Why? This is simply because the competencies were not addressed. The important thing to remember here is that the Office of Personnel Management (OPM) has been very specific about HOW it wants examples presented.

So, even though every example is different, every career is different, and there is no "cookie-cutter"

way to write an ECQ narrative, there are certain criteria that a strong ECQ should meet.

First, OPM wants specific examples presented in the Challenge-Context-Action-Result (CCAR) format. However, more importantly, OPM wants the examples to be expressed through the "lens" of the competencies. If these criteria (along with a few others) are not met, the board will probably reject the applicant's ECQs.

Let's get back to our example. It's not enough that this individual provided an example that clearly "proves" his/her leadership experience. Unfortunately, this applicant failed to tell the story though the lens of the competencies.

In other words, while providing a great story of leading large organizations through major challenges, this individual failed to describe how he/she built the team, developed individual members of the team, leveraged diversity, and managed conflict (the four competencies required for Leading People).

One of the best ways to ensure you address the competencies in any ECQ is to turn those competencies into questions, and then answer those questions in the "action" section of your narrative. Regardless of what a great leader you are, and how logical it seems that your "Leading People" examples demonstrate your leadership, go back to the competencies. If you don't weave those into the narrative, you are at serious risk of being rejected by the QRB. Here are some of the questions you might ask when writing up your Leading People narrative:

- What did you do, specifically, to build a more cohesive team environment? Did you hold weekly meetings or social gatherings, or provide incentives, awards, time off, etc.? (team building)

- Did you have to handle conflicts between two or more employees or offices? What did you do to resolve the situation constructively? (conflict management)

- Did you provide opportunities for or encourage staff to enroll in professional development opportunities or extend anyone's responsibilities to a higher level of job description or expectation? (developing others)

- Did you encourage female candidates in a traditionally male-dominated field or recruit to minority groups? (leveraging diversity)

- Did you select teams for projects that included a diverse mix of individuals—professionally, educationally, culturally, etc.? (leveraging diversity)

- Did you utilize intern programs, fellowships, or other professional development programs to recruit young talent? Did you then arrange for them to be mentored into the mainstream? (developing others/leveraging diversity)

ECQ 3: Results Driven

This ECQ is the ability to get the job done. It encompasses an ability to meet both organizational needs and customer expectations. Those who excel in this competency are able to effectively harness

risk assessment, technical knowledge, and problem analysis to create high-quality results.

The skills that make up the Results Driven ECQ are:

Accountability
Accountability is the ability to hold both oneself and others accountable for delivering timely, cost-effective, and high-quality results. The leader who demonstrates this skill is able to determine organizational objectives, set priorities, delegate tasks appropriately, and accept responsibility for mistakes. While doing so, this leader also ensures compliance with established rules and controls.

Customer Service
Customers include those both inside and outside of an organization. A leader who excels in customer service not only delivers the highest quality in products and services, but also successfully anticipates customers' needs and continually seeks ways to improve service and delivery.

Decisiveness
Decisive leaders are able to make effective, informed decisions, despite extensive data or information. These leaders recognize the potential implications of their decisions and are able to do so even while knowing some of their decisions may have negative consequences.

Entrepreneurship
In many respects, government agencies must operate

like businesses. Entrepreneurial leaders recognize this and are able to successfully exhibit a business mindset to take calculated risks, improve products and services, and identify potential opportunities suited to helping an organization meet its objectives.

Problem Solving

Problem solving is an important ability at any level of an organization, but it is a particularly vital skill for effective leaders. Leaders who excel in this skill are able to develop viable recommendations and solutions based on their abilities to identify and analyze problems and to create and weigh potential solutions to make the best choices.

Technical Credibility

Whatever the program area or field, the best leaders are those with a solid understanding of and ability to apply the requirements, principles, and procedures necessary for success in their fields. These leaders are experts in their industries, as well as knowledgeable of what works and how to best get a job done.

Writing a Results Driven Narrative

The Results Driven ECQ involves the ability to meet organizational goals and customer expectations. The competencies are Accountability, Customer Service, Problem Solving, Decisiveness, Technical Credibility, and Entrepreneurship.

Inherent to this ECQ is the ability to own and manage responsibilities and make decisions that produce high-quality results by applying technical knowledge, analyzing problems, and calculating/mitigating risks.

This includes the ability to make timely, effective decisions and to produce lasting results through the assessment and evaluation of programs and policies, as well as to hold yourself and others accountable. Here are some of the questions you might ask when writing up your Results Driven ECQ narrative:

> **Take Note**
>
> Regardless of how great you are at creating results, and how strongly you think your example meets the title of Results Driven, you must look at the specific competencies and ask yourself whether you can address most or all of them effectively.
>
> One of the best ways to do this is to turn those competencies into questions, and then answer those questions in the "action" section of your narrative.

- What is the topic of the example? Was this an opportunity to improve the organization's production, products, or customer service? (problem solving)

- What was the pressure to complete this project? Was it customer-driven? (customer service)

- Who were you accountable to during this initiative, and how did you ensure accountability at all levels? (accountability)

- Describe exactly what you did (your actions, decisions, communications, etc.) that moved the project, task, or problem to resolution or outcome. (problem solving)

- Were you ever responsible for any make-or-break decision that could have affected the project? (decisiveness)

- What actions did you take that demonstrate your mastery or specialized knowledge in your specific field? (technical credibility)

- In your results, can you describe how your actions and efforts positioned the organization for future success and growth? (entrepreneurship)

ECQ 4: Business Acumen

While entrepreneurship is a mindset and approach, Business Acumen is the knowledge and ability to leverage available resources to achieve organizational goals.

Business Acumen encompasses three major competencies:

Financial Management. More than generally understanding the financial processes of an organization, leaders possessing this qualification demonstrate knowledge and abilities in preparing, justifying, and administering program budgets as well as the ability to set financial priorities, oversee procurements, and monitor spending. Leaders successful in Financial Management know how to achieve the most with the least amount of funds.

Human Capital Management. Human Capital Management is a leader's ability to build and manage a workforce that performs well in a variety of situations.

This skill includes the ability to build an efficient workforce while taking into consideration factors such as budget limitations, organizational goals, and overall staffing needs.

Leaders who excel in Human Capital Management ensure high standards in recruitment, hiring, and follow-through while appropriately appraising, rewarding, and correcting workforce performance.

Technology Management. Successful leaders know how to efficiently use available technological resources. These leaders make the effort to remain knowledgeable on technological developments and are able to leverage appropriate innovations to achieve organizational goals without compromising information access or security.

Writing a Business Acumen Narrative

Business Acumen has three competencies (Financial Manage-ment, Human Capital Management, and Technology Management), but unlike the other ECQs, they don't always "flow" as naturally together.

In fact, many people find it extremely difficult to think of career stories that incorporate all three of the Business Acumen competencies. And even when they do, the stories tend to be overly dense and confusing because there's just too much information packed in there.

Here is a highly effective best practice and perspective to consider for Business Acumen: Imagine you are on the review board. You may be reading career stories from a senior military officer, a corporate executive, or a seasoned federal manager.

Moreover, the setting could be anywhere in the world, from the boardroom, to the battlefield, to countless other work environments.

Regardless of the applicant's background or the setting, you, as part of the review board, need to be able to see that the applicant is comfortable and capable in managing the financial, human capital, and technological aspects of programs and organizations. So, when writing your Business Acumen examples, think of this particular ECQ as three "mini-ECQs," instead of trying to combine the somewhat disparate topics of financial, human capital, and technology management.

The examples may have to be a bit shorter than normal, since all three still have to fit within the two-page limit. Additionally, the three CCAR examples can come from different positions or programs within the past 10 years, or they can come from the same position.

Ultimately, by taking this straightforward approach, you can more clearly present your top career stories while effectively addressing the Business Acumen competencies.

ECQ 5: Building Coalitions

The final ECQ is Building Coalitions, which encompasses the ability to build effective relationships internally and externally to achieve mutual goals.

External organizations include other federal agencies; state, local, and foreign governments; companies; non-profits; and international organizations.

The ECQ measures of success in Building Coalitions include:

Partnering

Leaders who are successful in partnering understand the need to create win-win relationships with others and work to develop such alliances through mutual collaboration. Rather than creating senior-subordinate relationships, leaders who excel in developing partnerships seek to build more equal alliances focused on achieving common goals.

Political Savvy

More than the knowledge of basic protocols, political savvy is the ability to understand and act on the nuances of human relationships. Politically savvy leaders are able to recognize internal and external politics and are accomplished at taking advantage of

those realities to meet organizational needs.

Influencing/Negotiating

Building Coalitions, whether internal or external, relies on a leader's ability to develop consensus around goals by persuading others. Leaders who are successful in influencing and negotiating understand the need to give and take in relationships in order to obtain the information and support needed to accomplish their missions.

Writing a Building Coalitions Narrative

In addition, if you use the five tips below, you will be well on your way to developing a strong Building Coalitions narrative that effectively demonstrates your executive potential.

1. Select an example that shows you working with stakeholders across multiple organizations, or at least multiple offices, divisions, etc. within your own organization. Use the Challenge-Context-Action-Result (CCAR) format to tell the story.

2. For Challenge/Context, clearly describe the stakeholder agencies involved, any politics or hidden agendas between them, and what goal or initiative you needed to rally them all around.

3. In the Actions section of the example, be sure to describe any partnerships you created, and how you communicated with stakeholders to bring them all together toward that common cause.

4. Next, describe how you overcame politics, and then cite one or two specific issues on which you had to negotiate to positively influence decisions and reach win-win compromises.

5. In the Results part of your example, describe what the group was able to accomplish together, as a consequence of your communications/involvement. Be as specific as possible and measure/quantify any details. Finally, be sure to describe how your efforts improved interagency relationships from a short- and long-term perspective.

Fundamental ECQ Competencies

These competencies do not need to be addressed directly, but are cross-cutting and should be addressed by your complete set of ECQs.

Interpersonal Skills

Treats other with courtesy, sensitivity, and respect. Considers and responds appropriately to the needs and feelings of different people in different situations.

Oral Communication

Makes clear and convincing oral presentations. Listens effectively; clarifies information, as needed.

OPM's "Guide to SES Qualifications" provides these definitions of the competencies and much more information. Simply conduct an Internet search for "OPM Guide to SES Qualifications."

Integrity/Honesty

Behaves in an honest, fair, and ethical manner. Shows consistency in words and actions. Models high standards of ethics.

Written Communication

Writes in a clear, concise, organized, and convincing manner for the intended audience.

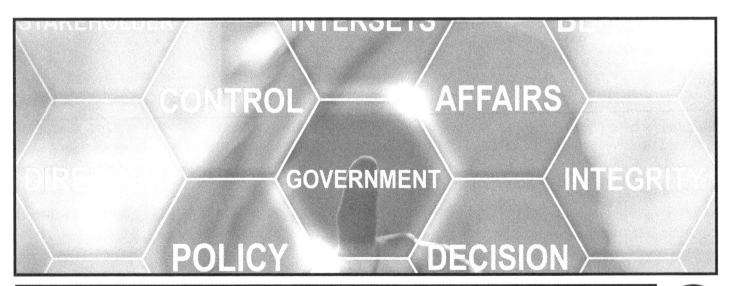

Brainstorming

Use the space on the following pages to jot down general ideas for each ECQ. For example: Assistant Deputy Director, 2017, leading diversity initiative.

At this point, you simply want to outline at least one example for each ECQ, and preferably two. The real value of this exercise is that once you have all of your potential examples organized in one place, you can easily decide if one might work better in another ECQ than you originally intended.

If your topic for Leading Change involves a lot of collaboration, negotiation, and building support while overcoming hidden agendas and internal politics, you might want to move that one to Building Coalitions and then come up with a new example for Leading Change. This type of brainstorming, before you begin the actual writing, is invaluable to the overall process.

As you brainstorm your topics, refer to the ECQ and competency explanations in the beginning of this Check Point and make sure you can address them in the examples you are choosing.

Finally, many professionals like you have found it extremely helpful to brainstorm their potential topics with a friend, colleague, supervisor, or mentor who has a clear understanding of their experience, leadership, and accomplishments.

If you would prefer to type out your responses, we have provided a Microsoft Word version of this Brainstorming Exercise on the CD.

LEADING CHANGE

Creativity/Innovation ■*External Awareness* ■*Flexibility* ■*Resilience* ■*Strategic Thinking* ■*Vision*

POTENTIAL IDEAS/SCENARIOS FOR SELECTING YOUR STORIES

■ Situations in which your efforts brought about impactful change in support or strategic goals, perhaps within and outside the organization.

■ Developing a long-term vision and strategic plan that challenged conventional ways of thinking and addressed shifting requirements such as economy, and political environments.

■ Balancing change and continuity while creating a healthy work environment and focusing on long-term goals.

■ Dealing effectively with pressure and maintaining focus and intensity while remaining optimistic and persistent, even under adversity.

■ Standing up a new organization; garnering support, resources, and staff from scratch.

■ Designing/implementing new, streamlined policies or business processes to improve operations, cost reductions, and overall performance.

■ Developing a new vision for an organization in disorder or shifting the organizational culture while overcoming resistance and obtaining buy-in.

■ Introducing automated programs, tools, and technologies to optimize business performance.

■ Leading a merger, acquisition, joint venture, or other business-building initiative.

Potential example 1:

Potential example 2:

LEADING PEOPLE

Conflict Management ■ *Leveraging Diversity* ■ *Developing Others* ■ *Team Building*

POTENTIAL IDEAS/SCENARIOS FOR SELECTING YOUR STORIES

- Turning around a dysfunctional staff by determining skills gaps, addressing those gaps through hiring and training and development, emphasizing team as well as individual performance, and making the group more professional and productive.

- Rallying your team around a specific challenge or problem while demonstrating your ability to build the team, develop subordinates, manage conflict, and leverage diversity.

- Building a new team and leading it successfully to meet or exceed high level goals.

- Creating an inclusive workplace that fosters the development of others, facilitates cooperation and teamwork, and supports constructive resolution of conflicts.

Potential example 1:

Potential example 2:

RESULTS DRIVEN

Accountability ■*Customer Service* ■*Decisiveness* ■*Entrepreneurship* ■*Problem Solving* ■*Technical Credibility*

POTENTIAL IDEAS/SCENARIOS FOR SELECTING YOUR STORIES

■ Major-scale programs/initiatives you directed that solved a strategic/organizational problem and positively affected your organization, either by improving business practices or through monetary savings or profit.

■ Problems you solved that increased productivity or resulted in other positive results, positioning your customers and the organization for future success.

■ Recognition for noteworthy or exceptional service and attention to customers, while holding subordinates accountable for quality results through budget adherence, milestone reporting, or other specific program oversight/management tools.

■ Stepping in and taking the initiative to solve some growing customer-related problem, while managing technical operations and keeping senior officials apprised.

■ Managing responsibilities and make decisions that produce high-quality results by applying "technical" knowledge within your own field of expertise.

Potential example 1:

Potential example 2:

BUSINESS ACUMEN

This is the only ECQ that doesn't call for two examples. This ECQ involves the ability to manage human, financial, and information resources strategically. It is as if you are writing three mini-ECQs under the Business Acumen umbrella, so please provide one CCAR story for each area below (3 total) on the next page.

POTENTIAL IDEAS/SCENARIOS FOR SELECTING YOUR STORIES

Financial Management:

- Leading the development of a creative budget strategy to get something funded that otherwise wouldn't have been funded.
- Managing a program or project that experienced funding problems, which involved examining priorities, adjusting work scope, implementing cost-saving techniques, and securing additional funding, to solve the budget crisis and to enable the program/project to meet milestones.
- Have you prepared, justified, and administered program budgets? In what amount?
- Have you made creative use of a procurement system, leading a source evaluation board under difficult circumstances, streamlining the use of contracts by a program, or managing the development of an important solicitation?

Human Capital Management:

- Leading a staffing analysis or recruiting drive to hire and train new staff and better align work with overarching strategic goals.
- Have you assessed current and future staffing needs based on organizational goals and budget realities? Did you develop staffing plans and/or realign human capital to optimize business practices?
- Have you acquired and developed staffs whose size, skills, and deployment met organizational needs? If so, how?
- Have you successfully recruited personnel and/or improved their performance within the organization?
- Have you been involved in improving traditional employee benefits?
- Have you introduced any innovative employee benefits and incentives (e.g., flex time, on-site daycare, etc.)?

Technology Management:

- Playing a lead role in developing and/or implementing some new technology or automated process in the workplace that leverages technology to improve business processes and increase efficiency.
- Have you expanded any information systems and technologies?
- Have you connected technology to critical functional business areas of accounting, finance, marketing, HR, and operations? (In other words, how have you expanded electronic government?)
- Have you integrated technology's vital role in helping your organization gain a competitive advantage?
- Have you led any technology projects to transform business operations or practices?
- Have you designed aggressive solutions to standardize business practices through leading-edge technologies?

Potential Financial Management example:

Potential Human Capital Management example:

Potential Technology Management example:

BUILDING COALITIONS

POSSIBLE IDEAS/SCENARIOS FOR SELECTING YOUR EXAMPLES

- A coalition you built from both internal and external agencies to create mutual benefit between all stakeholders, such as sharing resources and information.

- When you persuaded others, built consensus through give and take, gained cooperation from others to obtain information and accomplish goals, and facilitated win-win situations.

- A situation in which you mastered organizational politics using political savvy to both influence positive change and achieve career success at the same time, even when negative organizational politics were evident.

- A situation when you served as a uniting force, building alliances and overcoming politics/personal agendas to forge a group that was focused on a shared set of goals.

- A situation in which you had to use strong persuasive/negotiation skills to achieve an organizational goal or forge an interagency or multi-national agreement or Memorandum of Understanding.

- Describe how you've established partnerships to get things done that organizations working on their own could not have achieved, overcoming resistance to cooperate, perhaps as a member of a taskforce or working group, and playing the lead role in bringing members who previously could not agree to consensus.

Potential example 1:

Potential example 2:

Comparing Your Potential Stories to the ECQs

Now that you have some stories, it's time to decide which ECQs in which to display them. To help with this, we have turned the competencies to very simple, prompting "questions."

By comparing your potential topics/stories to the competency questions for each ECQ, you can decide if it is a good fit. After all, this is the most important assessment tool that OPM uses to decide if your ECQs are approved; are the competencies strongly and clearly addressed in the narratives?

It's a good idea to read the questions and ask yourself, "Will I be able to provide a few thoughts or a paragraph on most—if not all—of the competency questions?" Or, "Can I tell the story through this perspective that OPM wants to see?"

If the answer is no, then try to find another ECQ where the story might be a better fit. If the answer is yes, then the story is probably a good fit, so you can use the full ECQ builder to guide in developing your write-ups!

You can do this little analysis in several ways. First, you can use the ECQ builder on the CD and simply review the competency questions in the ACTIONS section of each ECQ.

For your convenience, those questions are also included below.

LEADING CHANGE
Creativity/Innovation | External Awareness
Flexibility | Resilience | Strategic Thinking | Vision

- What was your plan of action? **(Strategic Thinking)** Was the vision of this project established by mandate, or did you create the vision to improve a process or result **(Vision)**?

- Did it involve introducing any cutting-edge programs or processes that challenged conventional approaches? **(Creativity and Innovation)**

- What are the key national and international policies and economic, political, and social trends that affect the organization? **(External Awareness)**

- Did you encounter any unexpected obstacles or problems? [e.g., how did you adapt to new information, changing conditions, or unexpected obstacles? What did you do to overcome any setbacks and achieve buy-in from those resistant to change? **(Flexibility/Resilience)**

LEADING PEOPLE
Conflict Management | Leveraging Diversity
Developing Others | Team Building

- Describe how you brought the team together and built a stronger sense of pride and teamwork. Maybe you held weekly meetings, social gatherings, incentives, awards, time off, etc. **(Team Building)**

- Did you have to handle conflicts between two or more employees/groups? What did you do to resolve the tension in a constructive manner? **(Conflict Management)**

- Did you provide opportunities for, or encourage employees and staff to enroll in, professional development opportunities or extend anyone's responsibilities to a higher level of job description or expectation? Did you utilize intern programs, fellowships, or other professional development programs to recruit young talent? Did you then arrange for them to be mentored into the mainstream? **(Developing Others)**

- Did you encourage female candidates in a traditionally male-dominated field or recruit minorities, etc.? Did you select teams for projects that included a diverse mix of individuals—professionally, educationally, culturally, racially, etc.? **(Leveraging Diversity)**

RESULTS DRIVEN
Accountability | Customer Service | Decisiveness
Entrepreneurship | Problem Solving
Technical Credibility

- To whom were you accountable? Who was accountable to you? **(Accountability)**

- Who exactly were your customers, and how did you plan to improve service and support? **(Customer Service)**

- Describe exactly what you did (your actions, decisions, communications, etc.) that moved the project, task, or problem to resolution or outcome. **(Problem Solving)**

- Were you responsible for any make-or-break decision(s) that could have affected the project? **(Decisiveness)**

- How did you position your customer and/or the organization for future/continued success and growth? **(Entrepreneurship)**

BUSINESS ACUMEN: Financial Management

- Have you ever managed a large or complex budget effectively?

- Have you led the development of a creative budget strategy to get something funded that otherwise wouldn't have been funded?

- Have you managed a program or project that experienced funding problems—which involved examining priorities, adjusting work scope, implementing cost-saving techniques, and securing additional funding—to solve the budget crisis and to enable the program/project to meet milestones?

> There is not one right way to write an effective ECQ. How could there be, when such a diverse group of people is engaged in so many various career fields within the federal government?

Take Note

BUSINESS ACUMEN: Human Capital Management

- Have you led a staffing analysis or recruiting drive to hire and train new staff and better align work with overarching strategic goals?

- Have you assessed current and future staffing needs based on organizational goals and budget realities? Did you develop staffing plans and/or realign human capital to optimize business practices?

- Have you acquired and developed staffs whose size, skills, and deployment met organizational needs?

BUSINESS ACUMEN: Technology Management

- Have you played a lead role in developing and/or implementing some new technology or automated process in the workplace that leverages technology to improve business processes and increase efficiency?

- Have you connected technology to critical functional business areas of accounting, finance, marketing, HR, and operations?

- Have you integrated technology's vital role in helping your organization gain a competitive advantage?

- Have you led any technology projects to transform business operations or practices?

- Have you designed aggressive solutions to standardize business practices through leading-edge technologies?

BUILDING COALITIONS
Partnering | Political Savvy
Influencing/Negotiation

- Describe exactly what you did to form partnerships with key stakeholders, and why. With whom did you conduct briefings and other meetings? **(Partnering)**

- Were negotiations a part of this example? Did you participate in the negotiations? Who were willing partners and who had to be convinced?

How did you achieve buy-in from those resistant to partnership or compromise? **(Influencing/Negotiating)**

- Did any of the partners have hidden agendas? **(Political Savvy)**

- Were there any behind-the-scenes activities or backdoor politics of which you had to be aware? How did you overcome those? **(Political Savvy)**

CPG's Exclusive ECQ Builders do not guarantee that you will select good examples in accordance with the guidance in this book. Instead, the builders are designed to prompt you into the right way of approaching your ECQ narratives—to use the CCAR format, to stick to stories within the past 10 years, and to tell your stories through the lens of the competencies for each ECQ.

While these builders will help, there is no guarantee that by using them your ECQs will pass a QRB. We recommend that once you fill out the ECQ builders provided on the CD, you then copy/paste everything into a word-processing application, such as Microsoft Word, revising and streamlining as you do.

You can review sample ECQs on the CD and in the Executive Toolbox beginning on page 103.

ECQ Best Practices

CareerPro Global
YOUR CAREER IS OUR BUSINESS™

How To Write Executive Core Qualifications (ECQs) That the Review Boards Will Love!

CareerPro Global's writers and coaches have developed and refined these best practices while helping over 3,000 corporate, federal, and military leaders apply for Senior Executive Service (SES) positions

Use the 10-year rule: If an example happened more than 10 years ago, don't bother. The board won't like it.

Use the Challenge-Context-Actions-Results (CCAR) format: There are numerous ways to tell a story, but the Office of Personnel Management (OPM) wants your career stories presented in a logical format on the page, using Challenge-Context-Actions-Results. In addition, examples should include specific, impactful results.

Present executive narratives, not project management descriptions: It is easy to share detailed, technical write-ups of projects, but OPM wants specific career stories that are impactful and executive in scope. For instance, did you work with senior officials, cross organizational lines, and create results that have widespread and long-term strategic impact? It is also best to keep the reader in mind, and assume that they do not share your background. Simply put: express stories in a clear, concise way that any executive can understand and appreciate.

Use two examples per ECQ: OPM will accept one example per ECQ, but it is strongly recommended that you provide two each. Here is another tip: For ECQ#4, Business Acumen, think of it as three separate "mini-ECQs." The whole write up still needs to fit within two pages, but it is best to present one strong CCAR example for each of the following areas – Financial, Technology, and Human Capital Management.

Use the competencies as your guide: Don't overlook the critical importance of telling your career stories through the "lens" of the competencies. Instead, use the process below as a powerful decision making tool.

1 BRAINSTORM
With all of these best practices in mind, take the time to write down two potential topics for each ECQ (three for Business Acumen).

2 OUTLINE/COMPARE
Before you write your ECQs, you should outline your potential topics and then compare them to the competencies for each ECQ. Next, ask yourself, "Will I be able to address most, if not all, of these competencies effectively in my write-up?" If the answer is yes, you are probably on the right track. However, if the answer is no, or if it is unclear, then your topic may not be a good fit for that particular ECQ. The boards will be looking for evidence of the competencies in your ECQs.

3 DEVELOP
Once you have considered all of the best practices, and completed step one and two, you are ready to develop your ECQs!

ECQs & the Competencies

Leading Change	Leading People	Results Driven	Business Acumen	Building Coalitions
Creativity /Innovation	Conflict Mgmt	Accountability	Financial Mgmt	Partnering
External Awareness	Leveraging Diversity	Customer Service	Human Capital Mgmt	Political Savvy
Flexibility	Developing Others	Decisiveness	Technology Mgmt	Influencing and/or
Resilience	Team Building	Entrepreneurship		Negotiating
Strategic Thinking		Problem Solving		
Vision		Technical Credibility		

Fundamental Competencies
No need to address fundamental competencies directly, but they should be addressed over the course of the complete ECQ narrative...

Interpersonal Skills	Written Communication	Oral Communication	Continual Learning	Integrity & Honesty	Public Service Motivation

Likewise, OPM provides a number of tips to keep in mind when writing your ECQs and other narratives. We strongly urge you to read them and apply them:

Tips for Writing Effective ECQ Statements and Accomplishment Record Narratives

(from page 35 of *OPM's 2010 Guide to SES Qualifications*)

- Focus on leadership rather than managerial and technical abilities; all three are important, but leadership is most important.

- Follow the CCAR (Challenge-Context-Action-Result) model.

- Each ECQ or competency should contain specific, job-related experiences with specific accomplishments.

- Focus on what you have accomplished personally, but don't exaggerate.

- Show that you have the qualifications needed to succeed in the Senior Executive Service.

- Address the fundamental competencies over the course of the complete ECQ narrative.

- Never combine any of the ECQs or competencies.

- Never address an ECQ or competency by referring the reader to other parts of your application.

- Avoid using an identical example for more than one ECQ or competency.

- Avoid a "laundry list" of activities without context, actions, or accomplishments.

- Focus on your vision for the organization, not your personal vision.

- Focus on recent experience, education, and training. Some reviewers consider experience that's more than 10 years old to be stale.

- Highlight awards or other forms of recognition that relate specifically to an ECQ or competency (e.g., "Human Resources Manager of the Year").

- Include non-federal experiences (e.g., private sector, volunteer, and professional organizations) if they support the ECQ or competency.

- Include relevant formal education or training that has enhanced your skills in a particular ECQ or competency.

- Don't forget to include examples of special assignments and details.

- Include special qualifications if relevant to the position sought: public speaking, publications, languages spoken, membership in related professional organizations or scientific societies, or expertise in a technical area (e.g., budget, information technology).

- Show measurable results, especially in terms of improved customer service, increased efficiency, productivity, or money saved.

Senior Executive Positions in the Intelligence Field

SES positions in the Intelligence field are very similar to other SES openings, and call for a resume, Executive Core Qualifications (ECQs), and, sometimes, several Technical Qualifications (TQs).

However, if that isn't enough, quite often these vacancies also require applicants to respond to "Intelligence Community (IC) Senior Officer Core Qualifications" in a supplemental narrative statement. Specifically, applicants must provide essays that address the three Essential Factors below, which have been pulled directly from a recent job announcement:

IC SENIOR OFFICER CORE QUALIFICATION: You will be assessed against this Senior Officer Core Qualification Standard—Leading the Intelligence Enterprise—to determine your interagency or multi-organizational (business, mission, or professional) leadership competencies.

1. ***Collaboration and Integration.*** IC senior officers have a responsibility to share information and knowledge to achieve results and, in that regard, are expected to build effective networks and alliances with key peers and stakeholders across the IC and/or with other U.S. government (USG), state, local, tribal and foreign officials, as appropriate; actively engage these peers and stakeholders; involve them in key decisions; and effectively leverage these networks and alliances to achieve significant results. In addition, senior officers are expected to create an environment that promotes employee engagement, collaboration, integration, information and knowledge sharing, and the candid, open exchange of diverse points of view. Candidates assessed against this competency must demonstrate knowledge, skill, and/or ability to:

2. Build, leverage, and lead collaborative networks with key peers and stakeholders across the IC and/or in other government/private-sector organizations, or professional/technical disciplines to achieve significant joint/multiagency mission outcomes; and integrate joint/multiagency activities, effectively exercising collaborative plans that realize mutual, joint, or multi-organizational goals.

3. ***Enterprise Focus.*** IC senior officers are expected to demonstrate a deep understanding of how the missions, structures, leaders, and cultures of the various IC components interact and connect, as well as synthesize resources, information, and other inputs to effectively integrate and align component, IC, and USG interests and activities to achieve IC-wide, national, or international priorities. In addition, senior officers are expected to encourage and support joint duty assignments and developmental experiences that develop and reinforce an enterprise focus among their subordinates. Candidates assessed against this competency must demonstrate knowledge, skill, and/or ability to:

   a. Understand the roles, missions, capabilities, and organizational and political realities of the intelligence enterprise, and apply that understanding to drive joint, interagency, or multi-organizational mission accomplishment.

b. Understand how organizations, resources, information, and processes within the IC or interagency/ multi-organizational environment interact with and influence one another, and apply that understanding to solve complex interagency or multi-organizational problems.

4. ***Values-Centered Leadership.*** IC senior officers are expected to personally embody, advance, and reinforce IC core values: a Commitment to selfless service and excellence in support of the IC's mission, as well as to preserving, protecting, and defending the nation's laws and liberties; the integrity and Courage (moral, intellectual, and physical) to seek and speak the truth, to innovate, and to change things for the better, regardless of personal or professional risk; and Collaboration as members of a single IC-wide team, respecting and leveraging the diversity of all members of the IC, their background, their sources and methods, and their points of view. In addition, senior officers are also expected to demonstrate and promote departmental and/or component core values, which may be incorporated in writing, as applicable. Candidates assessed against this competency must demonstrate knowledge, skill, and/or ability to:

a. Promote, reinforce, and reward IC departmental component core values in the workforce and ensure actions, policies, and practices are aligned with, and embody, those values.

b. Ensure organizational strategies, policies, procedures, and actions give appropriate focus, attention, and commitment to diversity of people, points of view, ideas, and insights.

> The IC Senior Office Core Qualifications correlate with many of the 28 competencies in the ECQs. Our guidance is that, if you are part of the IC and you see Intelligence Office Core Qualifications Essential Factors in the job announcement, don't ignore them! More importantly, don't "recycle" the same examples from the ECQs or TQs. The hiring authority will almost certainly notice, and they won't like it.
>
> You must write and submit separate essays for each of these. Sometimes, they are restricted to two pages and sometimes, you are allowed even more space. Check the vacancy announcement, and call to ensure you meet all the specifications.

Writing Strong TQs

Technical Qualifications go by several different names: Mandatory Technical Qualifications (MTQs); Professional Technical Qualifications (PTQs); or Desired Technical Qualifications (DTQs). Regardless of the name, they are an integral part of the SES application and must be given as much time, attention, detail, and weight as the ECQs.

The TQs are critical in the first phase of the screening and interviewing process at the agency level. OPM requires that all narratives be written in the CCAR format.

Essentially, this means that OPM wants to hear detailed examples of your experiences as related to each narrative question from beginning to end. You should make these narratives as reader-friendly as possible. Speak in a clear, understandable language and leave out unnecessary acronyms; if acronyms are necessary, spell them out once in the beginning and use the actual acronym as sparingly as possible.

Select topics that are hard-hitting, took a great deal of effort and technical expertise to achieve, and are highly industry-visible. Think about your most difficult projects—the ones that kept you at the office until 2:00 a.m., the ones that involved bringing together numerous professional disciplines to achieve the mission, and the ones that saved or earned the most money for your employer.

In describing the Challenge(s), think about the biggest problems you faced in solving your problem, achieving your goal, or reaching your milestone. Who was in your way? Who did you have to support you? What were the risks involved and how did you decide which risks were worth taking and which had to be rejected? Where was the money to fund your efforts coming from?

In the Context, you want to set up the story: give the year and your role in the organization. Talk about how the problem came about and the impact or disruption it was having on your organization. Describe the organizational environment and culture. Was your work cut out for you? Did your efforts have adversaries? Was the funding you needed there? What was the external view of your organization by other divisions or outside entities?

The most important parts of the technical example

are Action(s) and Result(s). Action describes what you specifically did to address the Challenge/Context and to directly achieve the Result. Be sure to explain how you developed your strategic plan to achieve your goal.

Talk about your process in detail: Whom did you enlist for help and/or advice? How did you structure your actions? Was there any delegation involved? How did you maintain accountability for both tangible (money) and intangible (employee effort) elements? What sort of interagency communication did you employ, and how did you bring disparate parties together in agreement?

The Result should be reported in as many facts and figures as possible. Give percentages of items, like the reduction of employee attrition, the amount of money saved, the value of equipment that could be reconfigured and reused, the man-hours saved, etc.

Make sure that you end with a "bang"—that the result of your effort is far-reaching, extraordinary, and memorable.

Keep in mind that this statement is about you. While it is understood that managers accomplish tasks and goals through their workforce, use "I" instead of "we" as much as possible: say, "I supervised/oversaw/managed…" Your goal is to convince the hiring authority that you possess the necessary leadership competencies and are qualified to be successful in this executive position. Use the builder that begins on the next page to help you develop your draft TQ narrative. There is also a copy of the builder on the CD in the back of the book. As you did with the ECQs, we recommend you use the outline exercise on the next page to capture your examples before pasting them into a word-processing document such as Microsoft (MS) Word.

Tips for Answering TQ Questions

Be very specific. Provide your role, the date, location, and organization you are using for a topic. Begin every TQ with the overall environment of the organization that brought about the need to perform the action. Detail the approximate number of times or length of time that you have performed an action that supports the TQ.

Do not limit your TQ statements to any one particular experience or training in your current position. This is especially true if you have had limited exposure to a particular TQ in your current position, but have more experience in a former position.

Take Note
As you answer each question, give an example of a personal accomplishment in this category, and be sure to include detailed outcomes as a result of this specific incident and your efforts.

Answers should be specific and clearly reflect the highest level of ability. Quantify in numbers "What," "How," "How Much," etc., and mention the core of the accomplishment (e.g., Leadership, Industry Expertise, etc.).

Limit your answers to experiences from the past five to seven years. Include two examples or topics per TQ. Restrict the TQ to 8,000 characters (or 2 pages). Read the vacancy announcement closely— length and font restrictions will vary from agency to agency.

www.SESWriters.com

TQ Builder: Example 1

CHALLENGE: Describe a specific problem or goal and the obstacles, problems, and challenges you faced in achieving your goal.

_____

_____

_____

CONTEXT: Title of your job or role you are playing in this example. Talk about the individuals and groups with whom you worked, and/or the environment in which you worked, to tackle a particular challenge (e.g., clients, co-workers, Members of Congress, shrinking budget, low morale).

_____

_____

_____

ACTION: Discuss the specific actions you took to address a challenge. Describe your role and actions in resolving the problem or meeting the outcome goals.

_____

_____

_____

_____

_____

RESULTS: Describe results, outcomes, or long-term impacts of your efforts. At a senior level, you should be able to give more than one identifiable, measurable result from your effort.

_____

_____

TQ Builder: Example 2

CHALLENGE: Describe a specific problem or goal and the obstacles, problems, and challenges you faced in achieving your goal.

_____

_____

_____

CONTEXT: Title of your job or role you are playing in this example. Talk about the individuals and groups with whom you worked, and/or the environment in which you worked, to tackle a particular challenge (e.g., clients, co-workers, Members of Congress, shrinking budget, low morale).

_____

_____

_____

ACTION: Discuss the specific actions you took to address a challenge. Describe your role and actions in resolving the problem or meeting the outcome goals.

_____

_____

_____

_____

_____

_____

RESULTS: Describe results, outcomes, or long-term impacts of your efforts. At a senior level, you should be able to give more than one identifiable, measurable result from your effort.

_____

_____

_____

Check Point 4 Summary

By using the practical exercises throughout this Check Point, and then by using the ECQ and TQ builders on the CD, you should be well on your way to writing strong narrative statements that complement your resume.

Here's a helpful tip: Once you finish your ECQ and/or TQ narratives, go back and try to summarize some of your accomplishments in bullet format (CCAR). This will mean briefly stating the challenge, some of your key actions, and then some of the key results.

For instance, "Initiated, gained support, and led a major change initiative to overcome outdated strategic policies and business processes related to program assessments. Engaged senior staff in formulating a vision statement, then led in developing and vetting new policy and associated processes. As a result, put an updated program assessment framework in place within nine months, with full support at all levels. The number of annual program assessments increased from six to 16, and each one required only one week as opposed to the historical four weeks, which shifted the entire culture from stove piped operations to efficient coordination."

Next, integrate these summaries into the employment history (as accomplishments) and/or professional summary sections of your resume. This will create a more cohesive overall application package.

Now that you have your resume and narratives done, let's discuss next steps...

Check Point Notes

Check Point 5

Submitting Your SES Application Materials and Preparing for the Interview

SUBMITTING YOUR SES APPLICATION MATERIALS AND PREPARING FOR THE INTERVIEW

Attention to Detail is Critical

By now, you should have your SES resume, ECQs, and any TQs ready to blow away the competition. What's next? It's time to submit your application materials, and it's important to read each vacancy very carefully.

For example, one-inch margins and Times New Roman size 12 font are standard in most SES vacancies, and you will typically need to submit your materials in MS Word format. However, sometimes the agency will require that you convert some of your documents into .pdf format.

One agency may require a Five-Page All-Inclusive SES resume with ECQs and TQs included, and ask you to send in your application via mail. Another vacancy might require you to apply through USAJOBS and submit full-length narratives, but then direct you to a completely different system to upload your resume and narrative statements online.

Sometimes, there are actual mistakes in the job announcements, or there is contradictory information. For example, sometimes the vacancy will state that your ECQs cannot exceed two pages, but when you actually apply for the job, you find that you must paste your ECQs into an online field, and there are character restrictions you did not know about.

To overcome this type of confusion or inconsistency, you obviously need to read all sections of the vacancy announcement closely. The "Major Duties" will tell you about the position and provide the keywords and phrases to include in your resume.

The "Qualifications" section will describe any narrative statements that are required.

The "How to Apply" tab is typically (but not always) where you will find all the information you need to format and submit your materials. This is also where you will be told of any additional requirements, such as transcripts, performance reports, proof of security clearances, or professional references.

Nothing More, Nothing Less

Highly qualified people just like you have been disqualified because they failed to submit complete application packages, or submitted extra materials that were not called for in the vacancy. Check the vacancy announcement, and make sure you know exactly when it will close and that you fully understand the submission requirements. Submit your materials on time, and be sure you submit only exactly what the vacancy requests—nothing more, nothing less.

For example, if the vacancy does not ask for a cover letter or references, don't submit them, even if you have a glowing cover letter from a former President! Instead, if you feel strongly about the information in the letter, figure out a way to quote or describe the letter in one of your narrative statements, or in the resume.

Check Your Work…Then Check It Again!

You are presumably already working at or near the executive level, and now you want to enter the Senior Executive Service. You are expected to be able to communicate with a high degree of effectiveness and versatility, both verbally and in writing. Until you land the interview, you are being judged primarily on your ability to present effective written materials.

The resume must be accurate and concise, but it will typically be in bullet form rather than in complete sentences. Your ECQ and TQ narratives, however, are written in first person, and should clearly demonstrate your ability to write at an executive level (or lack thereof).

Accuracy is just as important as being thorough. If you submit all the proper materials, but they are improperly formatted and full of typos, the reviewer will notice. This type of sloppy presentation can, and will, have a negative impact on your submission. The people at the hiring agency won't appreciate it, and the SES members reviewing your ECQs certainly won't, either.

At the very least, we strongly urge you to have a couple of colleagues of friends proofread your work. Better yet, hire a professional editor, proofreader, or resume writer to review it. There is no shame in hiring a professional to help you develop your application materials (you can find more information on CareerPro Global's services at the end of this book).

Use your spellchecker. Research "English 101 writing tips" online. Read Strunk and White's *The Elements of Style*. Read Appendix C in OPM's *2010 Guide to SES Qualifications* (part of this section is listed on this page for your convenience).

The point here is to do everything in your power to ensure that once you have properly formatted and organized all of the required application materials, you also ensure the content of your materials is highly accurate, concise, and free of errors.

Here are some tips from *OPM 2010 Guide to SES*

Qualifications, the section entitled *English 101 Revisited, and Other Tips* on pages 36-37:

- Absolutely no typos or grammatical errors.

- Use personal "I" instead of third person.

- Write in short, complete sentences (subject, verb, proper tense agreement).

- Use common words and expressions instead of bureaucratic ones.

- Economize on words and expressions, but not to a cryptic extreme.

 I briefed Congress.

 I conducted a briefing to key Members of Congress and their staffs. (12 words)

- Avoid vague statements.

 I produce two weekly radio shows, one monthly television program, and a bimonthly newsletter for 10K employees in 12 regional offices.

I manage various communication processes to field offices.

- Avoid acronyms, unless you spell them out several times in the application.

FORMAT

- Follow the instructions in the announcement carefully; ignoring page limits or other formatting requirements may jeopardize your application.

- Material should be easy to read.

- Use paragraphs or bullets to separate items.

- Use headings and subheadings to indicate categories.

- Use all capital letters, bold, or italics to highlight important information.

- Leave some white space; don't type margin to margin.

- Avoid using small-size type.

- Don't make reviewers hunt for experience (e.g., "see attachments"). Put all relevant information in the write-up.

- Application should be neat, clean, and typed.

- Make sure photocopies are legible.

- Don't attach copies of training certificates, awards, or position descriptions.

- Number all pages.

- Don't assume spellcheck will catch all the errors; review every word.

TONE

- Be friendly and professional, not stilted, formal, or chatty.

- Avoid passive verbs; use active verbs with the personal "I."

 I established a new team structure that eliminated the need for six supervisors. (Only 13 words; concise, clear, good use of personal "I" with an active verb)

 The establishment of a new team structure was considered one of my best accomplishments in that it reduced the need for six supervisory positions. (too long—24 words; stilted, awkward sentence structure, too passive).

So, how do you navigate all of these different application requirements? If you are applying for only one SES position at a time, then it shouldn't be too difficult to follow the instructions in the "How to Apply" tab.

If you are applying for more than one SES position, however, we recommend that you create a tracking sheet (paper or electronic is fine, whichever you prefer) that lists the job announcement number, the job title, and the submission requirements. This is a simple way to stay organized and ensure you comply with all application requirements.

Although every vacancy announcement can be different, following the five steps below should give you a much better chance of submitting your application materials properly.

Five Major Steps to SES Application Submission

1. Read the vacancy announcement, then read it again.

2. Set up an account on the appropriate system (USAJOBS, Application Manager, etc.) and click on "Apply Online." Click through the steps to ensure you are preparing properly. Pay particular attention to whether you must use an online resume builder, or if you can simply upload your own resume. In addition, take note of the page where you must paste or upload your narrative statements and ensure you are developing your materials properly. Write down any questions or discrepancies you find.

3. Call and/or email the contact on the vacancy announcement. While you may have to be persistent to receive an answer, the Human Resources (HR) contact number is there for a reason. This is a major step in your career. Ask questions!

4. Give yourself time to properly develop your application materials. Submit only the exact materials the vacancy requests (nothing more, nothing less), and do it on time!

5. Call again as soon as you submit your materials (or the next morning if you're doing it last minute after hours). Ask the HR representative if your package is considered complete, and ask whether he/she has any idea on how long

the evaluation process will take. Finally, start preparing for your interview.

Federal Interviews

Congratulations! All the hard work of your job search has just paid off. You've met the agency's minimum qualifications and you've been offered an interview.

Are you prepared? This is an important question, because preparation is the key to a successful interview.

First, you want to consider the kind of information the agency is likely to seek. For example, employers want to know your motivation for employment, your ability to do the job, and how you will fit into the organization. Being able to answer probing questions in these areas will make for a successful interview.

While you already have some information about the agency, you may need to conduct further research in preparation for the interview. If you haven't already, look at the agency's website and review its purpose, mission, and strategic plan so that you are familiar not only with what it does, but also with the language it uses.

Although an agency will have a general idea of your qualifications from your resume and narrative responses, the interview helps the organizational representative to determine:

- Is there consistency between your written statements and a face-to-face presentation of yourself?
- Will you be able to meet the job duties?
- Do you fit in with the agency's culture and the personalities of current employees?
- How do you compare to others the agency is considering?
- How interested are you in this position and the agency?

While the agency directs the interview process, it is a two-way street. The organization is seeking the best employee, and the candidate is seeking the best agency and position. Remember that you have valuable skills to bring to the agency, and the interview allows you the opportunity to further demonstrate those skills and ask your own questions.

Preparing for the Interview

The federal government uses a structured interview process. This means that all candidates are asked the same questions, in the same order, and that all questions should be related specifically to the job.

Additionally, most federal interviews are conducted by a panel of two or more interviewers. Interviews may be conducted over the phone or in person; if given a choice, you should always opt for an in-person interview. Finally, most government agencies conduct only one interview, so it is important to make a strong and positive impression.

You should expect to be asked situational or behavioral-based questions. Situational questions are those that ask you to describe how you would respond to a hypothetical job-related situation. A behavior-based question asks how you have responded to a work-related situation in the past. In preparation for the interview, you should review the announcement and questionnaire and try to determine what sorts of situations and experience the agency is looking for and to be prepared with specific examples from your experience that address those issues.

Your examples should "tell a story" of how you used those skills, using CCAR (Challenge-Context-Action-Result). Use examples from past work experiences, internships, classes, activities, teams, and community involvement.

If possible, your examples should be recent, as the interviewer may want to ask you about specific details; it's much easier to provide details for a recent experience. In addition, be prepared to give an example of a time when you experienced a contrary outcome. (e.g., "Explain a situation that did not turn out as you planned. Highlight what you learned from the situation and what you might have done differently.")

You should also identify a few (two or three) of your best qualities that relate to the job and decide how you will convey these during the interview. Be sure to have examples (tell a story) that demonstrate these attributes. Finally, you should prepare two or three thoughtful job-related questions for the interviewer.

Take the time to practice how to convey your skills, abilities, and experience through accomplishments. Practicing with a friend who is familiar with the field, or even practicing in front of a mirror, can help you focus your answers and feel more confident during the interview.

On a similar note, practice by thinking of situational or behavioral questions that the interviewer is likely to ask you, and how you might respond. For example, "Think of a situation involving a confrontation with another staff member that you did not handle well, and how, in retrospect, you might have handled it better."

At the end of the interview, be sure to ask about next steps in the process, thank the panel members for their time, and reiterate your interest in the position. Finally, it is a nice touch to follow up your interview with a timely thank-you note.

Sample Interview Questions

Although the following questions have been fictionalized, they will nonetheless give you a powerful glimpse into what one federal agency recently asked their SES candidates during final interviews.

- This is a newly created SES position that will oversee two GS-15s who were previously running their own separate departments. As those department directors may become division directors, and division directors may become branch heads, and so on, there will likely be a great deal of unrest regarding titles, roles, and perceived stature. Please address what you see as the key challenges and how you would address them.

- You have been associated with (insert your organization name) in some capacity for a significant time. If you are selected as an SES, talk to us about the changes you foresee with integrating into our culture here.

- This department has offices across the world, and many of them have developed longstanding cultures wanting to "take care" of their own issues and not reveal negative issues to their chain of command. As the current leadership continues to work to change these cultures, we are uncovering challenging issues, such as inappropriate use of government computer systems. Talk to us about any related experience with this type of situation and what you would plan to do to address these challenges.

By considering these types of questions and applying them to the agency calling you for an interview, you can be even more prepared.

Interview Tips

Here are some interview tips to help you understand and ace your SES interview:

- Expect an interview, and practice your interviewing skills while you wait to hear back. Try watching yourself in a mirror and/or using a tape recorder. An excellent way to develop your interviewing skills is to conduct a "mock interview" with a family member, friend, and/or co-worker. You might also choose to invest in some professional interview coaching.

- Look professional. Appearance is an important part of the interviewing process, and conservative business attire creates a strong first impression. If you have questions about whether something is appropriate, it probably isn't.

- Think positive, and maintain a friendly, open demeanor. This projects confidence and enthusiasm.

- Be sure you have the correct time and clear directions to the interview. Obtain an agency contact's name, title, and a phone number in case of emergency.

- Arrive early. Allow plenty of time for traveling, parking, and going through security. For most government buildings, you will have to show photo identification and your belongings will be scanned. Assume that going through security will take at least 15 minutes.

- Be certain to bring a copy of your application materials, a notepad, and a pen to all interviews. You might also want to bring a list of references.

- If you must carry a cell phone, be sure to turn it off. Better yet, don't bring it at all.

Check Point 5 Summary

You've followed the steps in this check point. You worked hard on your application materials and you feel that they are strong and compelling, and truly demonstrate your qualifications for the job. What now? Now you have to accept that you submitted the best materials you could and simply wait.

It certainly can't hurt to follow up with the hiring agency, but you must use your best judgment because different agencies will be more receptive than others.

There is no right or wrong answer here. You might connect with an HR representative who is friendly and more than willing to let you know how long he/she thinks the process will take. Then again, you may speak with someone who is unwilling to give you any information. It is a good idea to email your questions, because then you have something set in writing.

Quite often, you will simply be told something like, "The review process is still ongoing, and you will be contacted if we would like to interview you." Sometimes, the entire process takes less than eight weeks. Other times, SES applicants wait six months .

We recommend that once you know your application was complete and submitted, you should remember that patience is a virtue. You should be proud of yourself. You navigated the complicated and challenging SES application process, putting your name in the proverbial hat.

You've done all you can. No amount of phone calls or emails to the hiring agency will change the effect of your application materials. Start preparing for the interview. Cross your fingers, take a deep breath, and wait for the good news.

Check Point Notes

ROADMAP TO THE SES CHECKLIST

If you did not know it already, you should now realize that the process of applying for and securing a Senior Executive Service (SES) position is a comprehensive one. By following the five check points in this book, the process should be much easier. Let's conduct a quick review, to make sure you understand each check point:

❑ **Check Point 1: Understanding the Senior Executive Service**
Do you have a good understanding of the SES?
Do you believe that you are qualified?

❑ **Check Point 2: Finding SES Jobs and Navigating the Hiring Process**
Do you understand the SES hiring process and the different steps your application will go through?

❑ **Check Point 3: Develop an Effective SES Resume**
Have you developed a compelling SES resume that complies with all formatting requirements in the vacancy announcement?

❑ **Check Point 4: How to Write Your ECQs and TQs**
Have you written strong ECQ and TQ narrative statements? Are they properly formatted?

❑ **Check Point 5: Submitting Your Application and Preparing for the Interview**
Did you follow the five steps to submitting your application materials?

Executive Toolbox

SES Application Samples and Templates

SES Federal Resume Template
(with instructions)

RESUME NAME
Address
City, State Zip
Home Phone:
Work Phone:
Cell Phone:
Email:

VACANCY IDENTIFICATION NUMBER:
JOB TITLE AND GRADE:

U.S. Citizen: Yes
Veterans' Preference:
Federal Employee:
Highest Grade Level and Dates:

AREAS OF EXPERTISE

- · · ·
- · · ·
- · · ·

PROFESSIONAL SUMMARY

Defines your "market niche," highlights your accomplishments, defines your mission, and creates interest.

WORK EXPERIENCE

FOR EACH POSITION YOU'VE SERVED IN THE LAST TEN YEARS, PROVIDE…

Position Title, Level	Dates
Organization	Hours/week:
Address	Salary: $
City, State Zip	Supervisor:
	Telephone: xxx-xxx-xxxx
	OK to Contact: Yes

Provide a brief summary of the federal agency, military organization, or private company for which you presently work and its mission and goal statement. Include if it is a Fortune 500 company, how many people it employs, if it is international, its annual sales, or other descriptive data. This can all usually be found in the company's website.

Professional Accountabilities:
Synopsis of your primary responsibilities/duties. It might help to think about:

1. What is the number-one function you perform?
2. What is the second most time-consuming function you perform?
3. What is the third functional expectation required of you?

From your analysis of the vacancy announcement, select two to six keywords/phrases that would best serve as your "headlines." Next, organize your duties/scope of responsibility into these headline categories.

Specific Accomplishments:
This is where you want to list your top three to five or more accomplishments from the position

EDUCATION

College Name, City, State Zip
Graduated: Date
Major:
Degree:
Number of semester/credit/quarter hours:
GPA:
Honors:
Relevant Course List:

OTHER QUALIFICATIONS

Job-related training courses:
List every training course completed in the past 10 years, including course hours and dates. Just one extra training course could be all that sets you apart from others applying for the same job.
Job-related skills (e.g., other languages, computer software/hardware, tools, machinery, typing speed, etc.):

List all languages you speak, understand, or can write. (Specify your ability level—novice, intermediate, or advanced for each element, if appropriate.)

If relevant, list all the computer hardware and software with which you are familiar:

Software:
Hardware:
Networks:
Databases:
Operating Systems:

Job-related certificates and licenses:
If applying for positions that require you to possess a license or certification, ensure to list all current licenses, certificates, and/or contracting warrants under the "Professional Licenses and Certificates" section of your resume. Identify the city and/or state of certification, name of certifying organization, and expiration date, if any.

Example: Certified Public Accountant (CPA), Illinois, 06-95.

Job-related honors, awards, special accomplishments, and additional information:

Include awards and honors that will demonstrate your motivation, dedication, loyalty, business acumen, community service, etc.

Professional and social affiliations:
Membership in professional associations conveys to the employer that not only are you a contributing member of your profession, but also that you have a desire to enhance your knowledge and skills for your own future and that you are committed to the future of your vocation. It's good to list the associations in which you have contributed time and effort. Avoid including associations in which you have had very little involvement, as this will take away from your other associations.

Hobbies and outside interests:
Do not include any hobbies and/or outside interests, unless the items complement the position for which you are applying. Avoid mentioning "controversial" causes with which you are involved, such as those related to religion or politics.

Blank SES Federal Resume Template

RESUME NAME
Address, City, State Zip
Home Phone:
Work Phone:
Cell Phone:
Email:

VACANCY IDENTIFICATION NUMBER:
JOB TITLE AND GRADE:

U.S. Citizen: Yes
Veterans' Preference:
Federal Employee:
Highest Grade Level and Dates:

PROFESSIONAL SUMMARY

WORK EXPERIENCE

Position Title, Level
Organization
Address
City, State Zip

Dates
Hours/week:
Salary: $
Supervisor:
Telephone: xxx-xxx-xxxx
OK to Contact: Yes

Duties and Responsibilities

Accomplishments

Position Title, Level
Organization
Address
City, State Zip

Dates
Hours/week:
Salary: $
Supervisor:
Telephone: xxx-xxx-xxxx
OK to Contact: Yes

Duties and Responsibilities

Accomplishments

Position Title, Level   Dates

Position Title, Level	Dates
Organization	Hours/week:
Address	Salary: $
City, State Zip	Supervisor:
	Telephone: xxx-xxx-xxxx
	OK to Contact: Yes

Duties and Responsibilities

Accomplishments

Position Title, Level	Dates
Organization	Hours/week:
Address	Salary: $
City, State Zip	Supervisor:
	Telephone: xxx-xxx-xxxx
	OK to Contact: Yes

Duties and Responsibilities

Accomplishments

EDUCATION

College Name, City, State Zip
Graduated: Date
Major:
Degree:
Number of semester/credit/quarter hours:
GPA:
Course List:

OTHER QUALIFICATIONS

Job-related training courses:

Job-related skills (e.g., other languages, computer software/hardware, tools, machinery, typing speed, etc.):

Job-related certificates and licenses:

Job-related honors, awards, special accomplishments, and additional information:

Five-Page All-Inclusive Resume Template

YOUR FULL NAME
Address, City, ST Zip
Day Phone: XXX-XXX-XXXX
Evening Phone: XXX-XXX-XXXX
Mobile Phone: XXX-XXX-XXXX
Email: name@email.com

Vacancy Identification Number: ENTER HERE
Social Security Number: XXX-XX-XXXX

U.S. Citizen:	Yes/No
Federal Employee:	Yes/No
Veterans' Preference:	Yes/No (If YES, include number of points)
Active Duty Military:	Yes/No
Highest Federal Rank and Dates:	GS-XXXX-15 (since MM/YYYY)
Security Clearance:	Enter, if applicable. Include types and valid dates

RELEVANT PROFESSIONAL EXPERIENCE

Job Title (Federal Grade, if applicable)	MM/YYYY to Present
Employer	Salary: $XXX,000 USD Per Year
Street Address	Supervisor: Name Here
City, ST Zip	Telephone: XXX-XXX-XXXX
	OK to Contact: Yes

Professional Accountabilities:
Brief description of the agency/mission. [May need to eliminate if you are short on room.]

TEAM BUILDING & DEVELOPMENT: Remember, for a "resume-only" application, hiring agencies generally want you to demonstrate each of the ECQs within your work history, but then again, they don't want you to list the actual ECQs. Instead, use some of the competencies or other similar terms to show the reader which ECQ you are summarizing, and then use a specific CCAR story to do so.

EXECUTIVE LEADERSHIP: Information, information.

COMMUNICATIONS: Information, information.

Initiatives/Achievements:
- Highlight 1
- Highlight 2
- Highlight 3
- Highlight 4

Job Title (Federal Grade, if applicable)　　　　　　　　　MM/YYYY to Present
Employer　　　　　　　　　　　　　　　　Salary: $XXX,000 USD Per Year
Street Address　　　　　　　　　　　　　　　　Supervisor: Name Here
City, ST Zip　　　　　　　　　　　　　　　　Telephone: XXX-XXX-XXXX
　　　　　　　　　　　　　　　　　　　　　　OK to Contact: Yes

Professional Accountabilities:
Brief description goes here. [May need to eliminate if you are short on room.]

INTERAGENCY ALLIANCES: Try to use ECQ competencies as headlines if you have appropriate experience.

EXECUTIVE LEADERSHIP: Information, information.

COMMUNICATIONS: Information, information.

Initiatives/Achievements:
- Highlight 1
- Highlight 2
- Highlight 3
- Highlight 4

Job Title (Federal Grade, if applicable)　　　　　　　　　MM/YYYY to Present
Employer　　　　　　　　　　　　　　　　Salary: $XXX,000 USD Per Year
Street Address　　　　　　　　　　　　　　　　Supervisor: Name Here
City, ST Zip　　　　　　　　　　　　　　　　Telephone: XXX-XXX-XXXX
　　　　　　　　　　　　　　　　　　　　　　OK to Contact: Yes

Professional Accountabilities:
Brief description goes here. [May need to eliminate if you are short on room.]

CUSTOMER-FOCUSED PROBLEM SOLVER: Try to use ECQ competencies as headlines if you have appropriate experience.

EXECUTIVE LEADERSHIP: Information, information.

COMMUNICATIONS: Information, information.

Initiatives/Achievements:
- Highlight 1
- Highlight 2
- Highlight 3
- Highlight 4

Job Title (Federal Grade, if applicable)
Employer
Street Address
City, ST Zip

MM/YYYY to Present
Salary: $XXX,000 USD Per Year
Supervisor: Name Here
Telephone: XXX-XXX-XXXX
OK to Contact: Yes

Professional Accountabilities:
Brief description goes here. [May need to eliminate if you are short on room.]

ORGANIZATIONAL TRANSFORMATION: Try to use ECQ competencies as headlines if you have appropriate experience.

EXECUTIVE LEADERSHIP: Information, information.

COMMUNICATIONS: Information, information.

Initiatives/Achievements:
- Highlight 1
- Highlight 2
- Highlight 3
- Highlight 4

Job Title (Federal Grade, if applicable)
Employer
Street Address
City, ST Zip

MM/YYYY to Present
Salary: $XXX,000 USD Per Year
Supervisor: Name Here
Telephone: XXX-XXX-XXXX
OK to Contact: Yes

Professional Accountabilities:
Brief description goes here. [May need to eliminate if you are short on room.]

FINANCIAL MANAGEMENT: Try to use ECQ competencies as headlines if you have appropriate experience.

EXECUTIVE LEADERSHIP: Information, information.

HUMAN CAPITAL & FINANCIAL MANAGEMENT: Information, information.

Initiatives/Achievements:
- Highlight 1
- Highlight 2
- Highlight 3
- Highlight 4

EDUCATION

Type and year of degree received: Type of Degree, YYYY
Major field of study: Major
Minor field of study: Delete this line if not applicable
College: College Name, City, ST
Total credits: XXX
GPA: X.XX out of 4.0

(Note: Credits and GPA are typically not required once a degree has been awarded. Check with the hiring agency and the job announcement for the specific requirements. Also, if your GPA was not exemplary, you might now want to mention it if you don't have to.)

Relevant Coursework:
List here if there is room; list here if there is room; list here if there is room

Type and year of degree received: Type of Degree, YYYY
Major field of study: Major
Minor field of study: Delete this line if not applicable
College: College Name, City, ST
Total credits: XXX
GPA: X.XX out of 4.0
Relevant Coursework:
List here if there is room; list here if there is room; list here if there is room

OTHER QUALIFICATIONS

Job-Related Awards:
Award Title, MM/YYYY
Award Title, MM/YYYY
Award Title, MM/YYYY
Award Title, MM/YYYY
Award Title, MM/YYYY

Career-Related Training:
Course Title, MM/YYYY
Course Title, MM/YYYY
Course Title, MM/YYYY
Course Title, MM/YYYY
Course Title, MM/YYYY

Five-Page All-Inclusive Resume Sample I: GS-15 to SES

MIRANDA DONI
2415 North K Street ▪ Doornik, MS 51237
Phone: 555-555-5555▪ Email: miranda.doni@email.com ▪ Security Clearance: TS
U.S. Citizen: Yes ▪ Highest Federal Rank and Dates: GS-15; 07/2015–Present

Applying For Job # 29-MMRKO3-44
Deputy Assistant Inspector General for Genetics Efforts

Highly renowned executive healthcare leader with 23 years of experience in establishing cutting-edge oversight programs in support of national and international medical programs. Hold exceptional knowledge of healthcare practices and operations, with a strong background of leadership in national professional societies and federal agencies. Maintain subject-matter expertise in genetics research ethics, regulations, and technologies.

~ Selected Areas of Expertise ~

Healthcare Inspections	Clinical Operations	Values-Based Care
Workforce Development & Mentoring	Policy Development & Compliance	Financial, Resource, & Personnel Management
Information Technology (IT)	Process Improvement	Federal Healthcare

PROFESSIONAL EXPERIENCE

04/2019–Present, Program Manager, Department of Medical Affairs, Crait, MD; Federal Grade: GS-15; Salary: $130,000 USD Per Year; Hours/Week: 40; Supervisor: Amylyn Holdo, Telephone: 555-555-5555; OK to Contact: Yes

Executive Leadership & Program Management: Direct a staff of eight senior medical practitioners and healthcare management leaders in the conduct of oversight inspections and audits spanning the full range of healthcare operations. Led the review and adjudication of 28 medical records in cases of potential patient harm within 6 months of assuming leadership of the organization.

Proven Ability to Plan & Direct Organizational Change: Drive compliance measures through comprehensive application of policies, regulations, and guidelines. Implemented new operational policies and training techniques to lead the organization to become the first hotline system to use the VA Office of the Inspector General matrix management strategy.

Leadership Development & Mentoring: Engage with nurses, physicians, nurse practitioners, occupational therapists, attorneys, and healthcare administration leadership on a daily basis. Assess organizational performance and coordinate training courses to improve efficiency in processing case files.

Strategic Planning & Policy Development: Develop strategies to ensure outstanding healthcare practices in a healthcare system executing an annual operating budget of more than $490M in support of 686K outpatient visits. Capitalize on expertise and professional networks in the healthcare executive administration community to identify and implement new methodologies, performance metrics, and reporting mechanisms to spur improvements in oversight and patient outcomes. Assemble and lead teams to solve complex problems involving scientific analysis, data assessment, and multiple sources of regulatory guidance.

Technology Management: Leverage multiple automated systems and IT network applications, including Share-Point, Skype, and video teleconference capabilities, to improve communications and streamline workflows.

Communication & Interagency Collaboration: Collaborate with the Council of Health Inspectors to implement Quality Standards for Inspection and Evaluation along with the Inspector General Act of 2017.

Selected Accomplishments and Key Results:

- Envisioned, organized, and led an organizational workshop to educate directors, associate directors, and healthcare staff about the new matrix organization approach to management structures. Led the organization to become the first in the VA to adopt new paradigm.

- Established and fostered a strong mentor relationship with two subordinate leaders and two health systems specialists to improve their mediation and communication skills. Resolved several interpersonal conflicts, leading directly to improved professional dynamics and productivity within the office.

07/2014–04/2019, Chief Nursing Director, Kamino Troop Medical Facility, Kamino, MD; Federal Grade: GS-14; Salary: $127,000 USD Per Year; Hours/Week: 40; Supervisor: Halle Burtoni, Telephone: 555-555-5555; OK to Contact: Yes

Executive Leadership & Program Management: Led an interdisciplinary team of 60 personnel comprised of federal employees and U.S. Public Health Service (USPHS) staff. Renowned as the organization's foremost leader on strategic vision, core mission, and operational policy evolution. Created and drove the continual analysis of key performance metrics through inspection and audit processes. Drove operations to review more than 200K healthcare records and 1.3K administrative operations documents. Served as the approval authority for more than $700M in grant funds supporting essential biomedical operations to increase available forces for active duty. Trusted as a leading expert on the Bioengineering Ancillary Creation for Troops Act (BACTA), with emphasis on Parts C, D, and F, to assess and adjudicate qualified funding recipients.

Proven Ability to Plan & Direct Organizational Change: Led constant process improvement initiatives to sharpen oversight performance across a wide range of operational recommendations and benchmarks proposed by the Government Accountability Office (GAO). Lauded by senior organizational leadership for revolutionizing use of data analysis methods and automated systems to improve healthcare outcomes and raise viral suppression rates.

Resource Management: Drove the establishment and prioritization of funding objectives for a $700M grants portfolio supporting more than 6K treatment sites throughout the U.S. Drove policy innovation to incorporate video teleconference, remote networking, and telework capabilities to improve operational efficiency and expand productivity. Served as a primary director of recruiting and hiring initiatives to draw top talent for Branch Chief and Senior Project Officer vacancies in the genetics research and propagation division.

Results-Focused Customer Advocate: Led clinical quality initiatives supporting the provision of direct care for more than 550K personnel under BACTA. Conducted visits to inspect processes, facilities, and administrative operations.

Communication & Interagency Collaboration: Spurred continuous process improvement and regulatory compliance through the development and presentation of clinical care training programs for more than 200 personnel.

Selected Accomplishments and Key Results:

- Seized upon a Congressionally mandated departmental expansion as an opportunity to overhaul the organization's mission statement and strategic outlook across six lines of business operations for the first time in 20 years. Coordinated directly with department heads to craft bold new vision, improving budget management and patient outcomes nationally.

- Instituted new industry best practices incorporating evidence-based methodologies to revitalize site visit operations and strengthen oversight of BACTA grant recipients. New policies saved more than $5M, directly contributing to the establishment of 500 new grants to expand gene therapy to 550K patients, drastically improving the national regenerated tissue rejection rate.

- Crafted innovative vision for the Order 66 program, implementing text-messaging technologies to remind patients to stay current with medication regimens. The system improved medication and program retention by 20%.

- Established a series of quarterly training sessions, leveraging network technologies to assist grant recipients and improve healthcare operations. The program provided training to more than 3K healthcare providers nationally.

04/2013–04/2015, Branch Chief, Mobile Hospital Facilities, Kamino, MD; Federal Grade: GS-1142-14; Salary: $118,000 USD Per Year; Hours/Week: 40+; Supervisor: Kit Fisto, Telephone: 555-444-2222; OK to Contact: Yes

Executive Oversight & Program Management: Served as a primary member of the cloning Senior Management and Leadership Development workgroup. Leveraged expertise in BACTA to drive improvement in oversight and management of operations. Steered formulation of fundamental budget and human capital management strategies. Personally conducted oversight of 17 administrative business lines of operation. Led the review of more than 3K healthcare records and 450 administrative reviews for 138 recipient agencies employing 1.2K healthcare professionals, administrators, and executives. Supervised the distribution and use of $125M in grant funding supporting more than 158K patients.

Versatile Leader & Team Builder: Led eight project officers in daily engagements with stakeholders and interagency partners, including GAO, National Institutes of Health (NIH), and Centers for Disease Control and Prevention (CDC), as well as five major universities and national non-profit healthcare programs.

Workforce Development & Mentoring: Led and interdisciplinary team of personnel comprised of federal employees and USPHS staff. Trained and mentored Contracting Officer's Representatives (CORs), project officers, and healthcare professional staff in management and oversight policies to improve capability to identify and recover misallocated funds. Drove operations to reestablish accountability of more than $180K.

Strategic Planning & Resource Management: Created, designed, and implemented research and design scenarios on best practices for decision making to support healthcare operations. Formulated, planned, and executed both the Part C Capacity Development and Part D funding process for over 220 applicants to successfully distribute more than $67M. Led the forecasting, programming, execution, and closeout of a $125M portfolio,

providing tissue regeneration and rehabilitation treatment to 158K patients across 138 facilities nationwide. Led recruitment and retention initiatives to sustain a high-performing corps of eight project officers.

Communication & Interagency Collaboration: Drafted official communications and responses to Congressional inquiries. Collated and formatted presentations of data in support of senior leadership efforts to advocate for the provision of human cloning healthcare services. Authored policies and program guidance for BACTA outreach forums.

Selected Accomplishments and Key Results:

- Directed senior healthcare project officers to increase the 5% monthly grantee-monitoring rate to 99% while simultaneously decreasing a staff backlog of items by 93%.

- Pioneered new policies and technical training initiatives to improve efficiency of oversight processes. Drove advancements leading to a document-processing rate of 1.6K annually, more than triple the rate of peer organizations.

04/2009–04/2013, Public Health Analyst, Division of Human Cloning, Coruscant, MD; Federal Grade: GS-1142-13; Salary: $98,000 USD Per Year; Hours/Week: 40+; Supervisor: Sifo Dyas, Telephone: 333-777-4242; OK to Contact: Yes

Selected Accomplishments and Key Results:

- Led strategic interagency and multinational engagements between federal, industry, and academic stakeholders to propel strategic growth of genetic research. Led development of the Mandalore Research Initiative, with combined budgets of more than $140M.

- Led a transformation initiative to revolutionize a failing genetics research program. Drove operations to produce more than 7K educational podcasts and establish functionality as a productive healthcare education institution.

EDUCATION

Doctorate of Nursing Practice, GPA: 4.0, Endor University, Endor, MO, 2012
Master of Public Health, GPA: 3.45, Plagueis University, Baltimore, MD, 2003
Master of Nursing, GPA: 3.76 (Summa Cum Laude), University of Endor, Endor, MO, 2001
Bachelor in Nursing, GPA: 3.52 (Magna Cum Laude), Windu College, Seattle, WA, 1996

Selected Professional Training & Certifications:
Board-Certified Nurse Executive, Advanced (NEA-BC), 2015
Board-Certified Adult Geneticist, American Nurses Credentialing Center, 2014
American Academy of Cloning Medicine Specialist (AAHIVS), 2011
Certified Advanced Regenerative Care RN (AACRN), 2010
HHS Supervisor Certificate (BC), 2009
HRSA Certified Project Officer, 2008
Certificate in Executive Leadership, Windu University, Seattle, WA, 2006

Registered Nurse (RN) and Adult Nurse Practitioner
(NP), 2005

Awards and Honors:

Presidential Volunteer Service Award, 2017
Jonas Veteran Healthcare Scholar, Cohort V, 2016-2018
Distinguished Alumni Award, Barnes-Windu College
Alumni Association, 2016

Five-Page All-Inclusive Resume Sample II: Corporate to SES

JONATHAN DOE
123 Alphabet Street • New Orleans, LA 70056
Day Phone: 123-456-7890
Mobile Phone: 123-456-7890
Email: info@careerprocenter.net

APPLYING FOR: SES 44-2011/ Asst. Inspector General for Audit (Info Technology Services)

U.S. Citizen:	Yes
Federal Employee:	No
Veterans' Preference:	No
Active Duty Military:	No
Highest Federal Rank and Dates:	GS-510-15, 02/2011-10/2019
Security Clearance:	Top Secret

EXECUTIVE SUMMARY

Multidimensional Information Systems Management executive with 30+ years of cumulative experience in Information Technology (IT), process improvement, business development, analysis, auditing, technology implementation, modernization, operations, and administration. Strategic problem solver who conceives innovative solutions while serving in a wide range of executive positions, including President, Vice-President, and Chief Executive Officer (CEO). Thirteen years of auditing experience within both the federal government and private industry.

COMPUTER SECURITY: As President of Doe & Associates, conducted computer security assessments worldwide for the Department of State (DOS) and computer audits at several U.S. Department of Energy (DOE) facilities. Provided computer security, risk analysis, internal control audits, and educational services to the federal government, telecommunications, and financial services companies, including the Bureau of Engraving & Printing, Government Accountability Office (GAO), U.S. Department of Agriculture (USDA) Graduate School, MCI, Bell South, Solomon Brothers, and Fortune 500 companies.

IT PLANNING AND MANAGEMENT: As Vice-President of Information Systems for Scranton Associates, Inc., championed the creation, development, and management of a full IT division. Managed numerous multi-million-dollar IT projects with companies such as U.S. West, Moorman Manufacturing, Standard Federal Mortgage, 1st Nationwide Mortgage, GMAC Mortgage, and the Frederick Telework Center. Adept at applying keen strategic vision to develop meaningful IT solutions that improve efficiency of operations.

EXECUTIVE AND STRATEGIC LEADERSHIP: Known for adaptability and flexibility in moving from one challenge to another and refining programs to better serve business needs. Built sustainable programs with multiple high-growth organizations by conducting strategic-level business planning and forecasting. Achieve diverse group alignment by building peak-performing teams in managing physical and data security and policy implementation.

AUDITING AND ANALYSIS: Served as Director, Computer Audits (GS-15) Inspector General's (IG) Office,

Department of Commerce, managing and supervising IG audits of computer-related operations. Acquired contracts to conduct computer security risk analysis at the Bureau of Engraving and Printing, Maritime Administration, U.S. Department of Housing and Urban Development (HUD), DOS, DOE, and other federal and commercial organizations.

COMMUNICATION/NETWORKING: Adroit communicator, collaborating with staff at all levels. Report findings clearly and concisely. Viable member of senior executive teams. An engaging speaker and facilitator known for building healthy, effective partnerships regardless of geographical dispersion. Superior ability to relay complex technical information and to foster interdepartmental coordination and team cohesion.

SELECT PROFESSIONAL EXPERIENCE

Chief Executive Officer (CEO)/President
Relevant Systems, Inc.
Macon, GA

01/2019–Present
Hours/week: 40
Salary: $200,000+ USD Per Year
Supervisor: Board of Directors
Telephone: none
OK to Contact: Yes

Relevant Systems, Inc. provides outsourced accounting and business services, application development, managed hosting, and professional services for government, commercial, and non-profit customers.

Implemented a broad range of strategic plans and initiatives, as approved by the Board of Directors.

EXECUTIVE LEADERSHIP: Planned, developed, and established policies and objectives for corporate office and four field offices. Provided executive management for mergers, acquisitions, and marketing initiatives. Monitored the company's performance on contracts with commercial firms and government contract with the HUD related to the management of the commercial multi-family housing program.

IT PLANNING AND MANAGEMENT: Developed and managed a multitude of IT projects, programs, and initiatives. Developed real estate advertising applications to the Rocky Mountain News and its real estate customers.

COORDINATION/NETWORKING: Coordinated effectively with commercial clients engaged in the mortgage industry, legal profession, and newspaper print media to ensure customer needs were met while growing revenue. Fostered and cultivated an environment of open communications throughout the organization.

Initiatives/Achievements:
- Selected as Entrepreneur of the Year for Emerging Business, 2000.

- Developed and implemented a fully automated, web-based system for a client's defaulted mortgage claim processing, ultimately aligning organization to gain $2.5M in new revenue.

- Leveraged new software to achieve more than $11M in new revenue.

CEO/Founding Member
Desert Technologies, LLC
Frederick, MD

01/2011–06/2019
Hours/week: 40
Salary: $125,000+ USD Per Year
Supervisor: none
Telephone: none
OK to Contact: Yes

Desert Technologies' strategic vision was to provide one-stop technology services to a broad range of clients, including security consulting, education, hardware, software development, cabling, networking, and Internet services and to further serve as the customer's Application Service Provider (ASP).

EXECUTIVE LEADERSHIP: Founded, staffed, and managed company to provide computer network services, Internet hosting, mortgage claims processing, computer security services, and computer retail operations to clients in the Washington Metropolitan Area, Denver, Oakridge, and Jacksonville. Grew the startup firm into a multimillion-dollar technology company.

IT PLANNING AND MANAGEMENT: Oversaw numerous software development projects, including an Internet-based, state management system for chronically ill DOD beneficiaries in partnership with Strategic Monitored Services that included electronic medical record applications. Applied an innovative concept to offer customers more cost-effective levels of technical support.

COORDINATION/NETWORKING: Created partnerships with several attorneys, accountants, and telecommunications providers to ensure we fully met all customers' needs. Negotiated contracts with computer distributors, manufacturers, and software companies; created a model work environment through maintaining the highest professional and ethical standards in dealing with technical, human relations, and organizational issues and problems.

Initiatives/Achievements:

- Revolutionized the delivery of IT services by consolidating services that customers had traditionally received from multiple companies.

- Built a new organization up to 35 employees and significant profit within 14 months.

- Managed the processing and filing of defaulted loan claims for 200 mortgage companies holding insured HUD, Veterans Administration (VA), and Private Mortgage-insured mortgages.

Vice-President, Information Systems
Lee Kelley & Associates, Inc. (LKA)
New Orleans, LA

01/2009–06/2011
Hours/week: 40
Salary: $90,000 USD Per Year
Supervisor: Joan Burton
Telephone: 123-456-7890
OK to Contact: Yes

LKA provides customized IT, budget and finance, and management services to government and commercial clients. With more than 30 years' experience, LKA delivers custom-built solutions to fit your mission.

Led a range of IT initiatives while developing a highly profitable technology business unit.

www.SESWriters.com

EXECUTIVE LEADERSHIP: Expertly managed a diverse group of information systems personnel, computer auditors, computer security analysts/computer programmers, and administrative staff located in offices throughout the U.S.

AUDITING AND SECURITY RISK ANALYSIS: Conducted information system audits and computer security risk analyses of several government organizations, including the DOE, CIA, Small Business Administration (SBA), and multiple commercial organizations. Maintained and utilized thorough knowledge of various computer security policies and regulations, including Office of Management and Budget (OMB) Circular No. A-130, Transmittal No. 3, Appendix III (Security of Federal Automated Information Systems), and Public Law 100-235 (Computer Security Act of 1987), Title 18 (Crimes and Criminal Procedure), Part I (Crimes), Chapter 47 (Fraud and False Statements), Sec. 1030 (Fraud and Related Activity in Connection with Computers).

IT PLANNING AND MANAGEMENT: Developed, implemented, and managed a wide array of IT support services and initiatives, including mortgage-related software, computer network services, computer security assessments, audits, and centralized computer hosting for commercial and government clients.

Initiatives/Achievements:
- Developed an automated system that modernized the mortgage claims auditing practice and streamlined submissions; increased efficiency by 65%.

- Achieved a 28% Return on Investment (ROI) in the IT business division in just two years and in expanding client base to include several Fortune 500 customers, such as GMAC Mortgage, Standard Federal Mortgage, U.S. West Communications, Moorman's Manufacturing, and Frederick County Government.

EDUCATION

College:	University of Montana, Missoula, MT
Major field(s) of study:	Business Administration/Economics
Type and year of degree(s) received:	Master's, 2003
Relevant coursework:	Accounting, Economics, and Data Processing

College:	Delgado University, New Orleans, LA
Major field(s) of study:	Business/Accounting
Type and year of degree(s) received:	Bachelor's, 1985
Relevant coursework:	24 hours of Accounting

OTHER QUALIFICATIONS

Additional Relevant Auditing Experience:
2006–2008; President; Doe & Associates, Inc.; Formed, staffed, and managed a company that provided computer security, risk analysis, internal control audits, and educational services to the federal government, telecommunications, and financial services companies. Conducted computer security assessments worldwide. Implemented and deployed a new quantitative risk analysis software program on the Department of State (DOS) mainframe computer. Implemented security control guidance in accordance with National Institute of Standards and Technology (NIST) handbooks and Federal Information Processing Standards (FIPS).

2005–2006; Director, IT Audits (GS-15); IG Office, Department of Commerce; Managed and supervised IG audits of computer-related operations. Created the first formal audit division that conducted reviews of computer operations and programs, including the modernization of the Federal Aviation Administration (FAA) Air Traffic Control (ATC) systems. Supervised a staff of auditors and prepared plans for conducting audits of data-processing programs.

Career-Related Training & Certificates:
Certified Information Systems Auditor (CISA), 2018
Computer Risk Analysis Course (Internet Security Technology), 2015
Wharton Information Systems Program (Government Accounting Office Program), 2013
United States Army Computer Programming Training, various courses and dates

Job-Related Honors, Awards, Special Accomplishments, and Additional Information:
Selected for Department of Commerce Executive Leadership Program, 2016
Entrepreneur of the Year, 2015
Selected for Leadership New Orleans Program, 2012

Publications and Articles:
The Federal Report, July 7, 2018, "Computers to Streamline War on Waste"
The Washington Times, July 8, 2017, "Inspector Is Honored for Probe"
Government Executive, Sept. 2014, "How DOT Is Pioneering in Federal Computer Use"
Government Computer News, Nov. 2014, "Microcomputers Invaluable Tool for Auditors"
OIG Update, "Microcomputers for Increased Productivity"

Sample SES Resume III: Corporate to SES

DAVID WILLIAMS
123 Anyplace Street. ▪ Anytown, USA 12345 ▪ Clearance: Active Secret
Day Phone: 123-456-7890 ▪ Evening Phone: 1234567890 ▪ Email: anyname@gmail.com
Applying for Job #VA-55489-BLS/Director, Resources and Logistics

HIGH-PERFORMING C-LEVEL EXECUTIVE WITH THE OPTIMAL BALANCE OF LEADERSHIP, TECHNICAL EXPERTISE, AND STRATEGIC PERSPECTIVE TO LEAD DOD PROGRAMS THROUGH CHANGE AND CHALLENGE. MORE THAN 25 YEARS OF EXPERIENCE NEGOTIATING, PLANNING, AND DIRECTING THOUSANDS OF GOVERNMENT CONTRACTS WORTH $250M+.

~SELECTED AREAS OF EXPERTISE~

Program/Project Management	Financial Management	Contract Management
Interpersonal Communication	Senior-Level Briefings	Contract Negotiations
Interagency Collaboration	International/Global Programs	Strategic Planning

PROFESSIONAL EXPERIENCE

"David is a wonderful boss. While working for him, I felt empowered to make decisions directly affecting the bottom line. Our company... delivered a quality product on time to happy customers. We did this largely due to David's superb leadership."

—JOHN ADAMS, SENIOR ENGINEER

09/2018 to Present; Co-Founder, President and CEO, Adventure Corporation, Missoula, MT; Salary: None (Compensation is tied to stock equity ownership); Hours/Week: 40; Supervisor: (Co-Founders) Jackson Ponkin; Phone: 123-456-7890; OK to Contact.

Adventure Corporation provides Intellectual Property (IP) products developed at the University of Montana for use by federal and state personnel as a covert, non-lethal laser weapon.

EXECUTIVE LEADERSHIP AND ADVISING: Provide ongoing executive leadership and guidance to a team of two PhD biomedical engineers, support staff of graduate students, and professional PhDs working in the community. Provide management oversight for funding, strategic planning and vision, and execution.

COMMUNICATION AND INTERAGENCY COORDINATION: Coordinate with a broad range of approximately 150 subcontractors, customers, and suppliers. Organize and lead high-level meetings with federal agencies and government prime contractors involved with the use of non-lethal, laser-directed technologies.

Select Value-Added Accomplishments:

- Established company and negotiated licensing for patented IP developed by co-founders, and tested by the High Propulsion Group.

- Developed productive relationships with stakeholders to coordinate development and deployment of non-lethal weapon prototypes.

01/2014 to 08/2018; Entrepreneur-In-Residence, University of Wisconsin, Jacksonville, WI; Salary: $10,000 USD per month; Hours/Week: 40; Supervisor: Dr. Shawn Petersen; Phone: 123-456-7890; OK to Contact.

One of nine CEOs selected to evaluate IP, and engage with faculty, entrepreneurs, and investors regarding commercialization opportunities at the University of Wisconsin.

Select Value-Added Accomplishments:

- Created sound business plans/structured proposals, and negotiated license agreements.

- Played a key role in more than 80 technology assessments and market identification.

- Successfully united a group of diverse stakeholders, overcoming lack of direction through effective communications and innovative use of new analytical decision-making tools; led the development and use of tools that simplified overall process and resulted in licensing of six new technologies.

- Overcame politics and pending legal battles among stakeholders on a complex battery technology licensing project; stakeholders consisted of a large, publicly traded multinational chemical corporation headquartered in Scandinavia, a large Australian power utility, and the University of Nevada; helped establish open communications that eventually led to the successful settlement of a complex battery technology licensing agreement.

01/2011 to 04/2015; Director of Quality Control, Creative Solutions, Oak Grove, KY; Salary: $150,000 USD per year plus bonuses, stock, and dividends; Hours/Week: 40; Supervisor: Rebecca Merlin Phone: 123-456-7890; OK to Contact.

EXECUTIVE LEADERSHIP AND ADVISING: Provided strategic planning, vision, and direction to a team of 60-80 personnel, not including contractors and suppliers. Managed a broad range of administrative duties such as commercial/industry approvals for facility and personnel clearances, manpower resources, job descriptions, and Statements of Work (SOWs).

FINANCIAL PLANNING, EVALUATION, AND OVERSIGHT: Provided planning, management, and oversight of personnel and departmental budgets of up to $25M. Managed projected growth and developed program budgets over $200M. Positioned the organization for growth on federal programs exceeding $250M. Directed and prioritized functional areas to maximize financial profitability and target new growth opportunities. Ensured division's compliance with Sarbanes-Oxley Act (SOX).

FEDERAL CONTRACTS AND SOLICITATIONS: Analyzed, evaluated, and responded to numerous solicitations for projects from various military commands and locations. Leveraged knowledge and educated team on Code of Federal Regulations (CFR), International Traffic in Arms Regulations (ITAR), and Export Administration Regulations (EAR). Negotiated contracts, managed supply chain subcontracts, and implemented new federal procurement channels by adding key General Services Administration (GSA) approvals for Information Technology (IT) and Security products and services within the federal supply schedules. Traveled to multiple locations, including the U.S., China, Thailand, Iceland, United Kingdom, and Denmark.

COMMUNICATION AND INTERAGENCY COORDINATION: Fostered, developed, and maintained relationships with, customers, and contractor personnel to broaden potentials for collaboration. Coordinated extensively with in-country contracting and government personnel. Coordinated with Board of Directors, law firms, accountants, and bankers to stage and address legal strategies, auditing, tax ramifications, and acquisition issues.

Select Value-Added Accomplishments:

- Provided management, strategic planning, negotiations, and oversight for hundreds of classified and non-classified Military Construction (MILCON) contracts.

- Initiated and managed sale of Creative Solutions to Microsoft (MS); led merger into $9B Automation and Control Solutions Division.

- Developed a new business model to governmental agencies within first 12 months; implemented the model across most divisions within 24 months; resulted in establishment of cross-functional, collaborative business relationships ranging from Defense and Space to Commercial Building Automation sectors.

- Conceived and directed a cross-functional change initiative to implement Total Quality Management (TQM) across the organization; shepherded a new corporate vision and business paradigm driven by external customer needs; greatly improved customer service and support.

06/2010 to 01/2011; Co-Founder, Quality Director, Smart Technologies, Inc., Kranston, OR; Salary: $150,000 USD per year plus bonuses, stock, and dividends; Hours/Week: 40; Supervisor: Eli Whitney; Phone: 123-456-7890 OK to Contact.

SMART Technologies is a global leader in security solutions for numerous federal agencies.

EXECUTIVE LEADERSHIP AND ADVISING: Led three- and five-year strategic planning and tactical execution efforts, driving organizational growth, profitability, branding, and marketing. Prioritized and led facility real estate leases, construction, corporate relocation, capital budgets, formalizing Human Resources (HR) management, business development, marketing, sales, and customer satisfaction programs. Led in the development and implementation of new policies, procedures, specifications, and guidelines.

FINANCIAL PLANNING, EVALUATION, AND OVERSIGHT: Managed revenues and budgets of $25M. Managed funding apportionment, obligating and expending funds on numerous governmental contracts. Responded to GSA quality and security reviews/audits.

FEDERAL CONTRACTS AND SOLICITATIONS: Established a new division for the installation, construction, and service contracts. Awarded numerous U.S.-based and international government contracts to provide products and services for U.S., foreign, and joint governments. Programs included specialized facilities, such as F15/F16 bases, missile defense sites, communications, over-the-horizon radar sites, nuclear weapons storage facilities, chemical and munitions storage facilities, documentation, and Sensitive Compartmented Information Facility (SCIF) sites. Managed programs with lower-level priority assets, such as depots, arms and ammunition, commissaries, and medical facilities.

COMMUNICATION AND INTERAGENCY COORDINATION: Fostered and cultivated strategic relationships and involvement on Signals Intelligence (SIGINT) projects with the U.S. military. Supported and served as representative to military commands and foreign ministries.

Select Value-Added Accomplishments:

- Managed hundreds of federal and MILCON electronic security programs within all branches of the DOD and various individual base projects and procurements, including a $300M small business award program.

- Led a major organizational expansion from a "services-only" company to a provider of both products and services; customers quickly embraced new approach, and sales activity grew rapidly, increasing pool of project opportunities from the $20M range to more than $120M.

- Established an innovative industry business model, which included partnering with "competitors" to win major programs; collaborative approach represented a "win/win/win" model, increasing revenues 100% in three years.

- Successfully grew company to become a global security platform, winning competitive bids for numerous major projects and programs with installs at various worldwide bases.

- Leveraged unique product certifications and technical capabilities (communications and encryption) to win award of a major program contract; oversaw operations and financial management, which involved coordination on manufacturing, quality and safety, and installation maintenance and support.

- Created rapid and consistent revenue generation within first month and remained profitable every month; averaged 30% annual growth rates over nine consecutive years; positioned the company as an acquisition target by multiple billion-dollar entities, eventually selling to Honeywell International, a $32B Fortune 100 company.

Additional Relevant Experience

2006–2010; Co-founded and organized Revamp digital, then utilized social media platforms to expand the brand, gain market visibility, and fuel overall growth; utilized Generally Accepted
Accounting Principles (GAAP) and established programs that increased revenues by 50% and reduced expenses by 30% within the first eight months.

2002–2006: Vice-President and General Manager, Overcome Corporation

EDUCATION

Bachelor of Business Administration, University of New Orleans, New Orleans, LA, 1999

Selected Professional Training:

Essentials of Finance and Accounting Seminar, 2018
Support Functions and Logistics Certifications, 2017
Inventory, Logistics and Supply Chain Management, 2015
Labor Management Relations and Electronics, 2015
Total Quality Management, Performance and Productivity, 2014
Ratio Analysis and Financial Statements, 2014
General Services Administration Federal Supply Schedules, 2012

Selected Awards And Recognition:

Entrepreneur of the Year Nominee, 2015
National Congressional Leadership Committee Award, 2010

Memberships And Speaking Engagements:

Utah ROTC/ Chamber of Commerce Guest Speaker
Entrepreneur Panel Speaker; State of Washington
Regional Center of Innovation and Commercialization Review Member
Member, American Society for Personnel Security

Sample SES Resume IV:
GS-14 and Navy Reserve Officer to SES

PETE TOWNSHEND
100 Quadrophenia Drive ▪ Accident, MT DC 59001
Day Phone: 420-444-9000 ▪ Email: behindblueeyes@gmail.com
U.S. Citizen: Yes ▪ Security Clearance: Top Secret/Sensitive Compartmented Information
Highest Federal Rank: GS-0801-14 (since 2015)

SEASONED EXECUTIVE LEADER WITH MORE THAN 15 YEARS OF PROGRESSIVELY BROADER EXPERIENCE IN DESIGNING, DEVELOPING, AND DIRECTING TRANSFORMATIONAL ENGINEERING AND TECHNOLOGY PROJECTS AND PROGRAMS, RESOURCES, STAFFING, AND BUDGETS.

SELECTED AREAS OF EXPERTISE

Operations Program Management ~ Coalition Building & Collaborative Partnerships
Quality Improvement & Change Management ~ Strategic Planning & Analysis
Policy Development & Implementation ~ Organizational Leadership & Human Capital Management
Business & Financial Management Systems ~ Engineering, Research, & Development
Monitoring & Performance Management

SELECT PROFESSIONAL EXPERIENCE

10/2017–Present, Director of Public Works, Headley Grange, Over the Hills and Far Away, Led Zeppelin Avenue, Washington, DC 20374; Salary: $100,000 USD Per Year, GS-0801-14; Hours/Week: 40; Supervisor: Jimmy Page, Telephone: 202-411-2732; OK to Contact

EXECUTIVE LEADERSHIP: Serve as the Public Works Officer (Professional Engineer) for Headley Grange—a 200-acre organization supporting 5K employees and their families; 20 mission and tenant units (geographically separated); various U.S. Army, Marine Corps, Coast Guard, and Joint Service Commands; and other Department of Defense (DOD) and federal agencies. Provide ongoing guidance and daily oversight to a diverse, multidisciplinary staff of 200+ engineering and contracting professionals (with warrant authorities from $5M to $20M) in the design, development, and execution of facilities and facilities services acquisitions. Assist in the formulation, development, and implementation of policies, procedures, and guidelines concerning the planning, design, acquisition, and execution of more than $100M+ in engineering, construction, environmental, and facilities services annually.

PROGRAM MANAGEMENT: Manage and oversee the full spectrum of engineering, facilities maintenance, and systems engineering services related to acquisition activities. Lead the development of technical requirements and specifications; design of projects; and development of acquisition plans, schedules, and cost estimates for proposed and authorized projects. Proven expertise in administrative and organizational leadership (internal controls, human capital management, budget management, information resource management, facilities, contracting, and business process improvement), with a demonstrated ability to lead complex organizations and programs at the highest levels while balancing short-term priorities against long-term goals, objectives, and customer expectations. Assess current business management structures and methodologies (cost, schedule, and performance) and provide Subject Matter Expert (SME)-level advice to improve enterprise-wide governance and accountability and to streamline decision making.

STRATEGIC PLANNING AND PERFORMANCE MANAGEMENT: Review the development of projects for technical soundness, cost-effectiveness, efficiency, and fulfillment of requirements. Forge positive partnerships to maximize resources, and ensure funds are administered appropriately and are free from fraud, waste, and abuse. Engage with stakeholders to define needs and to monitor and evaluate funded actions or projects. Evaluate best practices and evidence-based research to promote change, improve strategic-level coalition building, and develop consensus on complex and constantly evolving issues. Oversee the cost, schedule, and performance of multiple projects, lines of effort, and funding streams. Drive coordination to create a coherent and coordinated program to provide myriad facilities acquisition and facilities engineering services.

CONTRACTING AND ACQUISITION MANAGEMENT: Manage acquisition professionals and contracting officers in the development of acquisition plans, contract solicitation, negotiations, award of contract, and supervision of post-contract award activities. Authored contract clauses, contract language, and supporting acquisition documents, including Determinations and Findings, and Justifications and Approvals for complex and/or sensitive acquisition programs. Ensure acquisition actions and processes are executed in accordance with all Financial Improvement and Audit Readiness standards and other federal and military financial and accounting regulations and standards (laws, statutes, regulations, and case law).

HUMAN CAPITAL MANAGEMENT AND INTERAGENCY COLLABORATION: Coordinate with more senior warranted contracting officers when additional authority and/or capacity is required. Set and reinforce performance standards and conduct performance evaluations, ensuring goals are met and subordinates are held accountable for their performance. Review organizational structure, then implement realignments, staffing adjustments, and delegated authority levels, as needed. Keep executive leadership apprised of significant developments and potential program challenges; provide strategic process analysis; and escalate issues, when needed, or recommend alternative courses of action.

Selected Accomplishments/Initiatives:

- Successfully accelerated the development and movement to execution of the annual project and maintenance execution plan. Instituted an array of management controls that streamlined processes, resulting in program acceleration from consistently operating three to four months behind schedule to a program operating three to four months ahead of schedule. Successfully reversed a trend of returning 5 to 10% of annual maintenance account of $10M, and instead increased the amount of funding provided by higher headquarters (HQ) by more than 10% due to increased confidence in ability to execute. A total increase of 20% in execution capability has directly improved the material condition and readiness of the installation.

- Assessed existing financial expenditure practices as being at odds with regulations and established best practice. Developed and instituted appropriate management controls to ensure the proper obligation of expenditures to protect the organization's interests. Instituted weekly and biweekly financial management assessments to review all new funding and execution of funding already provided ($20M+). Instituted management controls that reduced annual total late Fiscal Year (FY) funding giveback to less than $100K from a previous high of $500K.

- Lead a multi-agency group of engineers and master technicians in identify root cause of unknown repeated and persistent electrical outages affecting family housing and 44 flag and General Officer houses (25+ in just over one year). Orchestrated systematic problem identification, hypothesis testing, and implementation that successfully resolved the issues.

01/2015–09/2017, Operations Officer, Peaches En Regalia Court, Aurora, CO; Salary: $100,000 USD Per Year, GS-0801-14; Hours/Week: 40; Supervisor: Frank Vincent Zappa, Telephone: 555-867-5309; OK to Contact

EXECUTIVE LEADERSHIP: Supremely trusted executive leader empowered to direct action on all matters as they relate to supporting operational goals and objectives focused on providing personnel support to North American Aerospace Defense Command (NORAD) missions. Led all engineering plans and disaster management for the sole unit providing support across the enterprise to anticipate, deter, prevent, and defeat threats and aggression aimed at the U.S., its territories, and its interests.

STRATEGIC PLANNING AND PERFORMANCE MANAGEMENT: Recognized Subject Matter Expert (SME) consistently sought out to lead complex or high-profile assignments. Assumed the duties of the unit's first Financial Integrity and Audit Readiness Programs Officer. Analyzed and evaluated programs, develop and implemented Standard Operating Procedures (SOPs) and guidance for all strategic planning, and make sound recommendations for the design of strategic plans and processes to synchronize actions with the organization's strategic goals. Managed the development and implementation of metrics to monitor and assess progress and effectiveness of strategic planning. Personally developed integrity and audit procedures to ensure unit compliance with all directives and that unit is audit-ready. Pioneered benchmarking and performance metrics to ensure the organization received the greatest operational support possible.

COALITION BUILDING AND HUMAN CAPITAL MANAGEMENT: Communicated effectively, both verbally and in writing, with a diverse group of stakeholders, senior officials, subordinates, and interagency partners to share best practices; to influence policy, programs, and initiatives; to reach consensus; or to collaborate on vital projects and initiatives. Negotiated to build consensus or overcome resistance to new or controversial ideas to further action items. Drove daily operations for a team of 40 personnel. Led, motivated, and developed staff; established performance objectives; and ensured all mandatory training is accomplished. Empowered employees to identify and implement best practices. Embodied and ensured understanding for and support of Equal Employment Opportunity (EEO) and diversity in all actions.

Selected Accomplishments/Initiatives:
- Provided leadership, guidance, judgment, and technical expertise during numerous national-level exercises (e.g. Watch Officer and team lead during MARS ATTACKS exercise 2015).

- Led the Command to its greatest (50%) year-over-year increase in operational support, achieving nearly 5K days of support from just 28 members. Ensured watches were fully staffed, enabling for robust decision support to executive leaders and enabling more timely response to threats to the nation, including emergency and disaster response events.

- Served as Engineering Desk Officer for Hurricanes Kravitz, Metallica, Hendrix, and Tommy. Coordinated support to civil authorities and served as Engineering Interagency liaison during national-level exercise WHITE STRIPES.

- Developed the initial program and project requirements documentation for the first set of Military Construction (MILCON) projects proposed on the Moon since the close of the Cold War. Authored project requirements documentation that resulted in obtaining current funding, permitting rapid execution of this significant national security project.

- Reviewed and provided commentary on numerous joint publications draft revisions and staff instructions for engineering and logistics concerns.

10/2010–12/2014; Operations Officer, Houses of the Holy Enterprises, Directorate of Logistics, Engineering, and Security Cooperation, U.S. Nirvana Command: $100,000 USD Per Year, GS-0801-14; Hours/Week: 40; Supervisor: Brian May, Telephone: 444-111-2222; OK to Contact

EXECUTIVE LEADERSHIP: Led the planning and management of multiagency joint personnel support to U.S. Nirvana Command (NIVCOM) foreign assistance, security cooperation, infrastructure, and logistics requirements. Served as Budget Officer and managed the preparation of the Commander's annual MILCON Congressional testimony to Senate/House Armed Services Committees and Appropriations Committees, including compilation and review of NIVCOM area of responsibility (AOR) project Program Objective Memorandum (POM) and program appropriations requests from external service agencies. Coordinated the operational employment of military engineering assets for foreign disaster assistance/recovery efforts.

STRATEGIC PLANNING AND OPERATIONS MANAGEMENT: Liaised with U.S. Agency for International Development (USAID) to formulate and execute foreign humanitarian assistance in support of overseas disaster response and management. Led 34 NIVCOM personnel in the development of the Operational Support Plan for the unit and the execution of 2K labor days of support. Ensured uninterrupted program execution across the AOR. Led the development of the newly published NIVCOM Contingency Basing Guidelines and led the development of a 20-week NIVCOM Action Officer Coverage plan using 11 personnel; efforts ensured uninterrupted service to NIVCOM's mission.

Selected Accomplishments/Initiatives:

- Served as Officer in Charge of the Guerilla Radio Detachment. Managed numerous issues expediting short-fused orders in support of Operation Bombtrack through the approval process and travel itineraries, ensuring members executed mission as planned.

- As Officer in Charge of the Guerilla Radio Detachment, flawlessly led and managed the unit's relocation to Coda, Texas. Coordinated training and mission support of all personnel.

- Developed classified and unclassified integrated program database and decision support system used by NIVCOM and U.S. Embassy-embedded Country Security Cooperation Officers working with the U.S. Department of State (DOS).

- Prepared annual budget submissions and managed budget execution for the unit's 21 personnel, and ensured all personnel fully supported the unit's supporting plan and tasking. Led the move of the NIVCOM Detachment to Kingston, Jamaica, smoothly integrating the unit into a new support center, and increased unit training and readiness, which significantly improved the unit's support of NIVCOM's mission.

10/2008–10/2010: Operations Officer, Babylon By Bus Inc., Wailers Way, CA; $80,000 USD Per Year, GS-0801-14; Hours/Week: 40; Supervisor: Ziggy Marley, Telephone: 678-098-1123; OK to Contact

EXECUTIVE LEADERSHIP: Provided operational and administrative control for the Master of Puppets Construction Team and three subordinate construction units (1K+ personnel) serving Navy, Marine Corps, or joint commands in contingency and peacetime missions. Led the training and operational employment of all assigned personnel. Managed all training needs; ensured all personnel were prepared to deploy to provide construction support to forward-deployed combined, joint, and agency Commanders. Deployed globally, providing

command and control of joint task forces, as assigned. Supervised development of unit operational orders along with monthly letters of instruction.

Selected Accomplishments/Initiatives:

- Planned and developed the FY 2011 training and employment plan. Ensured minimal resources translated into maximum readiness for a mobilization supporting Operation Valley Girl.

- Served as Operations Officer and Training Officer. Led subordinate teams through training plan compression and adjustment to meet readiness and ready-to-deploy requirements on a three-month accelerated schedule to meet the Afghanistan Surge acceleration.

- Visionary during a major training conference; de-conflicted multiyear and multiunit training requirements, leading to more effective delivery of combat deployment training to units and increased fiscal stewardship.

Additional Professional Experience

07/2008 to 08/2009: Director of Facilities, Mamma's House Industries, Portland, OR
07/2005 to 01/2008: Training Coordinator, David Bowie University, London, England

EDUCATION

Master's degree in Music, Willamette University Law School, Salem, OR, 2016
Master's degree in Business Administration, Weezer University, Salem, OR, 2010
Master's degree in Engineering, Soundgarden University, Seattle, WA, 2002
Bachelor's degree in Engineering, Radiohead University, Phoenix, AZ, 2000

Select Professional Certifications and Training:

Defense Acquisition Workforce Improvement Act (DAWIA) Contracting Level 3 (2016)
Certified Defense Financial Manager (2015)
Advanced Joint Professional Military Education (AJPME II), Joint Forces Staff College (2014)
Joint Professional Military Education I (JPME I), Naval War College (2013)
Reserve Community National Security Course, National Defense University (2013)
Maritime Staff Operations Course, Naval War College (2012)
Asia-Pacific Orientation Course, Asia Pacific Center for Security Studies (2012)

www.SESWriters.com

Five-Page SES All-Inclusive Resume Sample with integrated TQs

JOHN Q. PUBLIC
7 Seventh Street, Apt. 77 ▪ Beaumont, TX 77707
Day Phone: 707-717-7777 ▪ Evening Phone: 707-717-7778
Email: jqp@careerprocenter.net ▪ Security Clearance: Top Secret SCI
U.S. Citizen: Yes ▪ Highest Federal Rank and Dates: GS-15; 08/2013–Present
Applying For Job # DA-61-ABC-00112233
Senior Technical Director/Chief Engineer

Highly accomplished Engineering Executive with more than 30 years of government and industry experience developing and leading complex programs. Scope of responsibility includes planning, engineering, execution, and evaluation of cyber resiliency testing for Department of Defense-wide major systems and managing engineering development for hundreds of networks globally with 1.2 million end points. A venerable advisor, relaying solid advice and recommendations to executive leaders on programs of vital national security importance. Offering executive leadership and technical acumen to support critical missions in national defense.

PROFESSIONAL EXPERIENCE

03/2019–Present, Lead Engineer, Data Science Directorate, U.S. Army Network Engineering Technology Command (NETCOM), Fort Richardson, AK, Salary: $101,000 Per Year; Hours/Week: 40+; Federal Series and Grade: GS-0800-15, Supervisor: Robert Roberts, Telephone: 123-456-7890; OK to Contact: Yes

Executive Leadership & Program Management: Direct total lifestyle systems engineering on mission-critical, Command-wide systems, including the Fusion Center Common Operational Picture for the Department of Defense Information Network-Army (DODIN-A) via oversight of multidisciplinary teams of computer engineers, operations research analysts, and computer scientists. Manage multimillion-dollar engineering projects by a Federally Funded Research and Development Center to develop "big data" solutions in support of the NETCOM mission. Develop and implement analysis of systems for Network Operations (NetOps) and System Operations (SysOps) in Cyberspace. Make sound technical decisions affecting IT and cyber programs and budgets, architectures, and standards for Army and NETCOM programs.

Capability Management & Operations Oversight: Direct highly skilled, diverse team of military, civilian, and contractor specialists in engineering and provisioning mission command capabilities of NETCOM DODIN Fusion Center to meet objectives of world's largest tactical and strategic network supporting 66 Army networks and 1.2M end points.

Proven Ability to Plan & Direct Organizational Change: Historically, the process of entering crypto keys for Communications Security (COMSEC) devices had involved manual input across 66 U.S. Army networks. Led an innovative effort to modernize key management through a secure virtual private network from a central data center at the National Security Agency (NSA). Directed team in the development of an action plan for each unit, devised and conducted hundreds of site program audits, and trained crypto key account holders on the new system. To gain buy-in, held exercises ahead of each fielding, and opened a telephone bridge line to enable NSA Operations Center, Army Cyber Command, NETCOM, and other stakeholders to collaborate in real time during the crucial first crypto key installation at each location. Ultimately, 99.1% of all 1.9K accounts were migrated to the new system, resulting in the Army's ability to configure cryptologic devices remotely.

Leadership Development & Mentoring: Provide leadership, mentorship, training, discipline, and feedback to diverse, multidisciplinary team of technical experts in managing Network Operations and System Operations in support of up to 1.2M end users. Provide inclusive workplace and proactively support freedom from sexual harassment. Foster professional development. Facilitate cooperation and synergy and support constructive resolution of conflicts.

Strategic Planning & Policy Development: Apply decades of technical executive-level experience to innovate, develop, and implement strategic plans to improve capabilities and security of cyber operations throughout NETCOM and Army-wide. Interpret and implement existing policies, directives, and regulations pertaining to IT and cyber programs. Establish policy and operating guidelines to include planning, development, organization, management, direction, execution, and administration of IT and cyber operations, Army-wide.

Technology Management: Integrate vertically with Army Cyber Command and subordinate theater signal commands. Coordinate with higher headquarters (HQ), subordinate commands, and external agencies to monitor systems and collect, review and analyze information for analysis and big data visualizations that improve integration and nesting. Support the establishment of Data Science remote sites at the University of Hawaii and Air War College. Support and advise on NETCOM Commanding General on technical programs to resolve and respond to engineering problems and technology management issues across Army Cyberspace. Address engineering challenges in cyber-contested environments and with increasingly tight fiscal constraints to produce practical engineering solutions that preserve and increase combat power via electronic networks and big data analytics. Coordinate, refine, analyze, and relay advice in response to unique and recurring engineering challenges using modern big data analytics applied in the framework of the Military Decision Making Process (MDMP).

Communication & Interagency Collaboration: Communication & Interagency Collaboration: As overall Government Technical Lead, built a coalition of government, academic and industry partners, including 75 doctorate-level researchers. Created working group crossing multiple echelons of network mission command encompassing Army Cyber Command, NETCOM, and Sandia to define require¬ments and track achievements. Understanding researchers' appreciation of presenting their findings personally to NETCOM Commanding General, sponsored quarterly meetings to allow Sandia researchers to present their findings. Ultimately, projects totaling $102M annually were selected based on informed consensus and cost-benefit analysis.

Versatile Leader & Team Builder: Upon arrival, conducted robust inspections as part of worldwide standards and metrics compliance program for DODIN-A operations. Quickly identified 88K+ non-standard or out-of-compliance network device configurations. Standardized Tactics, Techniques, and Procedures across NETCOM subordinate commands. Drew upon 20+ years as Commissioned Officer in U.S. Army to create a cohesive team that could efficiently execute requirements. Developed and implemented mentorship and training programs and met with each person individually to hear their goals, their input regarding current operations, and their ideas concerning future operations. Held recurring team meetings and implemented a new system of reporting metrics to ensure subordinate commands could see how they compared against each other. Observed and addressed interpersonal conflicts among team members via mediation and team-building activities. Empowered subordinates to focus on internal requirements with less direct oversight. Introduced automation to streamline compliance reporting process via utilization of sensor array to identify standardization/ compliance issues automatically, built the capability to top-load and track trouble tickets into Remedy systems. Lowered discrepancies 64% in one year and enabled $7M annual savings in compliance costs.

Strategic Planning, Policy, & Interagency Coordination: Liaised daily with Commanding General on operational impact and proposed mitigation or elimination of global cyberspace threats and vulnerabilities. Applied comprehensive knowledge of Joint Operations and Cyberspace Command and Control Operations in order to support NETCOM in Army Cyber Command, DOD Cyber Command, Joint and Army enterprise working groups while assisting with development of Concept of Operations (CONOPS) documents and training for Enterprise Project Management and IT Service Management functions within directorate. Ensured unit maintained compliance with Federal Information Security Management Act (FISMA).

Selected Accomplishments and Key Results:

- Directed DODIN-A mission command surge support in response to threat escalation on Korean Peninsula; led Fire Team in engineering, launching, and managing Fusion Center.

- Modernized U.S. Army Cryptographic Key Management Infrastructure, resulting in $6M annual decrease in cost, and vastly improved agility in U.S. Army secure communications.

- Collaborated with Cyberspace Security Division to organize and launch robust plan to close residual Information Assurance Vulnerability Management (IAVM) reports, resulting in the closure of 73K IAVM vulnerabilities within nine months.

03/2011–03/2019, Test Director, National Cyber Range, Institute for Defense Analyses, Richmond VA, Salary: $170,000.44 USD Per Year; Hours/Week: 40+; Supervisor: Dr. Roseanne Rose, Telephone: 456-789-0123; OK to Contact: Yes

Operational Leadership & Program Management: Organized and executed cybersecurity test and evaluation for Under Secretary of Defense for Acquisition, Technology, and Logistics (USD [ATL]) to determine major weapons systems' vulnerability to cyberattacks. Led the multidisciplinary team in identifying and establishing efficient, in safe testing environment, and in devising realistic offensive and defensive cyber scenarios for testing systems, such as Acquisition Category I (ACAT I) and ACAT II systems.

Tactful Interagency Liaison: Coordinated with senior leadership and integrated product teams to outline goals and objectives, track progress, perform systems management, discuss and respond to evolving customer requirements, and support the warfighter. Liaised extensively with U.S. Navy and integrated product teams to plan and execute enterprise architectural design of U.S. Navy High Assurance Network supporting Joint Information Environment.

Selected Accomplishments and Key Results:

- Engineered and executed 14 major system acquisition cyber operational resiliency tests; led the adversarial Red Team that achieved 100% penetration on all tested systems and identified vulnerabilities to address on major weapons systems. (Results Driven)

- Researched and drafted cyber resiliency CONOPS for U.S. Department of Homeland Security (DHS), which aided greatly in increased DHS budget of $530M for local first responders.

- Organized quick reaction team for Arab Spring predictive analysis. Used mathematical models of social network traffic collected from classified sources to predict population unrest.

- Piloted text analytics research for the DIA; reduced time to categorize, summarize, and declassify documents from 30 minutes to 600 microseconds via machine learning.

- Designed and launched first cyber resiliency testing program for U.S. Navy via collaboration with three independent federal research centers, producing report used to build $965M Program Objective Memorandum (POM) justification for Navy Cyber Operational Testing.

05/2010–06/2014, Vice-President (Elected Office), Chicopee, MA Board of Public Works, Lowell, MA, Salary: $0 USD Per Year; Hours/Week: 20; Supervisor: Joseph Redsox, Telephone: 508-508-5085; OK to Contact: Yes

Executive Leadership & Program Management: As an elected official, provided executive-level oversight of electricity, drinking water, wastewater sewer and sewage treatment plant, and stormwater/flood control in support of region encompassing 8.5K residential homes and 45K residents. Continually monitored and evaluated plans, employees, and operations to meet standards and customer-service requirements.

Human Capital Management: Led, mentored, and trained up to 180 diverse, multidisciplinary city and contractor employees in implementing and executing utility services with annual revenue of $12M. Directed and organized employees; created employee work schedules; defined priorities and set deadlines; set and adjusted short-term priorities; identified potential problems and determined solutions. Conducted reviews, including qualitative and quantitative analysis of technical issues, policies, and cost/time estimates of person-hours.

Financial Management: Assumed leadership of public utility, which retained $20M in cash, yet issued $120M in debt. Identified and addressed systemic problems, which were causing financial risk via close analyses of program metrics, and interviews with city and contractor employees and residents. Recognized early on the opportunity to reduce rates for low-income customers and to ease debt concurrently. Devised and implemented $85M public debt reduction program, which also encompassed five-year $100M infrastructure renewal. Creatively applied provision within Clean Water Act to obtain federal grants, which matched each dollar the city spend with $6 from the federal government toward clean water programs, thus reducing the net cost of capital to 2%. Since capital costs were reasonable, held public hearings to reduce utility rates on all services. Reduced rates for electricity, clean water, and sanitation rates by 9% for 45K residents, and modernized 32 miles of utility infrastructure as a result of keen financial planning and oversight.

Selected Accomplishments and Key Results:

- Partnered with city and state-level public safety agencies to plan and construct new $5.2M fire station, thus providing emergency response for residents. (Building Coalitions)

- Elected to Finance Committee of Regional Medical Center; built a lasting partnership between utility services and Medical Center; instrumented construction of new $280M medical center and increased utility sales to the hospital by 200%.

05/2008–02/2010, Program Manager, Intel High Performance Computing, Kowalski Corporation, El Paso, TX, Salary: $435,267 USD Per Year; Hours/Week: 40+; Supervisor: June Cleese, Telephone: 444-777-2222; OK to Contact: Yes

Executive Leadership & Program Management: Oversaw High Performance Computing (HPC) engineering commitments to the DIA encompassing average of $160M annually. Directed Intel programs such as $25M Silicon Photonics. Managed several multimillion-dollar projects concurrently. Applied concepts and methods of operations research, campaign analysis, warfare simulation, statistics, accounting and other quantitative methods. Performed Contract Costing, Fair Value Assessment, Quality Assurance/Quality Control (QA/QC) to ensure customer satisfaction. Engineered HPC programs with NSA and 10 other intelligence agencies.

Technology and Human Capital Management: Performed range of technical and analytical duties focused on our customers' professional and scientific work. Used factor analysis and statistics to estimate Total Available Market (TAM) growth (added $3.5B TAM to 2013 business plan). Performed Earned Value Analysis of deliverables and milestones. Led engineers for circuit power estimation, performance simulation, and profit-loss estimation. Ensured staff was appropriately recruited, selected, appraised, and rewarded based on performance and contribution to objectives. Ensured system reliability and configuration integrity.

Tactful Interagency Liaison: Co-chair, representing industry, for Presidentially appointed commission on use of HPC for cybersecurity. Briefed Deputy Secretary of Defense, National Intelligence Director, and Deputy Secretary of Homeland Security on HPC technology.

Selected Accomplishments and Key Results:

- Raised market segment share in microprocessors engineered for supercomputers from 29% to 92%, dominating the industry and increasing revenue by $2.6B per year.

- Established Intel Corporation partnerships with DIA, Bank of America, and Target Corporation, enabling $200M in annual increase in sales revenue for Intel enterprise products.

- Negotiated DIA cooperative research contracts worth $8.14M, $4.6M, and $3.4M.

- Directly managed silicon photonics $4M Project SALAMANDER and $24M Project Zinc Valley. Results reported in Science Magazine.

- Wrote Procurement Strategy for $85M in joint DIA/Intel HPC Research and Development.

Additional Professional Experience:
08/1988–04/2008; Lieutenant Colonel, U.S. Marine Corps, Washington, DC. Received the Marcus Smith Memorial Award for Excellence in Analysis for team leadership in the Office of the Chief of Staff, U.S. Navy.

EDUCATION

Master of Science, Operations Research Engineering, Massachusetts Institute of Technology, Cambridge, MA, 1999, Honors: Summa Cum Laude
Bachelor of Science, Physics with Minor in Chemistry, George Mason University, 1990

Selected Professional Training & Certifications:
Microsoft Power BI, 2017; Johns Hopkins University Data Science Certificate, 2017 to Present; Big Data Analysis with R Language, 2017; Riverbed Network Analysis and Simulation, 2016; DOD, Defense Acquisition University (DAU), February 2014; Intel Corporation, Project Management Professional, January 2012; Intel Corporation, Contract Management, October 2010 and December 2010; National Charrette Institute, Certified Charrette Planner, May 2008

SES All-Inclusive Resume Sample without TQs

JONATHAN DOE
123 Alphabet Street • New Orleans, LA 70056
Email: info@careerprocenter.net • Phone: 123-456-7890 ▪ SSN: 123-45-6789
Vacancy Number: 123456
Deputy Officer for Equal Employment Opportunity (EEO) & Diversity

---

HIGH-PERFORMANCE EXECUTIVE WITH VISION AND ENERGY TO CREATE AND
IMPROVE EQUAL OPPORTUNITY, HUMAN RESOURCES, DIVERSITY, AND COMPLIANCE
PROGRAMS ON A STRATEGIC AND INTERNATIONAL SCALE.

KNOWLEDGE AND EXPERTISE FOUNDED ON MILITARY BACKGROUND, THREE YEARS AS
A SENIOR COMPLIANCE OFFICER IN THE FEDERAL GOVERNMENT AND A DECADE
OF CORPORATE EXPERIENCE IN…

- Diversity Initiatives
- Policy Development
- Critical Thinking
- Inclusion Strategies

- Affirmative Action
- Compliance Enforcement
- Change Management
- Enterprise-Wide Planning

- Policy Compliance
- Process Improvement
- Strategic Planning
- Grievance Resolution

PROFESSIONAL EXPERIENCE

12/2014–09/2018, Director, EEO Initiatives, Maxwell House Coffee, Athens, GA; Hours/week: 40; Salary: $157,000 USD Per Year (+ bonus and stock option); Supervisor: Larry Kelling, Telephone: 123-456-7890; OK to Contact: Yes

PROFESSIONAL ACCOUNTABILITIES: As Director of Equal Employment Opportunity (EEO) Initiatives, administered and directed EEO and diversity programs, providing leadership and driving change to ensure full and affirmative implementation of EEO principles for 235,000 employees in 48 countries.

EXECUTIVE LEADERSHIP & MANAGEMENT: Developed the strategy, vision, and annual operating plan, and then staffed the newly formed EEO Initiatives Department. Directed and prioritized the efforts of 17 personnel while administering a budget of $5.4M. Developed team members and utilized immersion training to ensure exposure to every relevant aspect of EEO compliance. Developed Annual Operating Plan and maintained budget discipline while delivering high-quality EEO compliance consultation and leadership. Initiated and disseminated critical reports and EEO initiatives. Developed methodology for Executive Diversity goals and led efforts to perform the first comprehensive analysis of compensation in the history of the company.

EEO & DIVERSITY PROGRAM MANAGEMENT: Oversaw development and administration of more than 7,000 Affirmative Action plans for all operating regions. Devised and implemented strategic EEO and diversity initiatives consistent with management's strategic vision. Developed regional operating plans to ensure compliance with global EEO regulations. Collaborated across cross-functional teams to develop and communicate the company's EEO compliance strategy. Articulated long-range plan for EEO compliance and its impact on overall employment strategy.

TRANSFORMING CULTURE & PROCESSES: Led major organizational change in response to growing federal non-compliance issues, ensuring compliance with U.S. employment law and directing a robust gap analysis to better identify any employment liability related to non-compliance with federal regulations. Determined worldwide compliance gaps, developed strategic compliance vision and plan, and then led execution of the operating plan to bring all of Starbucks' operating divisions into compliance with relevant employment regulations.

TEAM BUILDING & DEVELOPMENT: Challenged to overcome growing non-compliance; identified position requirements, wrote position descriptions, and recruited and hired a technically and culturally diverse management team and support staff comprised of 17 personnel. Overcame internal conflict and strengthened teamwork by fostering open communications and giving employees a sense of ownership in organizational strategy while aligning work efforts with overarching goals. Mentored and trained employees, developed standard operating procedures (SOPs), and provided developmental opportunities. Led staff through tasks previously considered impossible, bringing previously non-compliant organization to full compliance within one year.

CUSTOMER-FOCUSED PROBLEM SOLVING: Over time, a decentralized work environment created a nightmare in terms of regulatory compliance. Upon being hired and realizing there was no standardized process for data management in any of Starbucks' operating regions, developed policies and procedures to solve the growing problem by addressing data collection, input, and management at the organizational level. Led a complete re-survey of all 235,000 employees in 49 countries to determine their demographic data; positioned organization for continued success and improved customer service and delivery by leading the retail hiring solution team and participating on the acquisition leadership team that managed the rollout of a new Applicant Tracking System in all retail locations. Recognized with a Bravo Award and $10,000 on-the-spot bonus.

OPTIMIZING PEOPLE, BUDGETS, AND TECHNOLOGY: After being tasked with securing funding for new EEO Initiatives Department, developed a proposed budget, including specific milestones and associated timelines for success. Secured $1.2M the first year, $3.8M the next, and $5.4M the third year. Developed business cases, coordinated with procurement department to develop Requests for Proposals (RFPs), and clearly demonstrated the Return on Investment (ROI) for several other key initiatives, resulting in additional support and funding. Financial management and planning resulted in reduced compliance exposure and decreased risk of losing more than $500M in direct and indirect government business.

ADVISING & OVERSIGHT: Principal advisor to the Chief Executive Officer (CEO) and senior leadership team on all EEO and diversity-related issues worldwide. Coordinated with cross-functional teams in Global Staffing division to identify solutions; advise on how to effectively address the most critical compliance issues and risks. Established and implemented metrics for monitoring EEO-compliant processing programs.

PROCESS IMPROVEMENT: Reenergized EEO compliance programs across the board, resulting in CEO's full visibility and support of core initiatives. Developed and administered Starbucks' Alternative Dispute Resolution (ADR) program. Oversaw, reviewed, and approved all final actions for complaints of employment discrimination.

Select Value-Added Achievements:
- Developed a system that provided leadership with real-time metrics on the diversity landscape and potential impediments to EEO/fairness within respective countries/regions.
- Led major transformation and gained full compliance with all relevant employment regulations within 12 months of being hired.
- Created a Compliance/Fairness learning system to ensure "on-the-spot" training for staffing professionals and hiring managers; resulted in increased awareness and compliance with strategic diversity vision.

12/2012–12/2014, Senior Compliance Manager, Baker Laboratories, Springfield, VA; Hours/week: 40; Salary: $117,000 (+ bonus and stock option) USD Per Year; Supervisor: Lee Kelley; Telephone: 123-456-7890; OK to Contact: Yes

PROFESSIONAL ACCOUNTABILITIES: A global, broad-based healthcare company with 83,000 employees, devoted to discovering new medicines, new technologies, and new ways to manage health. As Senior Manager, Compliance, Diversity, and Inclusion, administered all aspects of the EEO/diversity and Alternative Dispute Resolution (ADR) program. Played a key leadership role in monitoring HR practices and policies; directing the creation of programs, processes, and tools that promoted and ensured workplace fairness and dovetailed with the company's Diversity and Inclusion (D&I) strategies.

INTERAGENCY ALLIANCES: Developed the business case for hiring veterans and then built a lasting coalition of VA-based corporations with a shared vision of improving access to corporate jobs for transitioning military service members, veterans, and military family members. As a result, partnered with state, local, and non-profit organizations to assist more than 6,000 veterans to embark on rewarding careers after military service.

EXECUTIVE LEADERSHIP & MANAGEMENT: Led a team of up to 12 personnel and administered an annual budget of $2M. Oversaw organizational recruiting and diversity strategy. Executed the D&I strategy while developing and maintaining a knowledge management process to identify, capture, and transfer enterprise-wide diversity and inclusion initiatives and programs. Promoted the creation of a discrimination-free work environment, allowing each employee to reach his/her full potential. Developed change and implementation plans for HR development projects that ensured transfer of capability and sustainability of HR programs, processes, and tools.

EEO & DIVERSITY PROGRAM MANAGEMENT: Directed the development of EEO/diversity strategies that supported the organization's current and emerging human capital needs and promoted anti-discrimination. Advocated and created strategy to enhance diversity of staff and increase cultural awareness. Ensured thorough and accurate tracking of applicants for monthly Affirmative Action/EEO reporting and oversaw local, state, and federal Affirmative Action reporting. Conducted and directed numerous discrimination investigations.

TRENDING, EVALUATION, & ANALYSIS: Performed statistical modeling and supervised PhD-level statisticians. Evaluated organizational policies to determine if they supported the goal of an inclusive and diverse workforce. Made viable recommendations regarding changes to HR policies, appropriate workforce-related programs, and business/procurement initiatives. Conducted demographic trend analyses.

ADVISING & OVERSIGHT: Advised business unit leaders on the implications of short- and long-term decisions, strategies, and large-scale change efforts. Counseled managers and employees regarding the intent, application, and compliance requirements of significant labor and regulatory laws, such as Family and Medical Leave Act (FMLA), Workers' Compensation, EEO Commission, and Americans with Disabilities Act (ADA). Served as expert resource and advisor to HR managers, helping them ensure diversity was embedded in processes and programs, especially those aimed at increasing upward mobility for high-potential employees. Educated managers and employees on HR policies, plans, programs, practices, processes, and tools (e.g., compensation, benefits, development projects, EEO).

Select Value-Added Achievements:
- Developed and implemented strategy that resulted in organization being selected as one of the best places to work by Fortune, Diversity Inc., and Working Mother magazines.

 www.SESWriters.com

- Initiated and led design and implementation of strategic diversity plan to drive business results and create a competitive advantage; resulted in a 2% decrease in employee turnover within an 18-month period.
- Discovered and investigated potential hiring and compensation discrimination allegations by implementing an "equity review" process; ultimately resolved compensation issues that resulted in $7M savings company-wide.

12/2008–12/2012, Diversity Manager, Absolute Consulting, Missoula, MT; Hours/week: 40; Salary: $88,000 USD Per Year; Supervisor: Cristal Deshowitz; Telephone: 123-456-7890; OK to Contact: Yes

PROFESSIONAL ACCOUNTABILITIES: Absolute Consulting employs 45,000 professionals in the U.S. with a single focus: serving their clients and helping them solve their toughest problems in four key business areas—audit, financial advisory, tax, and consulting. Hired to create and stand up Diversity and Compliance Department for a new consulting spinoff organization. At the last minute, senior management decided not to spin off from the parent company.

Select Value-Added Achievements:
- Entrusted and challenged to completely start the department from scratch, including hiring three subordinate managers, writing policy, and administering a budget of $900K.
- Communicated effectively, both verbally and in writing, with a diverse range of customers, supervisors, and colleagues.
- Coordinated and networked with Fortune 500 companies and governmental agencies, including Disney and GMAC, to develop their compliance diversity functions.
- Planned and implemented HR processes, plans, programs, and tools with business leaders to build and enhance organizational capability.

EDUCATION: University of New Orleans, New Orleans, LA, Master of Public Administration, 2003; Georgia State University, Atlanta, GA, Bachelor of Arts in English, 2001; Diploma, Shaw High School, New Orleans, LA, 1997

Job-Related Training: Situational Leadership, 2018; Attributes of Management Excellence, 2009; Leadership Styles, Starbucks, 2017; Servant Leadership, 2017; Project Management Leadership Group, 2015; Responsibility Assignment Matrix (RACI), 2004; Information Mapping, 2014; Management by Objective, 2012; Change Management, 2011; Advanced SPSS Training, 2010

Job-Related Honors & Awards: Bravo Award, Maxwell House, 2010; Senior Vice-President's Award, Baker Laboratories, 2005; Senior Vice-President's Award, Cingular, 2004; various U.S. Army awards

Cover Letter/Letter of Interest Sample

JOHN DOE
173 Pierce Avenue ▪ Macon, GA 31204
Day/Evening Phone: 478-742-2442
Email: info@careerprocenter.net

16 November 2019

Ms. Jane Smith
Human Resources Specialist
Organization Name
Reference: Vacancy Announcement XX-XX-XXXX/Attorney-Advisor (General Counsel)

Dear Ms. Smith:

Please accept the attached application and accompanying documents as an expression of interest in the advertised position for Attorney-Advisor (General Counsel). I believe I would be an asset to your organization for several reasons.

First, my diverse background crosscuts many different organizations, including government agencies, as well as various industries and all types of individual and corporate clients. Second, the combination of my expert knowledge of the banking industry, contracts, and general corporate and business transactions will provide your agency with a frontline perspective on complex issues involving the department, having represented clients for cases in which criminal investigations or illegal narcotics were involved. Finally, my strong commitment to public service, as evidenced by my service in the U.S. Navy and my previous five years as a federal attorney, are testament to my desire to serve my government and country to the best of my ability.

My relevant qualifications include the following:

- Significant experience in litigation involving various elements of corporate finance, such as loan workouts, corporate/personal bankruptcies, foreclosures, enforcement of loan guarantees, notes, and other financial instruments of failed institutions (2014–2019).

- Legal advice and counsel to executive clients and financial institutions on preparing internal policies and procedures for complying with federal bank, thrift, and Securities and Exchange Commission (SEC) statutes and regulations (2010–2014).

- Subject-matter knowledge and expertise on a wide a variety of legislation, such as Sarbanes-Oxley Act, evolving Homeland Security acts, and federal financial guidance.

I am very interested in exploring this new challenge and would welcome an opportunity to meet with you to discuss meaningful contributions I can make to the organization. I look forward to contacting you in the near future to determine the status of my candidacy.

Sincerely,
John Doe

Blank Cover Letter/Letter of Interest Template
(with instructions)

CUSTOMER NAME
173 Pierce Avenue ▪ Macon, GA 31204
Day/Evening Phone: 478-742-2442
Email: info@careerprocenter.net

16 November 2019

Ms. Jane Smith
Human Resources Specialist
Division Name
Organization Name
Reference: Vacancy Announcement XX-XX-XXX

Dear Ms. Smith:

Introductory paragraph: (Focus on the organization to which you are applying. Reference the position for which you are applying, and address the organization's needs, not yours. Capture the reader's attention by demonstrating that you've done your homework by studying the organization, what it does, and its customer base).
The second paragraph should tie your experience to what the organization is looking for in a candidate; this paragraph can focus a little more on you, but watch the "I" syndrome.

Be very careful not to start every sentence with "I." Be sure you convey what you can offer the organization, not what you want it to do for you (e.g., don't say, "I am seeking opportunities in which I can enrich my skills and gain experience in such-and-such…"). Rather, give a brief (very brief) synopsis of what you've been doing for the past five years and how your experience can further the organization's objectives.

Relevant qualifications include the following:

- Match your qualifications with their needs with some select value-offered career highlights or educational experiences.
- Quantify your accomplishments, whenever possible.
- Remember, this is your first impression. Keep it positive and active!

Your closing paragraph should reiterate how well you would fit with the organization. You should be assertive here; ask for action to be taken in the form of an interview or consultation.

Sincerely,

John Doe

Blank Cover Letter/Letter of Interest Template

CUSTOMER NAME
173 Pierce Avenue ▪ Macon, GA 31204
Day/Evening Phone: 478-742-2442
Email: info@careerprocenter.net

16 November 2019

Ms. Jane Smith
Human Resources Specialist
Division Name
Organization Name
Reference: Vacancy Announcement XX-XX-XXX

Dear xxxx:

Introductory paragraph:

Second paragraph:

Relevant qualifications include the following:

-
-
-

Closing paragraph:

Sincerely,

John Doe

Technical Qualification: GS-15 to SES
(with CCAR highlighted)

Note: A personal executive narrative statement can be written in countless ways, and each individual's career, disposition, writing style, and experience will be different. Be sure to include specific job titles and dates, and use the CCAR (Challenge-Context-Action-Result) format.

1. Skill in the defining, evaluating, and administering performance-based contracts for IT materiel and services.

(CHALLENGE/CONTEXT) As Director, Networking, Communications Infrastructure, Services and Operations (NISO), I am the Contracting Officer's Technical Representative (COTR) for a 10-year performance-based Information Technology (IT) contract valued at $627M. Because of my previous experiences and success in managing performance-based contracts, in June 2018, ITA's Executive Director personally chose me to lead and establish a structure framework for this large outsourcing effort. The contract was entering its second year, and the agency lacked adequate controls and oversight to ensure the contractor was delivering the services for which the government was paying. This contract was the largest outsourcing effort for ITA and was under scrutiny by the Pentagon community. Customers were skeptical regarding whether the contractor was being held accountable for meeting the required Performance Metrics.

(ACTIONS) I coordinated closely with a diverse group of personnel, including officials from General Services Administration (GSA), the IT departments from Headquarters (HQ), Air Force, Army, Office of the Secretary of Defense (OSD), and the Office of the Secretary of the Army (OSA) Budget Office. I developed a Concept of Operations that thoroughly explained my intended management processes and procedures, then provided it to both the government and contractor. For every task in the Statement of Work (SOW), I identified and assigned a government Performance Monitor with whom the contractor was required to work to resolve all issues. Further, I established weekly meetings to address any internal communication problems and monthly In Progress Reviews during which the contractor briefed the government on how well it was meeting the required Performance Metrics and budget cost. I reviewed all the required deliverables in the contract and closely evaluated how the information was being used by the government Performance Monitors to conduct their contract administration functions. I chose to restructure the Performance Metrics based on customer feedback and the "pain point" I identified.

For example, I readjusted the allocated percentage of the award fee pool. I wanted a strong initial focus on stabi¬lizing and standardizing operations, restoral times, and cost control. I updated the Performance Metrics on an annual basis, and incentivized and challenged the contractor. I collaborated with Gartner, Inc., to help me develop a Total Cost of Ownership (TCO) model for the services being provided by the contractor. In addition, I benchmarked costs against other Department of Defense (DOD), federal, and commercial organizations similar to my department. By consistently managing contract budget costs, I challenged the contractor to find more efficient ways to provide their service. To improve and refine the agency's overall contracting processes, I restructured the Award Fee Board Membership and appointed the Performance Monitors to serve on the board. This change sent a strong message to the contractor that it was important to work hand in hand with his/her government peers. I ensured feedback was provided to the contractor within 10 days after the Award Fee Board on items the government wanted addressed at the next meeting. Prior to my arrival, the contractor consistently achieved 100% on all Performance Metrics and never received feedback. The changes I implemented put the necessary oversight in place and allowed me to restructure Performance Metrics to better align them with the requirements of the contract, bringing increased creditability to the agency.

(RESULTS) My Concept of Operations was key in establishing the structure for how the government and contractor would work together in resolving any issues relating to the contract before elevating it to my level. Additionally, it explained everyone's roles and responsibilities and established mandatory meetings that promoted open communication and diversity with the staff. In fact, my ability to establish and foster a productive partnership between the government and the contractor was fundamental to my overall success in managing these contracts. I reduced the contract labor costs by $3M by removing non-value-added functions from the contract. I then conducted a 100% review of all hardware and software maintenance costs, identifying items that were no longer being used effectively. By leveraging such strict budget cost control mechanisms, I reduced the contract hardware and maintenance costs by $2M. Ultimately, I increased my mission from 56,765 network ports in 2017 to 97,900 ports in 2018 without increasing any contract costs. Customer confidence improved dramatically. Finally, I have been approached by peers, both internal and external to my agency, to share the challenges

anmethods I used to manage this Performance Based Contract so effectively.

2. Demonstrated knowledge of principles and practices of team building to create a team environment that fosters partnership, innovation, and continuous process improvement.

(CHALLENGE/CONTEXT). I have been building and leading diverse teams and educational organizations at various levels for the past 25 years. For example, in 2018, I became Educational Administrator for a large region of the Department of Education. A recent reorganization had divided Education Officers across organizational lines, and there was very little communication between these individuals. My goal was to create an environment founded on teamwork, in which team members felt a sense of ownership, and were engaged in a continual process of innovation and improvement.

(ACTIONS) I began to make contact and visit the 29 schools and 6 residential facilities under my purview. While forming partnerships with administrators, I took tours of their facilities, and helped them to complete needs assessments. I did not simply give deadlines, but rather cultivated the relationships and kept the administrators fully informed of any pressing issues. I also continued to provide outstanding assistance and support, consistently returning all calls and responding to emails within 24 hours.

Concurrently, I worked to form the needed teaming environment with my colleagues at the District Office. As a new member of the organization with a limited knowledge of its rich history, I had to be very tactful in making suggestions during administrative meetings. Since I transferred in from the West Coast, many stakeholders just assumed I knew nothing about life in the East. Over time, in formal and informal situations, I made it known that while I had been gone for a while, my roots have always been in the East.

(RESULTS) As a result of my ongoing team building and coordination, the culture and climate at both the district and school levels has become more collegial and collaborative. People reported feeling more empowered to participate in discussions and express their true thoughts about a given situation. As my credibility grew, I received more opportunities to plan trainings and workshops, and to run meetings and provide professional development. In this more engaged environment, the team's performance thrived. The number of educational assessments grew by 65% within my first year—the largest increase in the organization's history. Morale improved dramatically, and retention improved by 35% within the first six months, which all translated into a 90% efficiency gain in responding to customer requests.

(CHALLENGE/CONTEXT). Another example began in 2016, when I became the Chief of Staff within a Department of Education Regional Office in Ohio. I directed approximately 80 personnel across 9 schools in 4 states, encompassing more than 6,000 faculty and students. In addition, I planned and directed a variety of school/district management functions to include School Registration/Tuition programs; Student Transportation Services; Safety/Security; Logistics Programs Property Accountability; Facilities Management Financial Management; and Executive Services. When I arrived, there was no unity of purpose, and there were no standard procedures in place. My predecessor had been terminated, and I had no template to follow, only a clear directive from senior officials to make improvements. Most significantly, the staff members' attitudes were self-serving and complacent, thinking I would simply be another short-term leader. I took a number of actions to form a more engaged and effective team environment.

(ACTIONS) I began to simultaneously gather feedback regarding the culture and assess the efficacy and performance of all programs. I then engaged the team in developing protocols for how we should conduct business across various program areas. Next, I facilitated several book studies, and the resultant discussions allowed me to clarify values and emphasize what a healthy culture and strong work ethic should look like in our setting, without placing blame.

Meanwhile, I oversaw implementation of the completed protocols, and processes became tighter with each implementation. At the beginning of year two, I led efforts to revise our purpose as an organization and develop a vision and mission based on our core values. Anytime someone earned recognition, such as a citation or a time-off award, I presented the certificate to the individual in front of his/her peers.

(RESULTS) As a result of my team-building efforts during this period, the organization became much more effective and worked with a spirit of continual improvement. Due to clear standards and consistent leadership, morale improved, turnover decreased by 50%, and employee grievances decreased by over 80%. Finally, my team completed 6 strategic initiatives within the next 18 months, many of which directly supported the Secretary of Education's top priorities, while enhancing overall timeliness by 80%.

Technical Qualifications: Corporate to SES

1. Knowledge of planning, programming, and budgeting system for Military Construction (MILCON) and military component O&M funding; and knowledge of Government and international financial regulations, accounting standards and civilian personnel regulations, including employee appeal processes.

Over the past several decades, I have provided management, strategic planning, negotiations, and oversight for well over 1,000 classified and non-classified Military Construction (MILCON) and security-related contracts, projects, and programs for the U.S. government. Some of these initiatives involved the largest global Department of Defense (DOD) security programs protecting U.S. government, U.S. European Command (EUCOM), and North Atlantic Treaty Organization (NATO) facilities. The larger programs were typically Indefinite Delivery, Indefinite Quantity (IDIQ), multisite, multiyear (three to five years), multidisciplined in scope, and ranged from $1M to more than $500M in size. My experiences have provided me with an in-depth understanding of the federal contracting, planning, programming, and budgeting system.

For instance, I understand military component Operations and Maintenance (O&M) funding, which is an annual budgeted and funding approval process. Most O&M appropriations are subdivided into Budget Activities (BAs), such as Operating Forces; Mobilization; Training and Recruiting; and Administrative/Service Activities. Further, O&M funds carry a variety of restrictions such as Supplies and Materials (at certain thresholds), Defense Working Capital Funds (regardless of system unit cost), and Maintenance of Equipment for repair. Similarly, O&M funds often cover DOD civilian salaries, including personnel supporting or managing acquisition programs. There are some exceptions, such as personnel employed at facilities funded with Research, Development, Test, and Evaluation (RDT&E) funding. I am also highly familiar with the NATO Security Investment Program (NISP) and the National Industrial Security Program Operating Manual (NISPOM).

I effectively leveraged all of my skills and experience while serving as President and Chief Executive Officer (CEO) of Clearview, Inc. In this capacity, I spearheaded the strategic relationships and involvement with the various federal programs. In addition, I have led major programs and projects at all levels of DOD asset priority classification, which included specialized facilities such as F15/F16 bases, missile defense sites, communications, over-the-horizon radar sites, nuclear weapons storage facilities, chemical and munitions storage facilities, documentation, and Sensitive Compartmented Information Facility (SCIF) sites. I have also been involved in programs with lower-level priority assets, such as arms and ammunition, on post Banks, Post and Base Exchanges, Commissaries, and medical facilities. Given the scope, scale, and importance of these programs, my company had to embrace the standards and regulations that supported the mission and were accepted by the customers.

For example, the company was awarded a major contract for transporting weapons on trains due to our unique product certifications and technical capabilities. I oversaw my company's operational role, which involved extensive coordination on manufacturing, quality and safety, and installation maintenance and support. Beyond operational management, I also oversaw facets of the financial management effort on costing and allocation. As a direct result of my involvement, we were awarded a follow-on contract.

I have also managed numerous other MILCON electronic security programs. I adopted and instituted industry or governmental standards, such as Federal Acquisition Regulations (FAR), and Generally Accepted Accounting Principles (GAAP). Quite often, these standards further incorporated a host of other supporting standards such as Occupational Safety and Health Administration (OSHA) for safety and procurement quality requirements.

In each of these initiatives, I have been able to create outstanding results. My knowledge and leadership during more than 1,000 MILCON projects directly contributed to 30% year-over-year growth. Corporate quality can also be defined as customer satisfaction, and under my leadership, we experienced less than a 1/10th of 1% customer return rate. Yet another testament to my success and knowledge was our eventual sale to a billion-dollar Fortune 100 Corporation.

2. Ability to represent the U.S. in international forums, preferably involving NATO, and in formal arbitration proceedings; in addition, experience in developing and/or presenting Congressional testimony.

During my 25+-year career, I have participated in numerous large-scale U.S. governmental, international, and NATO program-level discussions, dispute resolutions, negotiations, mediations, and more formal approaches, such as legally binding/non-binding arbitration. Moreover, I have served in various roles, ranging from a Supplier and Quality Director, to Site/Project/Program Manager, to Senior Executive-level negotiator and final decision maker. While doing so, I have interacted with, presented to, and negotiated with European North Atlantic Treaty Organization (NATO) partners on security projects, including Embassies and military installations in NATO countries such as Belgium, Germany, Great Britain, Spain, Hungary, Iceland, Poland, and Turkey.

Additionally, I have presented to and briefed senior Department of Defense (DOD) flag-level officers, senior DOD Centers of Expertise staff members, Major Command staff members, and NATO Ministers of Defense personnel and staffs. These interactions ranged from one-on-one settings, to 10-50 member staffs, and even to large groups in the hundreds as a presenter or panel member at symposiums and conferences. Similarly, I have represented industry on panels to and in conjunction with senior staff members of U.S. government Centers of Expertise.

Every program or professional endeavor comes with its own circumstances and nuances, requiring independent review, analysis, and unique approaches. For example, in 2017, I was serving as CEO of Kraft Group during a complex testing and certification approval program. With a highly diverse group of stakeholders, this effort involved confusing and opposing points of view. More specifically, we had a product specification that was supported by Operations Orders (OPORDs), but that lacked sufficient detail to clearly define nuances regarding the OPORD. Additionally, the product specification lacked certain technical aspects of the testing configuration, procedures, and subsequent operator or supervisor actions.

To overcome these issues, I led the discussion regarding initially identified failures, met with the Testing Agency, and my company's staff personnel. I then led this group in reviewing, discussing, and dissecting all issues and concerns. After gathering all of the pertinent information, we placed the issues into categories and further classified them as "major" or "minor" issues.

Through effective communication, coordination, and negotiation, I achieved consensus among all parties. We still had several challenges to overcome, such as changes in the core specification, the Statement of Work (SOW), supporting documents specification, and Contract Data Requirements Lists (CDRLs). Moreover, we had to make cost modifications to the contract for additional funds for certain "agreed-upon development" that was outside the scope of the commercial product capabilities, but that were identified as unique requirements for the government. I led the group in developing an action plan to implement the changes, and responsible parties went about resolving the identified issues for retest. We updated the documentation and testing specifications, and even the OPORD. Next, we resubmitted these documents to the testing agency for review and approval, subsequently achieving full acceptance and certification of our product.

In another example, I was challenged to utilize my strong mediation and arbitration skills. I was serving as CEO and President of ShopSmart, Inc. in 2018, and it became clear that the responsible party (a shipping and storage company) lost a number of high-value pallets containing very specialized products. Initially, the company declined to accept responsibility, even though they could not account for the items. Regardless of my personal involvement and attempts to obtain resolution without taking legal action, the company seemingly had no intention of being held accountable for the loss of goods, likely due to the high value (in the hundreds of thousands of dollars).

Although formal legal action is always a last resort, in this case, I had no choice. I notified the customer, notified the supplier (shipping company), and began the process of formal legal action. Because of my efforts, and coupled with extensive documentation and even video proof, we quickly brought the shipping company to the negotiations table. Leveraging my communication and negotiating skills, we reached a mutually agreeable resolution without having to enter into a formal binding arbitration or further legal action.

Ultimately, I have been involved in a variety of contractual situations consisting of technical, schedule, financial, and even resource conflicts, all which could have turned into stalemates, finger pointing, and legal actions. To this day, I have never failed to overcome the issues and achieve a mutually acceptable agreement and roadmap for success. Due to the scope and sensitivity of many of the DOD programs and projects I have been involved with, there were seldom any formal awards or recognition. The satisfaction of service and the continued business relationship was considered reward enough. Nevertheless, on a few occasions, I received individual or team recognition from Major DOD Command-level staff, and from the Centers of Expertise. Because of the depth and breadth of my career, I can now confidently apply my skills and expertise to virtually any program, project, or position, confidently representing my organization to senior government officials in various forums, meetings, and arbitration proceedings.

Sample ECQ Narratives

While reading the following examples, please remember that this is only one way to write effective ECQs. Yours might be shorter, or a bit more robust. Everyone's career is different, and there is no "cookie-cutter" way to effectively address ECQs. Your own ECQs should be compelling and unique, and should directly reflect your own experiences and accomplishments. For your convenience, we have put captions within the first sample to show where the CCAR format is used, and to point out ways to address some of the competencies.

SAMPLE ECQs: GS-15 to SES (with annotations)

LEADING CHANGE

As Director, Financial Management (GS-0301-15) at the U.S. Department of Commerce in 2018, I demonstrated my expertise in leading major organizational change at the executive level. The department consisted of a headquarters (HQ) division and eight regional offices. When I took the position, I quickly realized that the budget-planning process was essentially non-existent and senior executives were only marginally involved in the overall budget formulation or planning process. The Office of Management and Budget (OMB) had recently implemented new rules/requirements designed to prevent fraud, waste, and abuse, and the senior executives and the Budget Officer were still adjusting course in response to these new rules **(EXTERNAL AWARENESS)**.

My multifaceted challenge was to develop an agency-wide budget-planning process that could be implemented to better align efforts with strategic objectives. Further, the Budget Officer left the agency with two weeks' notice, the agency was tasked by Members of Congress to provide three years of budget and staffing data within 48 hours, and the Fiscal Year (FY) 2019 budget call and mid-year budget allocations were due. Despite the absence of a Budget Officer, pending internal requirements, and major pressure from Congress on a short timeframe, I maintained a confident, positive outlook and focus **(FLEXIBILITY/RESILIENCE)**. The Chairman had entrusted me to change the way my organization conducted critical budget planning, and I began immediately to take action toward that end **(CHALLENGE/CONTEXT)**.

(ACTIONS) First, I studied the new budget rules, observed existing budget processes and internal controls, and examined budget programs in a number of other agencies. I solicited training needs assessments from senior executives and their administrative officers and distributed budget-planning documents to assist them in developing a viable budget allocation for the coming year. I soon realized that there was limited prior budget planning or exposure for executives in either strategic planning or the budget formulation process. I set out to educate and convince senior executives that the organization would be much more successful if it took on a stronger role in the budget process (and that it was critical in meeting the Chairman's vision for the agency) **(STRATEGIC THINKING/VISION)**.

I led a team of budget and management specialists in developing senior executive training on budget planning and allocation, specifically tailored to address the looming FY 2012 budget call. I then implemented a program to provide the training to senior officials, specifically focused on resources assessments, budget process and formulation, and retrieving real-time spending data within the agency's electronic budget accounting system using automated technology.

(RESULTS) Ultimately, I convinced fellow executives to play a more important role in the overall budget-planning process, and then provided executive-level training and insight to help them do exactly that. As a result of my leadership in creating this cultural change across the agency, the department now employs a simpler, fully automated budget-planning and formulation process. Moreover, senior managers have become totally engaged in the budget-planning process for their individual office allocations, and they clearly understand how their office budgets affect agency-wide initiatives. We met Congress' request to provide three years of budget and staffing data within 48 hours, and I assisted executives in developing and submitting the FY 2019 budget call and mid-year budget allocations on time.

Similarly, I brought about strategic change while serving as the Director for Administration for the Office of Personnel Management (GS-0341-15). My challenge was to overcome a strategic problem that affected all levels of the agency, and devise a plan to overcome lackluster or non-existent Human Resources (HR) services. The staff was comprised of a diverse group of lawyers and program analysts that reviewed the ethics programs for federal agencies, evaluating areas such as financial disclosure, Hatch Act Violations, conflicts of interest, and impropriety (EXTERNAL AWARENESS). Moreover, we reviewed public and confidential financial disclosure statements for political appointees and federal employees in sensitive/critical positions. The goal was to ensure there were no financial business relations (stock, company ownership, etc.) that would present a conflict of interest in performing their duties or derogatory areas that could create a negative perception. For the staff to properly conduct and provide such important oversight and services to federal agencies, the organization needed a strong internal HR foundation that likewise supported its own employees (CHALLENGE/CONTEXT).

For years, the HR staff had failed to provide employees with consistent or satisfactory customer service. Many personnel actions took much longer than necessary and the HR staff was perceived as complacent and reactionary. Further, employees were not held accountable for the quality or level of performance of their work, and many did not feel they were important to the agency as a whole. My vision was to influence positive change across the agency by developing and fostering a more proactive and empowered HR staff (VISION/STRATEGIC THINKING).

(ACTIONS) I took a number of steps to accomplish this. Specifically, I implemented a tracking system that allowed me to hold each HR staff member accountable for the quality and timeliness of his/her assignments. I instilled a renewed sense of purpose with the HR staff by reminding them of how their work propelled and affected the agency's goals and objectives. A number of longstanding personnel issues that had been compounded by time and did not have a simple or obvious resolution. To reenergize HR operations and create small victories, I focused the staff's attention on these issues first. For example, our payroll management team at the National Finance Center (NFC) was not providing timely or adequate advice, and this lack of guidance cascaded down to all levels. Because this issue involved a program administered by another Executive Branch agency, I leveraged executive contacts to resolve the problem. Based on my leadership and intervention, the matter was resolved within days and the HR staff was exposed to the valuable resources available within our own agency that would not have been previously considered in the problem-solving process. Using these new resources, the HR staff subsequently updated HR policies to increase efficiency through automation.

During this period, the Director and Assistant Director of HR were absent for medical reasons. I needed strong leadership in place to disseminate and enforce the changes I was implementing, so I utilized creative methods to overcome this obstacle (FLEXIBILITY). I approached the Bureau of Public Debt, since it was well recognized for its HR services, and secured funding for four contractors to augment the existing HR office. This was considered an innovative move, since the office had never done this before in its history (creativity/innovation). The presence of the contractors not only fostered short-term change in the HR Department, but also created long-term relationships that we continued to utilize, as needed, to either augment or otherwise improve HR services and delivery.

(RESULTS) Under my leadership, the organization's overall efficiency, along with the morale and productivity of the HR staff, increased dramatically. For example, service response time decreased/improved from a month (in some cases) to a matter of only days. Classification actions that typically took several months took only 20 days. Pay actions processing reduced from 7-10 days to only 48 hours. Overall errors were reduced by 45-55%. We simplified and streamlined important business processes by leveraging Information Technology (IT). The time saved due to improved efficiency was devoted to higher-profile areas. As a result of my efforts, I received an "Outstanding" rating and a cash award as part of my next official performance evaluation.

LEADING PEOPLE

I have been supervising and managing staff for more than 30 years, thriving at the GS-15 level since 2013, and have confidently led diverse groups of up to 235 personnel. As the Department of Justice's (DOJ) Chief, Policy, Development Division in 2017, I inherited a dysfunctional and demoralized team. The agency was in desperate need of a responsive Policy Office, and there was a leadership vacuum that had grown from the previous two years since the former Division Chief retired, and the group was left to fend for itself with no real direction. The team was dysfunctional because the team members lacked the skills to truly perform the duties they were assigned, there was no diversity on the team, and simple requests for policy interpretations that traditionally took two to three weeks to provide were taking three to four months for release (if they were even released at all). Managers, supervisors, and employees had no confidence in the policy guidance the division provided, and morale was at an all-time low because the team realized it was being devalued. I was determined to create a knowledgeable, responsive, customer-focused team that could respond to a department with more than 20,000 employees geographically separated around the world, including approximately 250 Human Resources (HR) specialists **(CHALLENGE/CONTEXT)**.

(ACTIONS) I began by reviewing the personnel records of all team members to determine their strengths and weaknesses, as documented in their performance records, resumes, and training documents. The team initially consisted of six female members and all but one was relatively new to the federal government. Fully supportive of diversity and Equal Employment Opportunity (EEO), I recruited another seasoned female HR veteran, a male with specialized skills the team needed, and a student who was inexperienced but promising and eager to learn in order to enhance the team **(LEVERAGING DIVERSITY)**. I then met one-on-one with all members of the team, actively listened to their personal goals and aspirations, and helped them to map out their five-year career goals. I also initiated weekly team meetings to clarify my expectations, maintain accountability, foster open communications, solicit team members' ideas, and create a safe environment in which success and mistakes alike could be seen as opportunities for improvement. I rewarded team members for their performance and contributions to the team and took appropriate corrective action, as needed, to address performance or conflict issues among team members **(TEAM BUILDING)**.

Not only was I focused on strengthening the overall team and creating a sense of shared goals, but I also discovered that the team was constantly challenged due to a lack of individual knowledge and specialized training. I quickly identified the strongest and weakest members of the team in terms of knowledge base, then paired them up to bridge competency gaps and promote cross-training and development. I established brown-bag study sessions twice a week and identified training opportunities for formal classroom instruction. Two members of the team were demoralized because they had been passed over for promotions on numerous occasions and had all but given up hope or a desire to do anything beyond the minimum. I established Individual Development Plans (IDPs) with each individual, including training opportunities, and encouraged them to stretch beyond their normal comfort level to acquire new knowledge, skills, relationships, and techniques to accomplish their personal and organizational goals **(DEVELOPING OTHERS)**.

One team member actually possessed much of the specialized knowledge that the team needed, but refused to share it because she felt that she was somehow increasing her value by keeping her knowledge somewhat obscured, and being very selective about when she shared it. Further, her disposition and attitude created a conflict with another employee. The two were vying for the same promotion and creating negative workplace tension. I was aware that the individual with the specialized experience was severely lacking in writing skills, so I used a creative and diplomatic technique to improve the team and overcome the conflict. I spoke with both individuals to ensure them that they could both reasonably expect a promotion and that they should be more focused on the team's interests and goals rather than on personal ones. Next, I convinced the individual who was withholding her knowledge that she was a vital part of our team and that we needed her to be more forthcoming. I then empowered her to lead others in achieving the teams' objectives by pairing her up with the strongest writer on the team and giving her assignments that displayed her knowledge. This approach worked beautifully. The entire team began to benefit from her knowledge, she felt like a more viable member of the team, and I captured her corporate knowledge in Standard Operating Procedures (SOPs) **(CONFLICT MANAGEMENT)**.

(RESULTS) As a result of my personally engaged and proactive leadership, within six months, I had formed a peak-performing Policy Office team that was well-trained, respected, and relevant in meeting the challenges head on. Prior to my arrival, it took the team an average of three to four months to release policy documents and guidance to an agency starving for direction; I reduced this time to two to three weeks. In addition, we issued policy notes at least once per month and responded to requests for opinions within 72 hours. The team quickly gained a new reputation within the agency as an effective Policy Office that possessed the skills and ability to respond quickly and appropriately to policy issues. Products released by the team were rarely—if ever—challenged, and when they were, the team had immediate, well-reasoned responses to customer inquiries. The team began receiving accolades for the level of customer service and responsiveness to their needs. I was formally and informally recognized for my efforts in turning around a team in short order and enhancing the overall office image within the intelligence, Inspector General (IG), and HR communities.

When I became the Senior Human Resources Policy Specialist, Department of Commerce in 2018, my 60-person HR team was in crisis mode and needed strong leadership and direction. It had failed a recent Office of Personnel Management (OPM) HR audit, and was not prepared for OPM's follow-up audit. Additionally, issues involving pay setting, promotions, reassignments, and details for the 3,000-strong workforce were not being properly documented or processed **(CHALLENGE/CONTEXT)**. To mitigate these concerns, I first reviewed the past OPM audit findings and then assessed current HR processes to see if the recommended changes or improvements had actually been implemented; they had not. **(ACTIONS)** Next, I determined the competency level of the entire team, met with each member of the team one-on-one to identify his/her strengths and weaknesses, and then created development plans. To overcome the prevailing lack of specialized HR knowledge and training, I immediately ordered copies of Title 5 of the Code of Federal Regulations (CFR) for each HR Specialist and conducted brown-bag lunch-training sessions on how to use and interpret the CFR. Likewise, I provided developmental opportunities and training sessions on a number of important HR areas and instituted SOPs. All team members were fully trained in their respective roles and responsibilities **(TEAM BUILDING/DEVELOPING OTHERS)**.

(RESULTS) As a result of my leadership in reenergizing the HR office, operations improved quickly and dramatically, and the office successfully passed the follow-up OPM Audit and retained its HR authority. We reduced errors in processing personnel actions involving critical issues, such as pay, promotions, and classification by 60%. The stovepiped business processes of the past were eliminated as I implemented a more streamlined service delivery model that reduced processing times by 40%. Aware of the major improvements, team members took pride in their work once more. Members of the team eventually requested and received reassignments to areas of interest, which greatly improved morale and the quality of customer service. Several of the employees I mentored have been promoted to new positions both within the organization and with external agencies. Customers have embraced the HR team more than ever before, inviting various members of the team to speak at their regular staff meetings to share evolving HR trends and activities. My performance and the team's overall performance were both formally and informally recognized by the Chairman of the agency and OPM.

RESULTS DRIVEN

As a seasoned executive who began my federal government career as a Division Assistant Chief (then Division Chief) with the Department of Veterans Affairs (VA) Board of Veterans Appeals, I find it extremely important to hold departments and agencies accountable for delivering their respective products and services in accordance with federal policy and overarching national objectives. As the Chief of Policy, Planning and Program Development with the Department of State (DOS) from 2015 to 2018, I oversaw a broad range of HR policies and initiatives while collaborating with approximately 40 senior managers and 250 HR Specialists in an environment that was highly resistant to change.

DOS' hiring timeline was 203 days, and I was given six months to implement the Office of Personnel Management (OPM) End-to-End (E2E) 80-day hiring model and comply with an Office of Management and Budget (OMB) mandate to reform government hiring across the DOS. I was fully accountable to the Deputy Under Secretary, Principal Deputy Assistant Secretary, and OPM. Likewise, I was committed to providing world-class service to our 20,000 customers, including employees, foreign service officers, political appointees, and senior executives **(CHALLENGE/CONTEXT)**.

(ACTIONS) To accomplish this strategic and herculean task, I partnered with key members of the DOS HR community to build support and promote a sense of ownership in the overall hiring reform process. Concurrently, I organized several focus sessions and led the development of an "as-is" current hiring model, including mapping of each step of the process to identify potential barriers along with methods to overcome each. For example, I believed that security clearance requirements were creating unnecessary delays in the hiring process. Even if an applicant was considered highly qualified, he/she had to wait 67 days for the security clearance to be processed before being hired. We were losing numerous qualified candidates, and the 67 days counted against our hiring timeline. My reasoning was that since 95% of all DOS positions required a Top Secret clearance, why not hire applicants based on their qualifications and an interim security clearance when possible? **(DECISIVE-NESS/CUSTOMER SERVICE)**.

This approach would increase the number of highly qualified hires, since we would not miss out on hiring these individuals because of security clearance processing. If the clearance was not approved, then the individual could be terminated. The end result is the same: a workforce of highly trained personnel, most of whom possess Top Secret clearance. By excluding this particular requirement on the front end of the current hiring model, we could instantly reduce our hiring timeline by 67 days. I gained support from the HR community, the Intelligence Community (IC), the Principal Deputy Assistant Secretary, and the Director of Civil Service HR to advocate this issue. During the focus sessions, I clearly explained the issue and my proposal with visual representations of the hiring timelines. I convinced OPM to permit DOS to exclude the security clearance process from the hiring model. Implementation of this change alone reduced overall processing times throughout the HR community.

Utilizing my vast knowledge of HR systems and processes, and based on the results of the focus sessions, I also directed the elimination of several duplicate processes (technical credibility/problem-solving). I partnered with stakeholders, classifiers, and systems developers to create a position description library used for all standard vacancy announcements, further reducing processing time. I directed that we refine the language used in the announcements to make them more user-friendly to applicants and that we implement an electronic four-point notice system to meet OMB's four-point notice requirement and achieve additional time savings in the process.

(RESULTS) My actions and changes created impactful results; DOS reduced its hiring processing times from an average of 203 days to 80 days, meeting both OMB and OPM requirements. Further, I positioned DOS for continued success by simultaneously enhancing accountability and customer service **(ENTREPRENEUR-SHIP)**. HR Specialists began to be held accountable for meeting specific deadlines for each step of the hiring process. HR managers were permitted to make effective hiring decisions to meet organizational needs, and we refined policies to improve overall performance. For effectively meeting the OPM hiring reform while addressing the department's strategic goal of providing timely recruitment actions, I received an "outstanding" evaluation and informal recognition from the IG Office for the support I provided to his team.

Prior to this position, I served as Chief of Staff within the Office of Government Ethics (OGE) from 2015 to 2016. When I arrived, the agency did not have a Continuity of Operations Plan (COOP) and was not prepared to respond to a natural or manmade disaster. I viewed this as a major deficit in terms of meeting organizational goals, and immediately set out to create a COOP and improve the agency's level of preparedness. I was accountable to the Deputy Director of Administration and the Director of OGE **(ACCOUNTABILITY)** to develop a viable COOP, and I felt strongly that an organization such as OGE with a public service responsibility must be highly responsive to customer needs (customer service), even in the event of a disaster (challenge/context).

(ACTIONS) I immediately began **(DECISIVENESS)** assessing the agency's program weaknesses and benchmarked various COOP plans of both state and federal agencies to determine viable options for the OGE (problem solving). Next, I surveyed managers, supervisors, and employees to determine their knowledge of emergency preparedness to focus my efforts on meeting their needs while developing the COOP. I then assembled a team of professional and administrative support members to lead the development of a customer-centered COOP strategy that was inclusive and responsive, and added value to the agency. Right around this time, the Administrative Officer went on maternity leave. She was one of the most respected leaders in the organization, and team members who were loyal to her suddenly lost interest in the initiative.

I overcame this challenge by delegating tasks, promoting inclusion, and driving progress and momentum toward our common goal. Specifically, I led the team in identifying the agency's Primary Essential and Mission Essential Functions, identifying essential personnel, determining proper delegations of authority, and creating chain of succession. We then documented the entire process to establish a historical record and a foundation for the COOP. I also identified an offsite secure location for essential senior officials and a computer backup system for vital records **(TECHNICAL CREDIBILITY)**. Additionally, I improved OGE's readiness by advocating for and leading the agency's first-ever participation in the Eagle Horizon exercise to test and validate the new COOP. In the past, OGE had not been required to participate in Eagle Horizon, which is an annual government-wide exercise designed to test agencies' ability to respond and reconstruct in the event of a natural disaster. To ensure OGE's future readiness **(ENTREPRENEURSHIP)**, I sought and received approval and commitment from the Director of OGE to participate in the ongoing national preparedness training; OGE is now a regular participant in such COOP exercises.

(RESULTS) Within 45 days, I trained evaluators, gained buy-in, and implemented the newly developed COOP. As a direct result of my ability to identify, gain support for, and address this complex, strategic issue, OGE now

has a functioning COOP in place that permits the agency to continue its defined essential functions in the event of any disruption of services. Additionally, all employees are now prepared to respond to any natural or man-made disasters. As a testament to its effectiveness, OGE's COOP has been used as a model for other agencies. I received a certificate of appreciation award from the Department of Homeland Security (DHS) and OGE for my involvement and leadership in the Eagle Horizon exercise.

BUSINESS ACUMEN

In the last four decades, I spent 20 years in the U.S. Air Force (USAF) and then climbed the ranks of Civil Service as a federal government employee. (financial management) In 2019, I was serving as the Deputy Director, Office of Financial and Administrative Management (FAM), which manages the Department of Energy's HR management, financial management, contracting, facilities, security, travel, and support services management programs. I was also the Deputy Chief Financial Officer (CFO) and Senior Contracting Officer, managing a $42M budget annually. In this capacity, I was challenged to ensure timely and accurate budget formulation and submission to OPM during closeout of prior-year procurement activities. Previously, these two activities were somewhat autonomous, but I actively involved and engaged Office Directors, Administrative Officers, and managers in the overall budget formulation process to clearly identify all funding requirements.

(CHALLENGE/CONTEXT) My situation was daunting. First, since end-of-year closeouts were taking place, managers did not want to be involved in the justification or formulation process. The agency was also seeking an increase in funding for mission-critical activities, including: federal employee case adjudications, human capital surveys, and mediation activities that are the core function of the agency, as mandated by statute. If I did not properly justify the budget and funding requirements, we ran the risk of being denied funding for these Congressionally mandated programs. In addition, the agency was in the middle of lease negotiations for two separate facilities that were due to expire within six months. If those leases were not renewed, the agency would have to spend $500K to move equipment, furniture, and employees to a new facility.

(ACTIONS) To ensure Administrative Officers received the financial, procurement, contracting, and administrative support they desperately needed during this critical period, I organized and chaired a monthly Administrative Officers' meeting to facilitate the free flow of information and synchronize efforts with geographically separated offices to provide efficient and responsive financial customer service. Collaborating extensively with the budget, contracting, and procurement officers, I established policies and procedures to ensure proper fiscal controls. To enforce compliance and progress, I directed internal control audits for all program areas to identify fraud, waste, or abuse involving the agency's contracting, procurement, travel, purchase card, and transit subsidy programs. During these audits, I identified weaknesses in two program areas and directed immediate corrective action, including certification of training for Contracting Officer's Technical Representatives (CO-TRs). I then met with Congressional staffers to explain, defend, and otherwise respond to questions regarding the budget and the agency's future financial needs.

(RESULTS) As a result, I obtained the full $45M in FY 2020 funding for agency programs and secured lease renewals for the two existing facilities, saving the agency $500K.

(HUMAN CAPITAL MANAGEMENT) I fully appreciate the valuable human capital provided by individual members of the federal workforce and consistently strive to recruit, hire, train, groom, and develop skilled professionals with the needed skills and specialized experience. I was promoted to GS-15 in 2018 as Director of HR for the Department of Transportation's (DOT) Surface Transportation Board. My challenge was to provide the full range of HR services with limited staff and budgetary resources (CHALLENGE/CONTEXT).

I needed a new strategy for HR service delivery, and since 58% of the organization's employees were eligible for immediate retirement (within 90 days), I set out to devise a strategy that incorporated specific plans to handle this potentially devastating loss of institutional knowledge.

(ACTIONS) I began by meeting with the key stakeholders to identify Mission Critical Occupations and the skill sets they needed to achieve organizational goals, then conducted a skills gap analysis based on the agency's Mission Critical Occupations, as defined by the stakeholders to identify positions the agency needed to fill immediately. My strategy also included a mentoring program for employees already on board, which provided retraining opportunities and ensured continuity of operations. At the same time, I established rotational assignments for current employees and identified the training needs required to fill the gaps left from projected vacancies. Recognizing the potential for the immediate departure of the most seasoned HR Specialist in the agency, I quickly recruited and identified two highly qualified HR Specialists to fill the void that would have been created had the Senior HR Specialist left prematurely.

(RESULTS) As a direct result of my human capital management: a) the agency provided a bridge between new employees and retiring employees to avoid the "brain drain" and loss of continuity associated with numerous retirements in a very short timeframe; b) offices were empowered to quickly recruit and identify new talent and bring them on board within 60 days; c) we provided training opportunities to current and new employees, maximizing current human capital resources while providing employees with developmental opportunities within the agency; d) employee retention increased by 25%; and e) based on the results of the next annual organizational assessment, productivity increased throughout the organization by 35%. Due to the positive human capital changes I made, 40% of those eligible for retirement decided to remain with the agency, received rotational assignments, and were often placed in new mission-critical positions based on their backgrounds identified during the skills gap analysis. Likewise, external candidates were identified, hired, and brought on board in a timely manner, allowing the agency to continue uninterrupted operations in all program areas. The long-term impacts were in salvaging corporate knowledge, executing a planned strategy that ensured a seamless transfer of information between employees, and empowering the agency to perform its mandated mission without degradation of services to the American public.

(TECHNOLOGY MANAGEMENT) During this same period, the General Counsel wanted a means to advertise positions to a wide audience of potential candidates, to quickly evaluate and identify applicants for attorney positions, and to maintain communication with them throughout the process. Moreover, she wanted to accomplish all of this without dedicating members of her staff on a full-time basis to evaluate applicants (CHALLENGE/CONTEXT). Working with the CIO and her team, I directed the development of an electronic application tracking and routing system to provide members of the General Counsel's Office immediate access to applications when they were received (ACTIONS). Additionally, the system would automatically send an email to the applicant once his/her application was received and would notify potential applicants electronically when their application was reviewed by members of the General Counsel's Office. I developed specific timelines for deliverables, and met with the Information Technology (IT) Specialist weekly to ensure all milestones were met.

(RESULTS) Once the system was implemented, I evaluated and validated the results of the new application process by developing an electronic applicant survey. The attorney application process time was reduced from days using the paper application process to hours using the electronic application process. The overall review process was reduced by 50% down from 60 days to 30 days maximum. The new attorneys were all selected and entered on duty within 90 days, helping the General Counsel to quickly eliminate the case backlog and provide prompt responses to individuals seeking relief from the Board. Applicants received immediate feedback from their initial application, and 85% of applicants surveyed indicated that the new application process was one of the easiest they had ever encountered.

During my service as a Senior Policy Specialist and negotiator with the U.S. Safety and Transportation Board (USSTO) in 2019, my challenge was to obtain special salary rates for more than 3,500 patent professionals as part of an overall recruitment strategy. Complicating this effort was the fact that all employees hired with specialized patent experience were eligible to become patent agents in the private sector after obtaining three years of patent experience. Many individuals took advantage of this option, thereby creating a revolving door for new hires. These employees could immediately demand six-figure salaries and a full benefits package; however, at the time, the agency could only offer its patent professional employees a medium income, benefits package, and a few other government benefits.

To make matters worse, the labor union was highly active and the relationship seemed to be adversarial by default. Regardless of what issue the USSTO brought to the table (including special salary rates), the labor union would report issues to the press amid negotiations. Needless to say, this was highly counterproductive and hindered my efforts to obtain special salary rates. Additionally, the union's actions placed the Office of Personnel Management (OPM) in a very awkward position by having the results of negotiations announced before they were final. The patent side of the USSTO wanted to go paperless, but the union was opposed because members thought that employees would be expected to process patents faster, creating more work in the same amount of time. There was already a backlog in patents. The USSTO obviously wanted to handle issues internally with the union, and wanted the labor union to stop involving the press. **(CHALLENGE/CONTEXT)**

(ACTIONS) I began by building productive relationships with the head of the agency, labor union officials, OPM, Public Affairs, and Human Resources (HR) officials by reaching out to them to share the agency's vision and goals regarding the special salary rates. I then communicated the requirements for obtaining special salary rates to the union and agency officials, advocating the agency's position to OPM and the union. My goal was to obtain buy-in, build consensus, and overcome objections raised by the union during the negotiation process to ultimately obtain special salary rates for affected employees.

As one of the key negotiators between the USSTO and the union, I was keenly aware of the politics at play. Some parties had hidden agendas and differing viewpoints; at the end of the day, however, we all wanted what was best for both the agency and its employees. To unify stakeholders, I partnered with management and union officials to identify their competing interests and balance the needs of both parties, provided insights on how agencies justify and obtain special salary rates, and facilitated the process with OPM. **(POLITICAL SAVVY)** During this period, I also partnered with economists at the Bureau of Labor Statistics (BLS) and collaborated with them to conduct extensive research for pay comparability for patent professionals or like positions in the private sector. **(PARTNERING)** I then developed a comprehensive business case for approval of the special salary rate that included adjustments in five different patent professional occupational series and provided pay parity for employees performing similar duties that would enable the agency to obtain the concessions sought from the union.

(RESULTS) Ultimately, I played a key leadership role in negotiating a win-win solution between all parties that included complex **(NEGOTIATING)**, often-daily negotiations over the course of several months and a number of concessions. Because of my direct intervention, diplomatic negotiation skills, in-depth knowledge of the organizational culture, and sterling reputation as an honest broker, I obtained special salary rates covering all 3,500 employees. A recruitment bonus I proposed for patent professionals was also approved by the head of the agency and the union as an additional incentive for the mission-critical positions. The USSTO was better equipped to recruit and retain the patent professionals that enabled it to grant patents in a timely and efficient manner, as mandated by Congress. Finally, my leadership and actions helped reduce the agency's attrition rate from 25% prior to approval of the special salary rates, to just below 10%. This alone was a significant achievement, since previous attrition rates had at one point spiked as high as 35% in the first two years of employment.

In 2017, I was serving as the Acting Director of the Merit Systems Protection Board, Office of Financial and Administrative Management. One of my greatest challenges has been implementing a replacement Voice over Internet Protocol (VoIP) telephone system and associated technology assets to replace the agency's antiquated phone network across nine geographically separated facilities **(CHALLENGE/CONTEXT)**. Further, this effort has been complicated by agency and senior executives' competing priorities, limited funding, end-of-year procurements, the latest technology, and the inability to upgrade the existing telephone system. The existing phone network has caused highly important contact with judges, appellants, appellant representatives, and officials from other agencies to be lost on a recurring basis, which has had a disastrous effect on the agency's overall ability to communicate with the public.

(ACTIONS) To mitigate these challenges and build a coalition of willing participants, I led and facilitated several meetings with senior leaders to discuss the financial and logistical aspects of this critical project. I also led and coordinated the efforts of Information Technology (IT) specialists, facilities management, and the procurement staff to benchmark other agencies with similar telephone systems. To build a business case, I partnered with experts from other agencies who had successfully completed similar projects to obtain guidance as well as discuss lessons learned and best practices **(PARTNERING)**. With this additional information and insight, I developed a realistic strategy to implement the conversion to the new telephone system, ensuring backwards compatibility with existing systems.

(RESULTS) As a result of my leadership in convincing stakeholders of the importance of implementing the VoIP system **(INFLUENCING/NEGOTIATING)**, I have gained approval for $400K and the agency is currently positioned to move forward with this critical and high-impact initiative. Although the effort is ongoing, the new telecommunications system will provide the public with more efficient access to agency personnel. For instance, there will be a main number for the entire agency with extensions for all employees throughout the U.S. Finally, the new telephone system will save money through more efficient, energy-saving technology and allow for more integration between agency telecommunications and computer systems.

SAMPLE ECQs: GS-15 to SES (EXAMPLE 1)

LEADING CHANGE

In 2017, I became the Interagency Plans Division Director within the Department of Labor (DOL). In this role, I was challenged to manage a $30M portfolio of programs and a six-member staff. My division was empowered to develop and implement individual and institutional capacity building programs that promote Science & Technology (S&T) for economic development. As I assessed the organization, I found that the division had worked autonomously for most of the previous decade, and this had fostered a culture of poor conduct and performance. The most egregious issue was a finding by the Inspector General (IG) that the staff had committed a misappropriation act violation prior to my arrival. Externally, the then-Assistant Secretary viewed the staff as the root cause of the problems. Thinking long term, I envisioned reinventing the division to an exemplar of fiscal management and performance.

First, I developed written documents that communicated my plan, mission, and vision. I also developed a set of clear performance expectations, and set in writing the culture and principles I wanted the division to embody. In my previous roles at the Department of Defense (DOD), I had grown accustomed to having multiple financial analysts and contract support to help me oversee money. I found none of that at DOL, so I leveraged my own training and knowledge to make it happen. Among many other changes, I hired an experienced Financial Analyst from outside the department. I worked closely with her to create a new financial system that would ensure fiscal compliance. In addition, I reviewed all of our grants and contracts, and found that many standard terms and conditions had never been inserted. This put the department at major risk, so I directed that the proper language be inserted immediately, even if it required modifying active agreements.

While directing all these program changes and engaging the staff, I also established strategic guidance and oversight. For instance, I created new Standard Operating Procedures (SOPs) for my four programs, which aligned daily activities with strategic goals and priorities. In the past, the status quo for awarding contracts and grants was arbitrary and based upon the review of a single staff member. Without review panels and pre-established review criteria, the system was prone to abuse. I instituted impartial review panels for all new awards, which created the governance framework and oversight we needed. It seemed as if everyone was resistant to my changes except my leadership, who hired me to do this very thing. The original staff viewed the new SOPs as "additional work," and the acquisition office did not want to modify contracts or grants because it was laborious. The prevailing approach was to simply award the money and provide little or no oversight. I explained the benefits of all these activities. In a creative and unprecedented move within the organization, I also required all of the staff to become certified Contracting and Grant Officer Representatives, and to take ethics training. Throughout this period, I kept my political and senior executive leadership apprised of my progress, and sometimes asked them to help me push through roadblocks at their level.

Ultimately, I turned my vision into reality, and the division underwent a major transformation on multiple levels. A year after I started, the Inspector General (IG) conducted a follow-up investigation. Because of all of the new processes and training, the errors from the previous management team were corrected and my senior leadership received a positive report. In previous years, the division awarded dollars at the last possible moment, but I greatly improved efficiency and we awarded dollars in the year of appropriation. No other office within the Bureau has ever been able to achieve that. By demonstrating sound financial planning and management, my division has gone from being given "leftover" money once per year, to being part of the department's baseline Congressional Budget Justification. As a result of all these changes, the culture went from an underperforming entity with a poor reputation, to being held up as a standard for others. With such an improved record and reputation, we no

www.SESWriters.com

longer receive the same level of scrutiny as other divisions. These efforts earned me a Meritorious Honor Award in 2017.

Another example took place in 2014, in my role as a Program Manager at the Defense Radar Agency (DRA). After years of substandard results, top officials in the Department of Defense (DOD) stripped the U.S. Army of a $110M medical research program and gave it to DRA. My $60M portion of the program was supposed to research and develop new drugs, and I was under tremendous pressure to modernize the program and make it productive. With a war raging and the threat of chemical weapons being used by terrorists, there was real interest among external stakeholders, such as the White House and Pentagon, for me to succeed. I soon found that the military researchers were using outdated scientific techniques and stovepiped processes, and were not taking advantage of modern advances. I envisioned a successful and efficient program that leveraged industry best practices, and set out to enact the needed changes.

The norm in the pharmaceutical industry is to screen thousands of compounds rapidly using a process called "high throughput screening." Promising compounds go on for further testing. Within the military labs, the staff was designing and testing only a single new drug at a time. To revamp these extremely slow and costly processes, I closed out $3M worth of defunct projects. I used that money to purchase access to several chemical libraries and the associated technology. Next, I incentivized the researchers by setting aside additional monies for them to use in the new facilities. After securing access to the right technology, I assessed the strategic processes we used to review and select proposals. Prior to my taking over the portfolio, the scientists writing proposals were often the reviewers. This needed to change, so I spoke with colleagues at the National Science Foundation (NSF) and National Institutes of Health (NIH), organizations known for excellence in scientific review. With their help, I eliminated conflicts of interest by designing a new review procedure and finding third-party researchers.

Next, I carved out part of my research budget to fund collaborations between university and military researchers. This novel strategy allowed me to expand the research dramatically. However, some of the "old guard" scientists did not like the idea of partnering with academia, and worried about sharing credit in publications. Stressing the need to keep up with evolving techniques technology, I nudged them out of their comfort zones by introducing the military and academic researchers. As expected, once the dialog began, many of them established strong professional ties built upon mutual respect. Similarly, my contract office resisted my strategy because the staff feared deviating from regulations. I read the Federal Acquisition Regulations (FAR), found the areas of flexibility I was seeking, and helped educate the contract office regarding why the collaborations I was building were well within regulations.

As a result, I completely modernized the program and created a culture of well-planned, aggressive, and customer-focused medical R&D. At the end of my three years on the program, I had 15 new drug candidates under formal consideration, and 6 were patented. The organization had patented zero new drugs in the previous 10 years. In addition, we had screened 20K+ candidates-up from a few hundred over the past decade-, and I increased the number of academics participating in my area of research from 10 to over 100. From a long-term perspective, the processes and tools that I put in place are still being used today, and the organization is much better suited to meet its constantly shifting requirements. Finally, I was named Civilian of the Quarter for my Division during this period, and my performance was a key factor in me being selected for an Executive Leadership Development Program.

LEADING PEOPLE

Since March 2018, I have been the Director of the U.S. Department of Agriculture's (USDA) Office of Scientific Research. In this position, I supervise and manage 19 Civil Service, Foreign Service, and contract employees across 3 cross-functional teams. My office's mission is to formulate, analyze, and implement policies and programs to promote science, technology, and innovation as tools for international engagement. As part of this mission, the bilateral affairs team is responsible for 60 government-to-government science relationships. When I arrived, the recently formed bilateral team included nine civil service employees, led by a Foreign Service Officer. The team lead was disgruntled because she had not been promoted, and her attitude fostered negativity and conflict in the workplace. Half of the team members were high performers, while the other half barely did anything. The strong performers' efforts were going unrecognized, and they were agitated that the team lead was not addressing poor conduct or performance. I knew that in a few months, the workload would spike dramatically as we prepared for a number of high-level meetings. I set out to form a more unified team that could work together to meet—and even exceed—program requirements.

Rather than creating a team structure or approach when she took over, the team lead had just started working on individual issues. This led to an ad hoc and ineffective way of doing business. Most team members were operating independently from one another, and there was no strategic oversight guiding program activities. To begin rallying the team and creating a sense of shared purpose, I worked with the team lead to develop a mission and vision statement. Next, I found she had been relying on the office-wide weekly meetings to bring the team together, but most people just sat in the meetings and said nothing. I worked with her to establish weekly meetings at the team level, and guided her in establishing Standard Operating Procedures (SOPs), task lists with clear deadlines, and rigorous oversight at her level as well as my own. I also worked with her to identify those staff members whose performance should be awarded. This process takes a bit of administrative work, and the team lead decided that it was not worth her time, given all of the other things on her plate. I worked with her to adjust that viewpoint, and we got half of her staff awards during the next cycle.

After building the overall team for a couple of months, and setting the conditions for success, I began to hold one-on-one meetings with each team member. I used this time to get to know them and learn about their career aspirations. I worked with the team lead to develop Individual Development Plans (IDPs) for all team members. Depending on individual needs, I sent some people to basic writing and public speaking courses, and sent others to high-level "stretch" assignments. For instance, Civil Service employees rarely serve overseas and generally lack an understanding of Embassy processes and politics. Since Embassy's are one my office's biggest customers, I secured three-month details for two of my most high-performing team members at U.S. Embassies in Jakarta and New Delhi for them to learn about the inner workings. Additionally, I continued to mentor the team lead by listening to her frustrations, and focusing on how her actions were being perceived. I also provided her some books from my leadership training at the DOD, and then discussed them with her.

To mitigate the culture of conflict and lack of connection between the team lead and her subordinates, I used the one-on-one time to delve into the issues at hand. With the insights I gained, I mediated individual meetings during which people could say what they thought to me and the team lead without fear of reprisal. I maintained an impartial demeanor and used "reflective listening" phrases, such as "What I hear you saying is…" In this way, I guided the discussion from a healthy venting session to an even more meaningful discussion on potential areas of improvement. In terms of diversity, when I began, all of the team members were all trained in political science and international affairs but lacked any scientific experience—a requisite for the office's success. I reduced that deficiency by hiring a PhD with research experience, and a highly accomplished engineer who had worked at Amazon. The new team members' perspectives helped the team to better communicate with foreign counterparts and colleagues at technical agencies.

As a result, the bilateral team's performance improved within a few months. I began to witness more interaction and desire for collaboration during and outside of meetings. Morale improved as well, because people were being rewarded and given opportunities to grow professionally. Those employees who participated in the stretch assignments were energized and excited, and their performance while on those assignments improved the team's standing and reputation. Productivity flourished within this engaged working environment. For instance, the team successfully developed over a dozen new scientific projects with foreign governments. In addition, within six months, the time required to get approval on formal communiques between state Headquarters (HQ) and the Embassies dropped from 10 weeks to only 3. Likewise, when I started, the team was averaging 12 bilateral meetings a year. By late 2018, that number had grown to 18, and in 2019, it will reach 25. The increase in workload is a direct reflection of the team's improved efficiency and output, and the team received a group award.

Another example began in 2018, when I became Supervisory Analyst within the Bureau of Land Management (BLM). I was the sole team member when I arrived, and my challenge was to stand up a new team within one year and expand the number of partnerships we had with domestic agencies and our counterparts in foreign governments. While identifying and hiring team members, I sought people with diverse backgrounds and perspectives. Not only would they need to understand all of the different technologies, but they would also need to be skilled in international affairs. After getting team members with the right skills on board, I held an offsite meeting to openly discuss our mission. I shared my vision of becoming the "go-to" team among interagency and international partners. I then built a sense of ownership and buy-in by leading collaborative discussions about how we would achieve that goal.

While we had strong collective backgrounds in arms sales, science, and international affairs, I determined that some team members needed a more balanced perspective. I created individual training/development plans for everyone on the team, including myself. For those with an international background, I sent them to conferences and crash courses on science that I found through professional societies. I also negotiated access to scientific journals and libraries at the National Institutes of Health (NIH). For my scientific staff, we took courses on negotiation and attended seminars at think-tanks like Center for Strategic and International Studies to learn more about international affairs. Although the team was coming together more each day, there was a lot of organizational conflict between my team and the three technical divisions. They really did not want us to provide them any oversight or guidance, and some were deliberately withholding information. I addressed this problem by requiring my staff to attend their weekly meetings, and made it clear that they were expected to participate at whatever level they could. I also volunteered my team to prepare the papers that senior leadership would use for high-level meetings with other departments or foreign governments.

Over time, my leadership paved the way for strong and lasting results. During the course of one year, the conflict with the other divisions all but evaporated, and I had positioned the team as the Subject Matter Experts (SMEs) on international affairs. Within that same year, my team had taken the lead on three new interagency Memoranda of Understanding (MOU) and five new international agreements. From an organizational perspective, my teams' success improved overall efficiency since the technical program managers were freed from these responsibilities. In addition, my team was called on to support a high-level official far removed from our chain of command. Our ability to bridge science and international affairs resulted in us not only advising this senior executive, but also traveling with her internationally since her staff did not have this hybrid capability. As a final testament to my leadership success, the Assistant Secretary of BLM requested me, by name, for a detail at BLM HQ.

In 2017, I became the Acting Chief of Staff in the U.S. Department of Agriculture's (USDA) Modernization Office. Whenever a domestic agency wants to sign an international agreement with a foreign government, the USDA coordinates a review to ensure everything is in order. This review is especially important for agreements that bind the U.S. government under international law. Named the "C-175" process after Circular 175, this laborious process requires consulting with more than a dozen different agencies before the DOS' lawyers even see it. My office receives more than 100 international science agreements a year, ranging from small projects to large and complex initiatives.

When I first arrived in the position, we had nearly 50 international agreements that had been languishing for more than a year, some for as long as two years. This meant that work that the science agencies wanted to do was simply not getting done. Most people inside and outside of the USDA had long since accepted this as "the way it has always been done." However, my external customers included technical agencies, such as the National Science Foundation (NSF), NASA, National Institutes of Health (NIH), and the U.S. Geological Survey (USGS). I was accountable to these agencies for ensuring the C-175 process was meeting their needs. Moreover, according to regulations, we were supposed to complete the process in two months or less. We were clearly not meeting that metric, and I refused to accept the longstanding complacency toward the C-175 process. With all this in mind, I wanted to improve how fast we processed these agreements so the international cooperation could occur in a more timely fashion.

To begin addressing this growing strategic problem, I first decided to contract with a Lean Six Sigma expert to analyze our business processes, so that I could develop viable courses of action. I observed as the consultant interviewed my staff, talked with the technical agencies, and followed the paper trail for these agreements through the bureaucratic process. He identified a number of problems leading to the backlog, such as scientists trying to write legal documents without the requisite technical knowledge. In addition, some members of the program staff some were not having their own lawyers review their documents before sending them to me. Third, my staff members were not reviewing the documents upon receipt, but simply forwarding them to our lawyers. Consequently, our lawyers were sitting on things for a long time because there was no consistency, and many of the products were poorly written and did not follow a standard format.

With so many failures in the chain, and reluctance by anyone to take it on, I had to be decisive. My holistic solution was to improve every step of the process that I possibly could. First, I initiated the creation of a handbook that clearly outlined our processes, addressed the fundamental difference between binding and non-binding agreements, and had some sample agreements that people could use as templates. To ensure the needed level of accountability and internal control, I changed our business processes by requiring that staff members closely review each document before sending it forward to the legal office. Additionally, I required staff members to attend training on the Fundamentals of International Law. I held informal meetings with customers and colleagues at technical agencies to make sure my products would meet their needs. On a monthly basis, I briefed my leadership to keep them updated on progress.

As a direct result of my leadership, technical program knowledge, and proactive approach to the backlog of international, within six months, I reduced the backlog from 50 to 25. Moreover, I had our lawyers sign off on the new C-175 handbook, and disseminated it among my staff and our interagency partners. In 2018, my staff reviewed and processed more than 175 international science agreements. I have cut the average time to process an agreement by 12 months to 6, vastly improving customer service and satisfaction. Over the long term, my efforts set customers and stakeholders on a path of success and scientific progress. Finally, my staff and internal stakeholders have the tools and resources needed to ensure proper oversight and quality.

A second began in 2012, during my time as Senior Program Manager within the Department of Labor (DOL). In the late 1990s, the U.S. and Australia signed a bilateral agreement to solicit and fund joint research projects. When I took over management of this international agreement, the program was receiving approximately 300 applications a year, each competing for a part of the $8M in total funding. The U.S. and Australian governments would each assemble their own application review panels with their own criteria. After months of working independently, the two sides come together to compare notes. As might be expected, this was highly inefficient and it was very common for the two sides to disagree on what projects to fund. Seeing a problem, I decided to develop a solution.

Taking this action on made me accountable to several DOL leaders, including two Assistant Secretaries—one Senate confirmed political appointee and a Senior Foreign Service Officer. I was also accountable to the two co-chairs of the U.S.-Australia Science Board, and to the Australian Minister of Science—a Cabinet-level position that reports to the Prime Minister and President. My customers included the scientists who sought funding, since they wanted a clear, understandable process. In addition, the U.S. Ambassador to Australian was a customer; she wanted a story of success to cite when talking to the Government of Egypt. I decided to improve this process not only to save precious time and money, but also because it would allow me to educate and encourage the scientific community to adopt some of our best practices.

I developed a multipronged approach to resolve the lack of communication and coordination between the U.S. and Australia. For instance, I replaced the NSF with a private research firm responsible for reviewing the documents and making recommendations. This streamlined approach gave me a single organization in the U.S. with which to work. I then proposed development of common application review criteria, and use of a common website for the proposal process. In addition, I proposed that DOL pay for recurring in-person meetings of the U.S. and Australian reviewers. The overarching goal of my proposals was to simplify business processes and foster information sharing. After soliciting and integrating input from customers and stakeholders, I presented the proposal to decision makers from both governments.

As a result, I gained full buy-in from customers and leadership from both governments. By designing a system in which the two sides agree to criteria, share their reviews, and then meet in person, I created a structure that has checks and balances needed for long-term success. Further, by asking the Australian to host the new website and host the review panels, I brought them into the solution and gained their support. In 2018, the first slate of proposals jointly reviewed was approved. Customers and stakeholders are extremely optimistic about this solution moving forward.

BUSINESS ACUMEN

In 2017, I was hand-selected by senior Department of Labor (DOL) leaders for a detail as Senior Analyst. My supervisor was supposed to be the primary advocate for the Science and Technology (S&T) program. However, due to a lack of advocacy and oversight, by the time I arrived, there was a real fear that the program could lose 20% of more of its $500M budget. I had to use my technical and business acumen to prevent any loss to the budget.

To begin assessing and identifying the problems, I coordinated a series of high-level briefings that brought together all stakeholders to review the portfolio. Not only did the briefings focus on the amount of money being spent on research in each of the technology areas, but I also asked program representatives to project the amount of money needed to commercialize those technologies in out years. By analyzing the financial reporting, it became clear that many of the high-level staff members were making plans and decisions without consulting the technical experts. Consequently, we had major misalignment between functional areas in terms of money and timelines. Meanwhile, I oversaw the efforts of my internal finance team in managing the fiscal aspects of

the portfolio. I directed the team to hold weekly meetings to review obligation and expenditure rates, as well as to keep me closely apprised. I routinely justified our spending and responded to questions from the Comptroller and Congressional (appropriations) staff. To ensure the program activities being reported matched what was actually taking place, I also spent a fair amount of time conducting site visits to military research labs and meeting with the researchers and lab administrators (typically O-6, GS-15 level). Additionally, I attended technical reviews of other agencies to identify ways to save money through collaboration.

As a result of my financial planning, management, and oversight, I used the outputs from the consolidated program review and financial projection to sharpen the program's contributions to the Future Years Defense Program (FYDP). The FYDP is a strategic planning process that included all of DOD's future staffing, resources, and programs for the next five Fiscal Years (FYs). By bringing all functional areas together in terms of financial and program planning, we demonstrated to the DOD Comptroller that our program was being managed competently and would provide capabilities for the military on the timelines they needed. Even amid major budget cuts across the government, we maintained the full $500M budget for FY 2012.

Another example began in January 2011, in my role as Manager of the Department of Agriculture's (USDA) Modernization Office. The Director is a Foreign Service Officer (FSO) who rotates every 18 to 24 months. Generally, FSOs have little to no experience managing Civil Service. I was expected to manage all personnel administration and Human Resources (HR) actions, including recruitment, retention, performance evaluations, professional development, and terminations for the 19-member staff. Through a combination of voluntary and involuntary personnel actions, nearly 25% of my staff left in early 2011. As I prepared to backfill the positions, I realized that our staffing analysis was out of date. In fact, as I read the Position Descriptions (PDs) of the people who had left, I learned that our HR support had hired people based upon inaccurate PDs without management's knowledge. Senior leaders and I were concerned that if we kept asking people to do things that were far outside of their PDs, we would become more inefficient and open ourselves up to lawsuits.

I began by developing a new staffing pattern/organizational structure and rewriting all of the PDs to better reflect actual duties and better match high-level program goals. I tailored the PDs to represent the unique mix of international relations, science, and financial management required in my office. Next, I presented the proposed staff positions within the organizational structure to my leadership and HR leadership. This posed a challenge, since the HR department preferred standard PDs and felt that they saved time. I developed a briefing for HR that explained how my strategy would allow my office to better meet customer needs and hire a diverse workforce.

As a result of my human capital planning and management, in December 2018, I had an approved staffing pattern and all-new PDs for my entire staff. Since then, I have already increased the intellectual diversity of my workforce. I have also increased the number of FSOs in my office by 25%, which improved our ability to interface with embassies and other parts of the department. Moreover, the new PDs will set a strong foundation for the future because my successors will have the flexibility they need to hire people without having to draft the PDs and get them certified. In terms of overall personnel administration, during my tenure, I have hired 18 people and removed 6 for cause. I have also placed staff members on performance improvement plans, sent employees to training, participated in Alternative Dispute Resolution (ADR) meetings with a mediator, and issued numerous awards.

In a final example, I was serving as Supervisory Analyst within the Bureau of Land Management (BLM). Beginning in 2014 and on into 2015, the General Services Administration (GSA) mandated that we shrink the square footage of leased space. As part of this requirement, my office and two others were selected for consolidation at a new location. The facility we were leaving lacked information technology (IT) infrastructure for classified and unclassified video and teleconferencing (VTC). The facility also lacked basic capability for presentations (no computers or projectors), and lacked the capability for simultaneous translations (used for foreign delegations who do not speak English well). As I assessed the new facility, I realized that we were getting little more than cubicles and basic phone lines. Seeing this move as an opportunity to improve business processes, I began to develop a proposal to purchase and install the required IT and presentation capabilities.

Working with my peers from the other two offices, I led the design of a comprehensive $750K IT plan for the new facility, which included VTC, new presentation equipment, and simultaneous translation hardware to assist with international negotiations. I then advocated for the plan in multiple meetings with the Bureau of Administration, and quantified how much time we were losing by having to use another facility's equipment, which were often overscheduled. Similarly, I described how hard it was to hold meetings with international stakeholders without the simultaneous translation technology. Next, I pointed out how the lack of basic presentation capability was inconsistent with the needs of a government office in the 21st century. Once the architectural drawings and IT proposals came in, I reviewed them, negotiated alterations, and continued to press for the capabilities I was proposing.

In the end, I gained support for the full $750K proposal and we took possession of the new facility in September 2014. In doing so, we went from having zero rooms networked for classified and unclassified VTC to four unclassified and one classified rooms. We also went from having zero rooms with presentation capability to having seven. We also ended up with a large conference room and modular equipment to support simultaneous translation. My use of technology to support critical business processes better enabled the organization to meet mission requirements, and fostered more VTCs with U.S. Embassies and foreign ministries. Many of our sister offices now come to our facility to use our new IT infrastructure.

BUILDING COALITIONS

In early 2017, I was serving as Director of the U.S. Department of Agriculture's (USDA) Office of Scientific Research. In this role, I was challenged to build a coalition of more than a dozen agencies to create a new Intellectual Property Rights (IPR) Annex as part of our Science and Technology Agreements (STAs) with foreign governments. STAs are one step down from treaties. They do not require Congressional action, but they bind the U.S. under international law. Each STA includes an IPR Annex that apportions rights, should any new invention come out of joint scientific research.

The IPR Annex is issued by the President's Science Advisor, who is the head of the Office of Science and Technology Policy (OSTP), a division of the Executive Office of the President. When I took on this initiative, the IPR Annex had not been updated in years, and was no longer aligned with domestic and international law and policy. Two attempts to update the Annex had been made, but both were unsuccessful, as no one could steer the group to a successful outcome. Once I started down this path, leadership began asking about it the initiative regularly. I was determined not to add my name to the list of people who had failed.

To establish the needed partnerships and collaboration, I formed a working group from the agencies who were using the STAs the most to conduct international research. Since the agency representatives were all lawyers, and I was the only policy expert in the group, I also brought one of my lawyers from DOS to co-chair the group with me. Initially, we held meetings every other month, and I led the group in reviewing past IPR Annexes and practices. We soon realized that the old policy using two separate IPR Annexes was not effective. When I recognized that we were going to promulgate a change to policy by developing a single product, I expanded the group to include the Department of Homeland Security (DHS), Department of Defense (DOD), Department of Energy (DOE), and several other smaller agencies. As momentum picked up on developing the new Annex, I began holding monthly meetings and circulating numerous drafts of the new Annex for review.

This initiative required me to negotiate and communicate on a number of highly complex cross-agency issues. For instance, when I brought DHS into the coalition, they raised concerns about how a change to the IPR Annex could affect the contracts they had in place with private industry. Seeking a win-win solution, I inserted some language into the draft annex that excluded the type of arrangements they were concerned about. At one point, I realized that a stakeholder's attorney had a hidden agenda. He had a view that was way outside the norm and was trying to use this IPR Annex update to get his idea signed off by the White House. Unfortunately, this idea would be unacceptable to our foreign partners.

Leveraging my experience in international relations, I diplomatically addressed this issue on several levels. First, I frequently reminded the assembled group that the purpose of the Annex was to craft a document that facilitated cooperation. Next, I recruited a third party that he respected to explain how his proposal would never be accepted by foreign governments. This tactic not only reinforced DOS' position, but it also demonstrated that we were not merely advocating for our own interests.

As a result of leading this coalition for almost three years, I delivered a new IPR Annex that was fully coordinated and even went through an additional review by the White House Legal Counsel. The Annex was approved in February 2017. In addition, the new Annex did away with two outdated Annex systems, which represents a major policy shift. This process improved interagency relationships by providing a structured venue to articulate and adjudicate contentious issues that had been lingering for many years. By leading the meetings, I created an environment for dialog among a diverse group of people that continues to this day. I received a Superior Honor Award, along with informal thanks from several stakeholder agencies for my deft handling of the proposal.

A final example took place in 2013, in my role as Supervisory Analyst within the Bureau of Land Management (BLM), where I served as a technical advisor. Our program was under pressure to cut costs, and the Science and Technology (S&T) portfolio was a prime target. I knew that several allied countries were facing similar issues. Each of these nations also invests in military S&T, so I decided to form a coalition among all five nations to save money, while maintaining our collective research capacity. I had less than a year to evolve my idea from concept all the way to implementation.

To accomplish this, I had to obtain buy-in from the Ministries of Defense from the other four nations. I began by seeking buy-in from the U.S. side using a two-pronged strategy. First, I briefed SES and political leadership about how my proposal would save money and strengthen international partnerships in a new way. Next, I briefed the program managers on how this strategy would protect their investments in certain technologies, as long as they were willing to share some information. After gaining support from U.S. officials and program managers, I had to go and do the same thing overseas. During that year, I spent almost 25% of my time shuttling between the five countries and communicating with our foreign counterparts.

My plan required each nation to share its S&T requirements, and what it was doing to meet them. Next, we all conducted an honest assessment of our capabilities in the pertinent S&T areas and created a matrix. Using this matrix, we then compared our capabilities and made collective decisions on which organization was best suited for certain areas of research. This process became contentious at several points, such as when I had to convince the U.S. to stop testing certain compounds to treat chemical agents that affect the lungs. I minimized conflict and built alliances by knowing my audience and being able to speak their language. For instance, I leaned heavily on my credentials as a scientist to point out how this approach would lead to better data when talking to other scientists. I further explained how the improved data could help in gaining regulatory approval in the future. Conversely, when talking to the budget personnel on both sides of the Atlantic, I focused on how my strategy would save money.

As a result, I successfully brought together five research communities for a common cause, and we saved $20M in the first year following my collaborative and multinational approach to S&T research. Additionally, my versatile communications and sound reasoning avoided hostile or political agendas. Building upon the productive relationships we had formed, coalition countries began including one another on major programmatic reviews.

SAMPLE ECQs: GS-15 TO SES (EXAMPLE 2)

LEADING CHANGE

In 2018, I began my current position in the Department of Agriculture as the Senior Policy Advisor. In this role, I oversee high-level initiatives and directly advise the Deputy Assistant Secretary (SES) for Finance on a broad range of policy, planning, organizational management, administration, and technical matters during the initial stages of replacing an outdated Time and Attendance (T&A) system. Throughout the country, some disastrous outcomes took place, such as many employees not receiving a paycheck. When senior leadership gave organizations the option of not utilizing the system further, the majority of facilities decided to return to using the old system and it appeared that the initiative would no longer be a viable solution.

From an external perspective, however, this highly visible $49.3M initiative had major payroll implications for over 300K employees and all five labor unions. Moreover, the Government Accountability Office (GAO) and our financial statement auditors cited the limitations of the existing T&A system as a top priority that we needed to resolve. With pressure mounting, the senior finance executives decided to change the leadership on the initiative, and this is when I was hired as Program Manager. Making my own strategic assessment, I believed that the new system could indeed serve the agency for many years to come, as it offered the promise of centralized, standardized, and more accurate T&A management. My vision was to engage the staff at all levels and resolve the technical issues, all while navigating the agency through this critical transformation initiative.

Fully aware that many team members, executives, and users felt excluded from the process, I first formed a cross-functional team comprised of members throughout administrations and staff offices. Through various planning sessions, I shared my vision with the staff, mapped out a plan, assigned responsibilities to address any technical issues, and worked to completely change expectations from the previous program leadership. I then led the staff in conducting focus groups with all stakeholder groups to gain their buy-in and to ascertain firsthand accounts and lessons learned. Next, I assimilated all of this information and insight into a comprehensive change management plan and continued to socialize the initiative across the organization. For instance, I directed the creation of a robust marketing campaign to reassure our customer base that the system had been fixed and was now ready to be used for T&A.

While I was making strong progress, I also faced pushback from some members of the workforce and the unions, who did not want to go down this road again without major changes. Specifically, the National Nurses United blamed some of their pay issues on the system. Remaining flexible in my communications and approach, I established a biweekly conference call and coordinated efforts with our Help Desk to research and document the source of any issues. The union president soon stated that the majority of the issues were not system-related issues, but procedural in nature. My transparency and responsiveness sparked a renewed sense of confidence among stakeholders, and I was able to finalize the terms of a Memorandum of Understanding with two of the unions for redeployment. Building on this success, I completely overhauled the training strategy from a "train-the-trainer" approach to sending Subject Matter Experts (SMEs) (myself included) out into the field to conduct training for timekeepers, supervisors, and payroll technicians. In addition, I assigned a representative to work at each field site to facilitate the transition, creating a bulwark of support at the user level. This strategic decision served as the catalyst for changing the prevailing mindset from doubt to optimism, as stakeholders appreciated having someone present at their facility during the actual transition.

As a result, I gained the needed support and reinvigorated the previously failed efforts with the relaunch of the program within eight months. In doing so, my team updated the system with over 150 enhancements through 6

---

releases using an iterative software change management approach. Since that time, we have added an additional 54,000 users at various locations. We now have automated workflows, better transparency, and increased internal controls that support more accurate and timely pay for employees. With these and other streamlined business practices, this implementation has created $320K in annual cost avoidance. My collaborative approach to technical and cultural change has been lauded by many senior executives and staff as the model for future system initiatives. We received consistent exceptional reviews and accolades from users deploying to the system, including a Presidential Award for two of my trainers that were nominated by our user base. The system should be fully implemented across the Treasury within two years and will provide even broader benefits to employees, along with cost avoidance of $14M per year.

Another example occurred in 2013, while I was serving as Senior Staff Accountant within Customs and Border Protection (CBP). Congress implemented the Troubled Asset Relief Program to address the subprime mortgage crisis and to restore confidence in the housing market. My organization was accustomed to changes on the Daily Treasury Statement (DTS), as each day's strategic report had to account for numerous financial changes, accounts, and spending. But this new legislation was complex in many ways and required detailed financial reporting immediately upon distributing the first payments within the program. The high-level vision was to set up a new federal agency (the Federal Housing Finance Agency). As part of this effort, my challenge was to add new formal reporting lines to the DTS. This was an enormous undertaking, which I needed to accomplish while I maintained daily operations of government financial reporting. Many stakeholder and external agencies were doubtful that I would be able to reflect the many changes necessary to show reporting so soon.

Snapping into action, I researched and documented every aspect of the legislation so that I was well informed when discussing our plan with other business units. While working with other divisions and senior executives to develop the overall strategic plan for establishing the new agency, I proposed several innovative program changes. For years, the DTS Operating Cash Balance was reported only in two categories, but neither of these balances accurately reflected money set aside for this new legislation. Seeking a better way to report this and maintain transparency regarding the program, I proposed the creation of a new type of account to reflect the balance for the new legislation. I then sought and gained support from senior leadership through various meetings and briefings, and we called the new account the "Supplementary Financing Program." Next, I worked with various divisions and executives to decide how to report the new entity and the other payments related to the program. I encountered resistance from some stakeholders who simply wanted to add the new reporting to an existing account, but in partnership with other colleagues, I convinced them that my approach would provide more transparency and control of the federally mandated reporting.

As a direct result of my efforts, we successfully reported the new financial information within two weeks of the legislation. Not only did the new reporting strategy represent a major paradigm shift, but it also demonstrated the flexibility and agility of the financial management system and experts. We were no longer simply viewed as accountants who followed everything to the letter, but as strategic problem solvers who could adjust quickly to new legislation. Senior executives looked to the team and me as authoritative sources on the legislative impacts and came to us for support on many new issues as we continued to report on this account for years to come. My accomplishments were noted in my annual performance appraisal with an "outstanding," and my overall team received a certificate of achievement from executives.

LEADING PEOPLE

In 2015, I was serving as a Division Director within the Department of Defense (DOD). My team was comprised of 15 personnel spread across an office in Maryland and another in West Virginia. I soon realized that I had inherited a number of leadership challenges. I had arrived in the midst of a merger between two major organiza-

tions that caused over half of the team to leave altogether. Even in the midst of declining resources, my division was expected to continue providing critical guidance to the federal financial community. Battling both feelings of anxiety about their future and the demands of upcoming deadlines was a combination that seemed insurmountable. I set out to form a strong and unified team that could not only survive, but also thrive and grow through this experience.

Initially, the team was skeptical of me, and there was an underlying tension in almost every interaction. To build trust and rapport and open the lines of communication, I scheduled individual sessions with each team member. I gave each team member the opportunity to vent in a safe space, and encouraged him/her to speak their minds. Many team members were willing to share what they had heard about me and what they assumed I was going to do with the division. This provided me a great opportunity to dispel the rumors, build a foundation of support, and address each concern up front. My team included people from their mid-20s to late 50s, with varying ethnic backgrounds, educations, and levels of expertise. Seeking to leverage our inherent diversity of thought, I established recurring staff meetings and encouraged healthy discussion and group problem solving to find the best solution.

Traditionally, the division relied on experts in a given area (most of which had now left) and did not solicit input from other team members. As the staff saw that I would consider their viewpoints before making decisions, they began to take more ownership in our collective success. In addition, it was important to set expectations and develop the remaining team members. I strove to create an atmosphere of high productivity by ensuring staff understood the importance of their assignments and how they fit into the overall goals set by higher headquarters (HQ) and other policies and requirements. Meanwhile, I developed performance plans and worked with individual team members to ensure a clear understanding of division and individual goals. During mid-year evaluations, I provided each individual with constructive feedback and coaching. In these sessions, I also established training plans and offered advice on how to achieve their career aspirations. Additionally, I directed a team in providing extensive training for the new staff in the Parkersburg office on critical new systems and procedures.

Under my leadership, morale improved and productivity spiked. The team continued to develop and publish policy and procedures related to reporting and accounting. For instance, I led the team in issuing the full annual update to a major policy on time. Working closely with the Office of Management and Budget (OMB), we also incorporated and issued three official bulletins related to program changes and OMB directives within 30 days. On another level, my division served as a trailblazer for the newly formed Bureau of the Fiscal Service as a model of functioning in collocated sites. Finally, I assisted other divisions affected by the merger by coordinating "Working in a Virtual Team" training.

Another example occurred in 2017, when I became the Director of the Accounting Division. In this role, I led a team of 24 professionals organized under two branch managers. My division collected, monitored, and analyzed agency data in support of the release of the Monthly Treasury Statement. Unfortunately, when I arrived the division was suffering from a negative reputation among executives and other divisions. In addition, the branch managers were displeased that they had previously applied for the Director position and were not selected. Nevertheless, the division had monthly operational deadlines to meet, along with added pressure to assist in developing a new strategic financial management system. My goal was to empower and rally the team in tackling these and many other challenges.

At the most basic level, I strengthened the team through regular staff meetings, where I shared my vision, encouraged participation, and stressed everyone's unique contributions. I also created several process improvement teams to remedy customer service and performance issues. Within only a few weeks, the team began to respond to my guidance and showed progress in improving internal processes, performing government-wide cash reviews, and serving as Subject Matter Experts (SMEs) on the new financial management system initiative. I hosted an Employee Appreciation Day to express gratitude to the staff for all of their hard work. In addition, I used "on-the-spot" and incentive awards to recognize high performers and celebrate success.

While the process improvement team approach helped to hone important skill sets and understanding of the larger mission, I also wanted to develop individual team members. During required coaching sessions, I ensured staff was aware of their level of performance on the process improvement teams and offered suggestions to improve. Likewise, I held my subordinate branch managers accountable for developing their respective teams, and I even included this in their annual performance plans. Throughout the year, during coaching sessions and mid-year and performance appraisals, I offered mentoring to push team members to new heights of performance and professionalism. I also focused team member and intern training for the coming year on project management, data analytics, and other areas in anticipation of potential future organizational changes.

My team was highly diverse, including GS-4s up to GS-14s of various ages and cultural backgrounds. I also had a number of technical specialties, such as administrative assistants, interns, financial program specialist, staff accountants, senior staff accountants, and branch managers. However, many team members were eligible for retirement, and I noticed that we lacked a strong base of younger entry-level accountants. Further, one of my branch managers tended only to select individuals that matched her own personality. This did not help to build a well-rounded team with differing viewpoints to obtain optimal decisions. I allowed both branch managers to recruit new talent using an intern program and inserted myself into the process of reviewing possible candidates. We selected two candidates who served as great assets to each branch and who would eventually provide continuity when retirements occurred.

Both branches provided systems development support, while maintaining daily business operations. I soon learned that the systems development process had often been contentious and left many to believe that the operations SMEs were not qualified to provide assistance in the process. In order to minimize the growing culture of conflict, I directed the integration of systems development team members from another division into the business operation areas. I also participated in the workgroup and encouraged staff to actively participate in the development sessions, ensuring both sides had a voice and all remained focused on the needs of the division. Through these sessions, I forged a sense of shared purpose and mutual respect and bridged the gap between the system development project team and my two branches.

As a result of my sustained leadership, the team soon realized my commitment to our overall success and brought a renewed vigor to the next round of process improvement efforts. Within six months, I had a business continuity plan in place and branch managers began to see how their teams improved through the experience. I also led my newly empowered team in the development of scope, design, and requirements for seven cash management modules in the new financial management system. In addition, I led in piloting and then implementing a telework policy and alternate work schedule. Both of these initiatives helped me to test the new business continuity plan, while raising morale and providing team members with more flexibility.

RESULTS DRIVEN

In 2016, I was serving as Program Manager within the Department of the Interior's (DOI) Government Wide Accounting. The organization had a material weakness (major audit finding) regarding transfer of funds between federal agencies. The finding had been in place and unresolved for 15 years prior to my arrival. In the U.S. government's consolidated Financial Report, the Government Accountability Office (GAO) encapsulated the strategic problem as "the federal government's inability to adequately account for and reconcile intragovernmental activity and balances between federal entities." Our primary customer here was the American public as we

endeavored to improve the government's financial reporting. I was directly accountable to the Fiscal Assistant Secretary (SES), who challenged me to make meaningful progress toward resolving this longstanding issue.

This extremely complex initiative required extensive collaboration across government-wide accounting business lines and the entire federal financial community. I immediately set about coordinating a cross-functional team of federal and nonfederal personnel. I then led the team in developing a strategic roadmap and framework that would eventually lead to removal of the material weakness by the GAO. Within this plan, I developed strategies and methodologies to address the material weakness and other reporting challenges associated with the Financial Report. I also directed the team in rewriting effective and efficient financial management standards, policies, and practices that enhanced government-wide reporting.

Next, I wanted to add in additional layers of transparency and accountability to avoid this kind of material weakness in the future. After a short pilot program, I directed the creation of standard metrics and performance scorecards to demonstrate progress. I then issued the results of the scorecards to the 39 verifying agencies along with a quarterly government-wide scorecard.

The scorecards not only stated the material differences but also documented corrective actions and suggested action items to be performed by the agency. As the scorecards highlighted issues, the agency could react in a much more proactive manner and better prepare for the next audit.

Throughout this period, I had to make difficult choices that not everyone agreed with. After considering all sides, in each instance, I aligned my decisions with interagency agreements and ensured agencies had the needed tools and resources. I continued to engage with stakeholders to take ownership and make this a priority within their respective strategic plans. Along these lines, I presented briefings as the Treasury representative at various conferences, including the Council of the Inspectors General on Integrity and Efficiency (CIGIE) Conference, the Association of Government Accountants Professional Development Conference, and the department's own Financial Management Conference. Within four months, I had a fully developed and collaborative plan in place to overcome the material weakness.

As a result, my plan received approval form the highest levels of the department. As part of the ongoing strategic initiative, I led the revision and issuance of a comprehensive guide to reconcile and reduce intragovernmental differences between trading partners. In addition, the Quarterly Scorecards paid huge dividends in the full year of full utilization by the 39 reporting agencies. Four out of five audited categories experienced an approximately 20% decrease in accounting reconciliations during intragovernmental reporting totaling more than $20B. I also introduced additional preventative controls that give agencies more lead time to access the needed data and create more accurate reports. While the material weakness has not yet been removed, GAO lauded our significant progress, and I feel that the agency is now on a clear path toward resolving this complex finding.

Another example began in 2015, during my time as the Program Manager in the Office of Financial Planning and Strategy. In this role, I was challenged to create an overall strategy for modernization of major financial management systems across the federal government. There were over 24 major federal agencies and 100 federal agencies with possible modernization requests. Further, all of these agencies had to be transitioned to one of four Federal Shared Service Providers (FSSPs). Our customers included the FSSPs, the Office of Management and Budget (OMB), Department of the Treasury, and the federal agencies themselves. I was fully accountable for mapping out the next 10-year window of system implementations for the federal government.

I first directed development of a questionnaire to collect information from each agency, which provided an overview of the agencies' current financial management system environment. Among other things, we gathered detailed information on current systems, timeframes for modernization, alternatives to those modernization plans, and how to address interdependencies and schedules for implementation. On a broader level, all of this information painted a compelling picture of each agency's plans and emerging requirements over the near term (one to five years) and their future state (over six years). Next, I collaborated with agencies to create a one-page summary for each proposed modernization initiative, which articulated the business case to modernize. In addition, I prepared an overall strategic plan and a 10-year timeline to improve the government's financial management capability through the use of improved technology.

As a result, my plan and recommendations were adopted by senior executives and OMB. The roadmap has already paved the way for many related initiatives. For instance, the Department of Transportation's (DOT) Enterprise Service Center upgraded their system. While monitoring and supporting these and other initiatives, I realized the need for a fifth FSSP to support the overall plan. I then coordinated to have the U.S. Department of Agriculture's National Finance Center added as an FSSP. Finally, the FSSPs themselves are now better equipped to prepare several years in advance for the needs of their future customers.

BUSINESS ACUMEN

In 2017, I was serving as Program Manager within the National Science Foundation (NSF). In this role, I had oversight of the $3.3M Intra-Governmental Transactions Project (IGTP), which involved issuing strategic policies for intragovernmental money transfers. The support contract had been initiated by another office within Treasury, and when their funding dried up I was asked to assist the Office of Financial Innovation and Transformation. I knew that this would require top-level support, so I set about developing a justification/business case to validate the need for continued support. In reviewing the IGTP strategic plan, it was determined that additional contract resources were needed as the full-time workforce was focused on operational activities and year-end reporting. In looking at the current contract and determining present gaps, I was able to ascertain the level of resources needed to complete the project. Certain directors did not support my efforts and felt that their particular divisions should take over. I worked to find common ground and gain their support during staff meetings. I then presented the business case to senior executives in written and verbal formats. During this period, I also continued to maintain internal planning meetings and continued collaborative sessions with agencies to build upon the established framework for the initiative.

As a result of my financial analysis and planning, my budget justification was quickly approved by senior executives, and I began to document a Performance Work Statement that outlined existing and future requirements for a potential contractor. After awarding the contract, I led the IGTP and used key contractor support to finalize the policy rewrite still in use today. I later went through a similar process and garnered funding for a $1.8M-a-year initiative to develop standardized reporting financial metrics across almost 40 federal agencies.

Another example began in 2016, when I was serving as Director of the Special Projects Office. Senior executives had created the new office to handle a range of responsibilities and cover operational gaps across the Office of Finance. My office would assist with special projects, as needed, under the direction of the Deputy Assistant Secretary. Moreover, the office would facilitate collaboration among the other divisions to meet agency goals. Starting from scratch, I established the office with a small staff. I then developed a mission and vision and began to share it with stakeholder agencies. I then completed an organizational needs assessment to determine the level of staffing needed to handle the offices' current and pending workload. I then developed a human capital strategy that called for the addition of seven full-time employees in the short term to handle enterprise-wide initiatives. I oversaw efforts to develop position descriptions and classifications, along with GS-14-level vacancy announcements. In addition, I led in recruiting and hiring the initial seven division employees. These individuals had varying backgrounds and requisite skill sets, and I developed them through clear performance expectations and support. I also established ongoing coaching sessions to help with a myriad of interpersonal and professional issues.

As a result of my human capital management, within four months, the new office began to show progress on various initiatives. For instance, the Secretary tasked my team to collect information and to write Congressional testimony for hearings on Government Purchase Card activity. I also led the team in reviewing and editing white papers to ensure they adequately addressed corrective actions and incorporated leadership's finance goals. One of these was a white paper on reimbursable expenses, which the Secretary used to raise awareness. Additionally, my team managed an initiative to ensure compliance with an Executive Order related to PIN technology implementation. Senior executives continue to leverage my fully staffed and flexible division to help track and resolve areas of process improvement.

A final example took place in 2018, in my role as Senior Policy Advisor for the NSF. In this role, I led a major initiative to implement the Time and Attendance (T&A) system, a web-based software that is currently replacing an outdated system. Due to the complexities of pay issues, senior executives did not want to proceed until they had detailed requirements in hand. I directed my team in planning, developing, testing, and implementing system requirements related to iterative system releases. To systematically implement the needed technical changes, I established a change control board comprised of key administrations and staff offices. While engaging with this board on how to best improve the system on the strategic level, I incorporated perspectives from stakeholders into my recommendations for improving the user experience. I also formed a team of Subject Matter Experts (SMEs) from various organizations and regions of the country to develop technical requirements. On several occasions, I brought the geographically separated team members together at a central location to gain agreement on requirements and to conduct user acceptance testing. During this entire period, I communicated with the vendor daily to set expectations and ensure any risks and mitigation strategies were properly documented.

As a result of my leadership on this high-visibility technology initiative, I have led in making more than 150 system enhancements within the past two years. The system was first deployed across the organization, and then to an additional 20,000 employees, without missing a single payroll payment due to system issues. The Interim Chief Financial Officer has publicly recognized me for restoring the credibility of the system.

BUILDING COALITIONS

In 2017, I was serving as Program Manager within the National Safety Transportation Board (NTSB). As federal agencies led their own financial management system modernization efforts, many projects were unsuccessful and led to significant costs, time overruns, or even complete failures. Similarly, agencies often configured systems to their own specific processes, which only drove up upgrade and maintenance costs. Amid these challenges, I was chosen to lead the Federal Agency Migration Evaluation (FAME) initiative to address the ongoing challenges. This involved working with the Office of Management and Budget (OMB) and other stakeholder agencies to migrate technical services to a Federal Shared Services Provider (FSSP) that would offer standardized solutions.

I led my team of federal employees and contractors to build the needed partnerships and coalitions across the federal agencies and implement FAME. For instance, we participated in strategy sessions with other stakeholders to establish strategic goals and operational milestones. I then focused my team on collaborating closely with each agency to identify their specific system needs and help them through the FAME process. Next, I helped facilitate an "Agency Day" during which Treasury, OMB, and FSSP leadership provided information about the benefits and implementation best practices of Shared Services. This forum enabled federal agencies to interact and learn from FSSPs and from other agencies going through the FAME process.

Even as momentum and support grew, many agencies were still reluctant to lose control of how their financial systems would be built, and they expressed their lack of confidence with the identified FSSPs. I patiently worked through the details with stakeholders to demonstrate the merits of the FSSPs. After much negotiation, I gained consensus on an FSSP to host their new financial management system. Shortly after this, it appeared that one particular agency had an agenda to discredit the FSSP in order to be allowed to use a commercial provider. Among other behaviors, at times, they made unrealistic demands and demonstrated a lack of cooperation during the process. I avoided counterproductive politics by focusing stakeholders on what would serve the greater good. Over the course of several meetings, I negotiated a win-win solution and linked the agency with their new FSSP.

Under my direction, the team forged productive relationships with stakeholder agencies and came to genuinely understand their needs and objectives. In addition, my team completed the FAME strategic implementation plan and accompanying guidance to assist agencies in developing standard templates and other reusable documents. As I successfully implemented the FAME process with the Department of Commerce, Department of Labor, and Department of Homeland Security, agencies began to accept my role as supportive rather than intrusive. My team advised nine agencies by helping them to analyze their needs and select the best FSSP. In the longer term, the FAME strategy created government-wide results by reducing the risk of failed system implementations (cost avoidance).

A final example also comes from my time as Program Manager. In 2010, many federal agencies were struggling to determine the correct account and transaction for a particular type of financial transfer. My idea was to create a TurboTax-like tool to simplify the process and help agencies determine the correct account and transaction. With this in mind, I led development of a tool called the Transfers Logic Model (TLM).

Once the tool was complete, I provided a demonstration to OMB and solicited their feedback. Up until this point, the OMB budget methods specialists were the authority to address these types of questions, and they were not ready to endorse a tool that they did not develop. After stating for months that they did not have the needed time or resources, they conducted a review. They found several extremely minor flaws, and the team leader was willing to throw away the whole product for one issue. To minimize personal agendas and egos, I found better ground with the team's higher-level manager. This individual was intrigued with the tool and agreed to review it personally. I established a meeting date, briefed him on every aspect of the tool, and then answered all of his questions. This comprehensive review of the tool during these meetings with the OMB official proved to be beneficial to the implementation of the tool in the federal financial community. Since OMB did not develop the tool, the review was very exhaustive and took place over a series of meetings over several months. Along the way we identified and negotiated other ways to improve the tool, including correcting some accounting entries. The tool was also adjusted to reflect budgetary transactions, as it previously only addressed proprietary transactions.

As a result, the OMB official decided that my TLM concept and strategy was ideal for helping the government execute policy related to the specific accounting transactions in question. I made several changes based on his input and then implemented the TLM with full OMB endorsement. This initiative helped resolve the complexity of these types of transactions in an automated fashion, utilizing a tool that simplifies the process by asking the user questions and leading them to the correct accounting entry. Because users could tell that the tool was designed to make their lives much easier, this initiative improved our relations and reputation among partners and stakeholders. The TLM tool is still being used today and can be located on the Bureau of the Fiscal Service website. Not only do accountants and budget analysts use the tool frequently, but it was also immediately used as a teaching tool for new accountants. The tool also decreased the dollar amount of accounting discrepancies by $10B (down 39% from the previous year). OMB recognized my team's accomplishments, and the TLM model has since been used in other business areas to implement policy changes.

SAMPLE ECQs: GS-15 to SES (EXAMPLE 3)

LEADING CHANGE

In 2017, I was serving as Senior Program Manager (GS-15) within the U.S. Department of State's (DOS) Agricultural Support Office. I assisted in leading 86 regional employees, and directly supervised a Disaster Response Team comprised of a matrixed group of skilled personnel from across 15 different program areas. During disaster relief and support operations, the office played a key role in the external emergency management community, working with many federal and state-level agencies to provide residents in affected areas with food and nutrition. This work was highly visible to the public, the media, and our stakeholders, and I wanted to ensure we could deploy quickly when disasters hit. Within a short time period, the Coordinator and several key staff members retired or moved to new roles. The Disaster Response Team (DRT) had used the same structure and operating model for more than 12 years by this time. Taking a long-term, strategic view, I envisioned assessing and revamping the overall Disaster Response Team (DRT) and operating model so that the office could play a viable role in disaster relief for years to come.

First, I met with Program Division Directors who provided many of the team members during disaster responses. Speaking with them, I identified several key areas ripe for improvement, such as communication between the team and the many stakeholders involved. The directors and other supervisors were often not included in the initial "alert" when the team deployed, which delayed their ability to reassign and manage the day-to-day work of the deployed staff in their divisions. In addition, team members were not trained to fill in for others on the team, when needed. I then developed a strategic plan that included development of current Standard Operating Procedures (SOPs) to address each issue. For instance, we coordinated with the National Weather Service so that all DRT members, the Program Division Directors, and the Public Affairs (PA) Team would receive automatic weather alerts. Key players would now be kept aware of any impending weather events before they escalated and required them to deploy their personnel. I also included requirements for each team member to be properly cross-trained to fill in for others. In a creative move, I then developed a Backup Coordinator position to serve as a point of contact for communications with our deployed staff and our PA team.

While putting the right framework and controls in place to ensure my changes took hold, I was also seeking out new team members to fill the critical vacancies. Serving on the DRT was voluntary because it often required additional travel and after-hours work. Although the agency paid for the travel and offered overtime and comp time, it was still difficult to build interest among staff members. Many of them knew that the work that they were assigned in the office would still be there waiting when they returned, and most of that work was time-sensitive with short deadlines. I knew that if I could change this business process, I could build more interest and quell the growing negative perception and resistance from program directors as well as team members. Remaining flexible in my communications and approach, I set up a protocol with the program directors that ensured team members' work would be appropriately reassigned to other staff when they were deployed. Another concern was that team members had to use their office-issued laptops and personal phones when deployed. To overcome these obstacles to success, I worked directly with our Budget Officer to purchase and issue additional laptops and iPhones for all of the team members.

As a result of these and many other changes, I alleviated the staff resistance and attracted a fresh group of volunteers. Within 45 days of starting this initiative, I had a fully staffed DRT in place, along with new SOPs and equipment, and a new cross-training program. The team's integral role in the larger mission became very evident when we experienced record-breaking snowstorms and power outages in New England. The newly revamped team was deployed five times to assist several thousand affected people in nearby states and local communi-

---

ties. This resulted in nearly $2.5 M in food commodities shipped to these communities. The team's efforts were recognized with several awards, and this period represented a cultural shift in the agency. Not only did Program Division Directors and potential team members value the team more, but stakeholders were more confident in and appreciative of the team's capabilities.

Another example began in 2015, while I was serving as Senior Budget Director for the Department of State (DOS). Among my many responsibilities, I oversaw the Support Services Department that provided a range of program support to our 110-member regional staff. The regional staff oversaw and administered 15 different programs that provided access to low-income people at risk. In conducting my own strategic assessment of the internal and external environments, I determined that the Support Services Department had no internal controls in place for providing services, and had become very inefficient and obsolete. For instance, there were no centralized systems to make and monitor purchases, compare costs, or track incoming or outgoing deliveries and inventory. I formed a vision to restructure the Regional Support Services Department in order to maximize customer service, efficiency, and accountability.

I met with the Regional Administrator and our four directors to discuss and assess their expectations for the department, and to formulate my strategy. I needed new technology in place, and a new Administrative Assistant position to handle daily duties and low-level purchases (under $500). Since the agency was under a partial hiring freeze, I took a creative approach to gaining the needed resources, and reached out to a local college and coordinated an agreement for a second-year business student intern to assist with the restructuring. I also proposed a personnel solution to the Union President and Regional Director, and then quickly advertised and filled a new Administrative Assistant position internally. Next, I contacted the regions and learned that one was testing a pilot for a new automated purchasing system. The staff and Budget Officer pushed back on the idea of participating in the pilot because of uncertainty about how the program worked and whether they would be able to confidently use it. To gain their support, I arranged for staff from the other region that had developed the program to visit our region and demonstrate the program and provide training.

As a result, the Support Services Department was running more efficiently within just a four months cutting our ordering and delivery time nearly in half. I also engaged our intern in redesigning our supply room to reduce the overall size by 75%, and developing a new inventory tracking system. Regional staff members appreciated these changes, as I greatly reduced their wait times in receiving purchase orders by two to three days. They also saw a noticeable improvement in the overall customer service and interactions with the Department. In July 2015, our region received a "clean" audit with no findings during a Quality Control review focused on purchasing and procurements. This was due to the protocols that we had put in place for segregation of duties and second-level process oversight. Finally, senior officials lauded the new electronic purchasing system as a best practice, and the Regional Administrator recognized me with an Extra Effort Award. We also received similar "clean" audits in 2016 and 2017.

LEADING PEOPLE

For the last 25+ years, I have served in a range of progressively broader assignments within the federal government, leading multifunctional teams of up to 110 personnel. For example, in 2016, I was serving as Senior Program Manager (GS-15) within the U.S. Department of State's (DOS) Agricultural Support Office. In this position, I oversaw a Regional Management Team consisting of four directors and seven deputy directors, each of whom led approximately eight personnel. I quickly identified a number of leadership challenges. An agency restructuring led to having three new deputy directors with limited or no first-level supervisory experience or knowledge. By the time I arrived, the region had seven active Union grievances or complaints and three Equal Employment Opportunity (EEO) complaints. Employee morale was also at an all-time low, as reflected in the agency's 2015 Federal Employee Viewpoint Survey (FEVS). I was determined to build a cohesive and effective team that could meet and exceed the region's strategic goals.

I facilitated an offsite meeting with my management team and established monthly "workshop" meetings during which to discuss specific supervisory issues, such as approving travel and leave requests, telework arrangements, T&A issues, and the use of comp time and credit hours for employees. I designed these workshops to provide a safe and collaborative atmosphere. Based on the feedback and participation of supervisors, during the workshops, we established Standard Operating Procedures (SOPs) to address their shared issues and challenges. I was also focused on developing the individual members of my team, and met with each individually to discuss his/her training needs and career goals, and to develop Individual Development Plans (IDPs). I then met with our Regional Human Resources (HR) Liaison and drafted a three-pronged plan to improve professional development. As part of the plan, I arranged a mandatory two-day supervisory training session that included an overview of the union contract, examples of grievances, complaints and unfair labor practices, the labor management bargaining process, EEO complaints, conflict management, and best practices. I also positioned myself as a supportive mentor, and assisted team members with a myriad of interpersonal and professional matters. For instance, I mentored one of the directors for 12 months, supporting his long-term career goals.

The team was almost evenly spread between women and men, and included a great deal of varying ages, backgrounds, levels of education and experience, and technical specialties. I embraced this inherent diversity, and took every opportunity to leverage and expand upon it. For instance, I served as the second-level hiring official for the three new deputy directors that were hired, and helped to achieve almost 50% minority representation across the team. Even while getting the right people and training in place, we still had a major issue with internal conflict. Upon carefully assessing the seven formal grievances, I found that all of them had come from three directors in particular. I engaged with the union to try to resolve the grievances, and then met with each director to discuss the issue. Two of them readily admitted that they could have handled the discussions better, but the third director was defensive and adamant that she had handled each situation properly. I continued to discuss the issues openly with all directors during the workshops, and eventually gained the third director's buy-in and participation with the union.

Within four months, all team members had received supervisory training, which had a positive effect on customer service and communication. Within six months, the culture of conflict had all but vanished, and all of the Union grievances and complaints were resolved or closed. Morale and employee engagement improved dramatically. The 2016 FEVS showed an 8% improvement in employee satisfaction and trust, and there have been no additional Union or EEO complaints filed. Building this unified Management Team was also critical for our success in being able to fill 24 new Program Specialist positions in our region in 2016. Finally, two other regions have adopted my training model, and a third region has expressed an interest in doing so.

A second example also comes from 2016, during my time as Senior Program Manager. As part of my duties, I oversaw the Regional Public Affairs (PA) Division, comprised of a PA Director and three GS-12 PA specialists. After a six-month vacancy, the agency hired a new PA Director who was unfamiliar with our programs and operations. Further, the PA specialists had always worked independently, with each specializing in exclusive areas, such as media relations, publications, and Congressional/public inquiries. Essentially, the team was divided and underperforming compared to its counterparts in the six other regions. To begin turning the team around, I assessed each person's strengths and weaknesses, their interests, and how they viewed their role within the organization. I also worked with the new PA Director to set new performance goals, such as increasing the number of events and publications on which the team assisted. Next, I established new protocols to improve interaction and information sharing between PA and program divisions, such as new daily briefings with the Management Team, including the PA staff on program-level meetings, and a new SharePoint calendar and electronic library. I then used the weekly meetings to monitor progress, discuss issues, provide support, and implement cross-training.

To gain another measure of performance, I also met regularly with Program Division Directors to gauge the PA staff's engagement in their meetings.

Meanwhile, I worked with the PA Director to develop IDPs for each team member that addressed the skills we identified for improvement, such as written communication, photography, and public speaking. I also arranged for a Director from another region to mentor the new PA Director on daily operations and best practices. The team had strong diversity, including two men, two women, and a Latino American Outreach Coordinator (GS-301-12). The Outreach Coordinator had been reassigned from a previous role as a Program Specialist (GS-201-11) in another division as part of a settlement for an EEO complaint. Although he was readily accepted by the team, his particular outreach initiative had been discontinued. He felt strongly that he should be reassigned as a PA Specialist (GS-1035), which would be more beneficial for his career in Public Affairs (PA). I met with the Union President and agreed to a desk audit, which clearly demonstrated that the employee was performing most of the work of a PA Specialist. His position was formally changed, resolving the growing tension around the issue.

As a result, the PA Director and his three staff members evolved into a highly effective team that worked very well with program divisions in the region. In just over nine months, the Regional PA Division met and exceeded all of its Fiscal Year goals, and reduced its overall response time for public inquiries by 30%. Specific accomplishments included issuing more than 30 media advisories and press releases, and pitching over 300 media engagements to editors. In addition, the team's media efforts resulted in more than 100 interviews and media placements for the Agency's Under Secretary. Further, the team increased the visibility of our programs and priorities while providing media and logistical support for an unprecedented 80 regional events, and by making presentations at two healthcare summits with state and community partners. Today, the Regional PA Team continues to be recognized by senior agency officials as one of the most productive and best-performing out of seven regions.

RESULTS DRIVEN

In 2015, I was the Budget Director for the U.S. Department of State's Outreach Office. I was directly accountable to the Regional Administrator (SES) for ensuring the proper use and accountability of approximately $12B across 15 different programs. My internal customers included the Regional Management Team and the seven regional program staffs we supported. My external customers included state-level partner agencies for Health, Social Services, Education, and Agriculture. Following an agency-wide position management study, the office had recently undergone a major reorganization intended to elevate the roles and responsibilities of each position, and more closely align them with similarly located positions in the national office. The divisions in the regions were the only ones that did not go through this same restructuring process. Before long, the workforce spread across the regions began to raise many questions about fairness and consistency, as well as the perceived value of the work they did for its customers.

During a meeting with the agency's senior executives at our annual conference, I took the initiative and raised concerns about the impact of the agency's new regional restructuring initiative on the morale of the staff in the regions, as well as current and future staffing. The seven other directors agreed to conduct an analysis of the Regional Operations and to provide feedback and recommendations to the Associate Administrator to address and mitigate these concerns. Further, my colleagues all requested that I take the lead on this initiative. Between August and December 2015, I led the group in conducting a thorough analysis of the organizational structures, core responsibilities and functions, partnerships and relationships, and potential improvements to service delivery. As part of this analysis, we gathered critical feedback, data, and technical information from internal and external customers, such as the General Services Administration (GSA).

I also created subgroups to lead various focus areas, and to present their findings to the larger group for feedback and editing. This approach helped me identify best practices that we could adopt for a national model. The analysis showed that all of our regional divisions operated similarly, with the same core responsibilities and functions, including accounting, auditing, contracts and procurements, facilities management, records management, budgets, and technical assistance. Next, I directed the overall group in creating a report with our findings and recommendations. Among other things, we recommended aligning the Regional Division with the model used in the newly structured Regional Program Divisions. We also recommended dividing the regional structure into two branches, with each focused on either internal or external customers. Assimilating all of our findings, I made a formal presentation to senior officials and stakeholders.

As a result, senior officials supported all of the group's recommendations, which were eventually forwarded to the agency's Human Resources (HR) Department for a formal position review. HR agreed with our recommendations after a lengthy review, and forwarded them to the Agency's Senior Executive Council without any significant changes. The Council also agreed with our recommendation to reorganize the Division under the Department of State (DOS) administrators. My leadership also positioned the USDA, its employees, and its customers for long-term growth and success. Not only did the group's work serve as the crucial step in completing a major reorganization, but it will also define future expectations and responsibilities of employees in the Regional Divisions. Consequently, this will help the divisions continue to attract and retain skilled staff, and contribute to overarching goals effectively and efficiently.

Another example occurred in 2014, while I was serving as Director of Operations within the National Science Foundation (NSF). In this capacity, I directed a team of approximately 10 personnel engaged in a variety of program areas, such as workforce planning initiatives, training, budgeting, staffing and personnel, Information Technology (IT), contracting and procurements, and overall program administration. I also provided operational and administrative oversight for approximately 100 employees in 4 program offices in the region. HUD's mission is centered on ensuring safe, affordable, and adequate housing opportunities. Due to staffing losses, rising costs, and unforeseen construction issues, a total of 83 initiatives were behind schedule (more than four times the number of backlogged projects than in any other region). I was directly accountable to senior officials for solving this strategic problem and improving support to the customer who relied on these housing programs.

I coordinated an offsite "retreat" to focus on the issue with the Regional Director and our State Office Directors. I facilitated discussions with this group to identify the number of projects in the pipeline that were "at risk," the reasons for the delays, and the options available to us for addressing the problems. I quickly realized that all of the projects identified were in the same office, and that the level of staff in that particular office was not sufficient to handle the underwriting and construction oversight required for these projects. This lack of expertise created a situation that continued to increase the number of backlogged projects each year. Taking decisive action to solve this problem, I set out to leverage all of our staffing resources and skills around the region. After gaining support from all of the State Office Directors, I led in devising an innovative regional plan of action that called for the creation of a Regional Task Force comprised of staff from all four program offices. Rather than addressing each project individually, under the new model, the program offices would approach the issue as one holistic process that affected them all. Each office would be held accountable to do its respective part, and then pass a given project on to the next office. I would monitor the process and ensure accountability at my level, and report progress up to senior officials.

As a result of my technical knowledge of these critical housing programs, the Regional Task Force was a complete success. Under my direction, the regional program offices completed half of the projects in the pipeline within 12 months, and the rest in the following year. In all, we completed 83 projects worth more than $98.4M in grant funding within 18 months. The Regional Task Force was recognized as a best practice, its members all received Extra Effort Awards, and I received two separate Special Act Awards.

BUSINESS ACUMEN

In 2017, I was serving as Budget Director for the U.S. Department of State's (DOS) Outreach Office. My primary responsibility was to ensure the proper use and accountability of approximately $12B in program funding for 15 different programs. More than 1,500 employees throughout seven different regions were involved in this mission, each compensated with salaries and benefits from one of 14 different budget accounts. To ensure compliance with their specific budget accounts, senior managers used their own "Charging Plan" spreadsheet programs. There was no consistency in how these were used to accurately manage program budgets and staff ceiling numbers, which led to imbalanced funds at the end of the Fiscal Year (FY).

To address this issue at the strategic level, I assembled a task force of 15 Funds Officers, Budget Analysts, and Financial Management Directors from the Regional Offices and the National Office. I then led the group in conducting an analysis of its division and regional financial processes, and then developed a standardized set of Standard Operating Procedures (SOPs) that integrated best practices from across the regions. Next, I broke the task force into two groups. One group drafted a detailed set of SOPs for the new procedures and protocols, the new Charging Plan template, and a summary report detailing the work of the group. The second group researched our agency regulations related to certifying and obligating federal funds and internal controls. The second group would also provide Quality Control for the first group.

As a result of my financial management, within four months, I signed off on the Task Force's final report and recommendations. I then presented the plan to the Chief Financial Officer, and gained full approval. The new financial management model and tools improved budget accuracy and balance of end-of-year funding. Using this new system, I was able to identify and return $145K in unused program funds to our national office in 2017, which were eventually reallocated to another region to cover a shortfall. Under the new procedures, every division and region would use one standard Charging Plan spreadsheet to track all staffing and funding. The Funds Officers would also be required to follow a strict set of protocols for completing the Charging Plans and certifying that they matched the salary data from the agency's accounting system. My new model was quickly recognized as a best practice, and became mandatory as the new standard for budgeting all of our salaries and benefits.

Another example took place in 2014, in my role as Acting Supervisory Analyst within the Department of the Interior (DOI). As part of a major reorganization a few years prior, approximately 30 positions in the agency's seven regions were significantly restructured and reclassified to be more responsive to the needs of the agency's mission and external partners. Because these were considered "new" positions, the employees needed to reapply and compete for positions that they were already filling. By early 2014, the directors (GS-15), deputy directors (GS-14), and team lead positions (GS-13) were filled. In our region, we still needed to fill 24 Program Specialist (GS-12) positions, including 13 incumbent GS-11 employees and 11 new hires. This situation posed many challenges, such as some GS-11 program specialists lacking the required competencies for the new GS-12 positions. Another challenge was that some of the employees in our region wanted to transfer back to their previous branches. I met with our program directors and proposed that we develop a Regional Hiring Strategy. I also offered several key ideas, such as allowing interested employees to request a lateral reassignment to a new branch. These would be handled as direct reassignments, which did not need to be advertised and competed. I also suggested that we announce the newly upgraded positions as career ladder positions (GS-11/12). This would allow everyone to at least qualify at the GS-11 level, and demonstrate their competencies for the higher grade later. I gained consensus among program directors, and then from the Human Resources (HR) Director and Union President. I then tasked our HR Liaison to develop a Memorandum of Understanding (MOU) with the union to manage the reassignments.

As a result of my human capital management, within two weeks, six GS-12 employees submitted requests to be reassigned. All of them met the criteria and were approved, but only three elected to go through with the move after their interviews. All three employees were reassigned to their new branches, and within two months, we had advertised, interviewed, and transitioned all incumbent GS-11 program specialists into their new positions. Ten of them were selected at the GS-12 level, and three were selected into GS-11/12 career ladder positions. We also filled seven of our vacancies with GS-11/12 position. To fill the remaining four vacancies, I utilized direct hiring authorities, such as the Schedule A Program for persons with disabilities, returning Peace Corps employees, and the Fellow Experience Program.

A final example occurred in 2012, in my role as Director of Administration within the National Transportation Safety Board (NTSB). In our region alone, we conducted approximately 70 Management Evaluation (ME) reviews annually, which involved reviewing onsite records, procedures and protocols, funding systems, and other program-related data. We also worked with the Office of Inspector General (OIG) to resolve approximately 10 audits each year. I found that we lacked a way to systematically coordinate these program activities at the regional level, which led to a lack of consistency in planning, budgeting, scheduling, and documenting all of these activities. When the agency introduced Microsoft (MS) SharePoint, I immediately realized its potential for program management and oversight. To overcome a lack of available internal staffing and resources, I coordinated with a local college and gained the support of a communications student intern with the requisite skills to help me research other government and commercial websites, and then develop our own.

Within four months, the Regional SharePoint site was complete, and served as a "dashboard" for accessing information and collaborating during program reviews. Through the use of a shared calendar to track all program reviews (and associated documents) across the region, it was much easier to find opportunities for sharing staff and resources. As a result, program reviews became much more efficient and cost-effective. In some cases, we were able to combine reviews and reduce the number of staff needed often saving several thousand dollars in travel costs per year. The various links in the site also made it much easier for employees and managers to check the status of an ME or audit, which reduced response times for addressing corrective action plans and audit findings by an average of several days each month. This initiative did not cost the agency anything, aside from the time invested, and was later recognized as a best practice.

BUILDING COALITIONS

In 2018, I was serving as Budget Director for the U.S. Department of State's Outreach Office. The employee satisfaction scores in the 2017 Federal Employee Viewpoint Survey (FEVS) were a main focus of senior leadership. When I arrived, scores were the lowest in the regions, and had declined by more than 15% from 2016. The challenge for me in my new position was to develop a regional plan of action to turn this around in time to have noticeably improved scores for the next FEVS.

Throughout the next couple of months, I partnered with employees, the Regional Management Team, and the Union and then co-hosted a series of "listening" sessions and town hall-style meetings with our employees. I also tasked our directors with reaching out to our state partners for feedback about their interactions with the staff and the overall level of satisfaction with our customer service. The common theme was that the employees did not feel that they had the resources and support to properly perform their work, and they did not feel empowered to make decisions that had a direct impact on their work. Assimilating all of this information, I formed a workgroup of our employees and began to develop a Regional Cultural Transformation Plan that supported top priorities. My plan included several goals and objectives, and focused on five key components for success: employee trust, respect, transparency, accountability, and results.

By January 2018, the workgroup had developed an initial series of recommendations that included a more focused onboarding process for new employees, more frequently structured all-employee meetings during which employees could contribute and make presentations about their work, more consistency in how supervisors conducted mid-year and final employee performance reviews, and more opportunities for training and career development. Due to the complexity of these recommendations, the amount of work that would be required in order to develop these ideas, and the varying opinions from the workgroup members on how to adequately address the issues, I decided to expand the coalition by engaging even more employees in the process. I then established four separate workgroups, each tasked with addressing one of the following focus areas: leadership, communications, employee engagement, and training and career development.

Some members of the original workgroup were originally resistant to conceding some of the control that they had obtained from being in the first workgroup. Likewise, some felt that their initial work was not appreciated and that their ideas would never be implemented. To minimize personal agendas and counterproductive politics, I appointed the original group members as co-facilitators for the new groups. I had to manage a plethora of different opinions and approaches. To develop consensus in a diplomatic manner, I led a negotiating process that identified what initiatives were necessary (not just desired), available resources, and tradeoffs. To further strengthen the coalition, I established and led weekly meetings with the co-facilitators of each workgroup, the Union President, our Regional HR Liaison, and the Regional Management Team.

My interagency communication and coordination led to highly impactful results. By forming a broad coalition with the Management Team and the staff to address the organizational problem, I created an atmosphere that fostered trust and respect. The workgroups developed more than 50 specific ideas for making improvements in each of their four focus areas. The region saw an overall increase in employee satisfaction scores in the 2018 FEVS by almost 10% from the previous year—an amazing accomplishment, considering that employee satisfaction scores actually decreased overall. The region also met or exceeded all of its program goals and objectives in 2017, which had not been the case in 2013. On another level, bringing together all stakeholders of these parties for a common goal improved relationships and overall cohesion.

A final example took place in 2015, in my role as Budget Director. During the school year, approximately 21M children qualify for free or reduced price meals at school based on the income level of their households. My agency administered a program to address the needs of these children and teens during the summer months when they do not have access to meals through their schools. Historically, the average daily participation rate during the summer months was only 4M children and teens. Senior officials in my agency established a new national goal to serve more than 200M meals during the summer months. I also wanted to expand with more sites in rural areas. To accomplish this, I sought to build a coalition and leverage the resources of key external stakeholder agencies.

I contacted the Regional Directors from several associated agencies, and convinced them that our program would be a good fit and help the families living in their residential housing projects. I then appointed one of my Program Directors to lead in developing a workgroup with our staff, our state-level representative, and staff members from stakeholder agencies. I then directed him to form a plan with specific goals and timeframes for my approval. The states remained guarded and reluctant to committing resources. To help push through this roadblock, I participated in one of these meetings with the Regional Directors. I won their support by asking other stakeholders to share their successes with the program, and through give-and-take. More specifically, I allowed the Regional Directors to set their own goals, and the amount of time and resources that they would be willing to commit. After gaining consensus across the group, I continued to oversee the initiative from the executive level and kept the Regional Directors updated.

As a result, stakeholders committed to establishing 21 new rural housing sites, with the potential of feeding nearly 2,500 children and teens. Based on approximately 46 weekdays (M-F) during the summer months, this meant an additional 115,000 meals. Building on this momentum, I expanded the coalition and developed many other sites and sponsors in the region, as well.

SAMPLE ECQs: GS-15 TO SES (EXAMPLE 4)

LEADING CHANGE

In July 2016, I became the Director at Captain Schwartz Veterans Affairs (VA) Hospital. In this role, I was "second in command" of a 147-acre medical care facility with 471 operating beds, 6 Community-Based Outpatient Clinics (CBOCs), a $600M annual budget, and more than 3,500 employees. Upon conducting my own strategic assessment of the environment, I quickly identified an area that was ripe for improvement. The hospital's medical and non-medical equipment was generally in a state of disrepair. Some organizations may be able to operate with computer equipment, telephones, furniture, and perhaps some limited facility space. However, with more than $135M worth of equipment at any given time, it was obvious that our hospital relied heavily on its equipment to carry out its mission of caring for our veterans.

Historically, the hospital had lacked a preventive strategy and had spent $39M on equipment in annually, most of which did not need to be replaced yet, according to the manufacturer. This approach left the hospital with mostly aging and unreliable equipment. The frequent operational breakdowns had strategic and systemic impacts on areas such as staff frustration, operational efficiency, and patient satisfaction and safety. In addition, external stakeholders within and outside the VA system were very aware of our equipment and related problems. Believing that I could drive the needed changes, I formed a vision to dramatically shift the way the hospital maintained its equipment, which I knew would require a new mindset and various process changes across the organization.

I created the Aged Equipment Initiative to serve as a framework for change. I then held meetings with the Chief of Logistics, the hospital's senior leadership team, and the 31 Service Chiefs to share my long-term strategy for a viable prevention program. I then directed my Chief of Logistics to formulate a plan to spend the annual equipment budget on aged equipment first. Since this approach replaced longstanding business practices, I was not surprised when the Chief of Logistics was initially resistant. He still could not see the logic of replacing equipment, oldest to newest, to reduce breakdowns, and, in fact, did not perceive an overall problem with equipment breakdowns across the hospital. Remaining flexible in my communications and approach, I gained his support by citing how much recent issues had interfered with patient care, increased costs, and upset staff members and patients.

With this broader perspective of how the operational issues would play out at the strategic level over time, the Chief of Logistics agreed to support the initiative. Knowing that he preferred autonomy in getting things done, I built on this success by delegating him to oversee the Aged Equipment initiative under my direction. I guided the Chief of Logistics and Service Chiefs in carefully prioritizing all of the hospital's equipment purchasing needs for the next five years. To further expand support for the initiative, I also directed he work with Subject Matter Experts (SMEs) from the different business areas in deciding what needs to be replaced. For instance, SMEs shared that microscopes actually last much longer than the manufacturer's recommended replacement date, so I integrated this into the overall plan. I maintained top-level support during this period through providing frequent updates to the leadership team, including the Hospital Director, and updated the Service Chiefs each month.

As a result, my Aged Equipment Initiative virtually eliminated the unreliable aged equipment (and related breakdowns) in the hospital within one year. Using a more deliberate and systematic approach to the inevitable changes caused by aging equipment, I reduced the amount of money needed to replace equipment from $39M the year before my arrival, to $3.58M in 2016 and $6M in 2017. In terms of a cultural shift, the medical staff now spends more time providing direct patient care, which leads to better health outcomes for our veterans. Non-medical staff, such as the Operations and Maintenance department, also benefited greatly from this new paradigm. For instance, prior to this initiative, they spent an estimated 50 hours annually repairing just one type of old equipment. Now, they spend that time completing preventive maintenance work orders that prevent equipment emergencies from occurring in the first place.

Another example occurred in 2017, also in my role as Director. The internal climate was very negative and cynical at the time, with low employee satisfaction scores and many people voicing their intent to find jobs outside the hospital. It did not help when both the Hospital Director and higher-level Network Director (more than seven hospitals in the region) retired with very little notice and no planning. Media outlets were quick to run negative stories about VA and Hines. External stakeholders, such as Veterans Service Organizations (VSOs), began questioning hospital leaders about the allegations they read about in the media. Despite high scrutiny and staff complacency, I set out to improve both the organization's internal environment and external reputation.

I solicited input from the senior leadership team, from employees, and from veterans at town hall meetings. I then assimilated all this feedback into a strategic plan that focused on three key areas that had been identified as weaknesses/opportunities for improvement on the latest employee satisfaction survey (Praise, Workgroup Communication, and Conflict Resolution). I then planned, gained support for, and implemented several initiatives to support this overarching plan. For instance, I created a Human Resources (HR) program that allowed supervisors to immediately reward/recognize/praise employees for outstanding work with On-the-Spot Awards. In a creative move, I also instituted a "10-minutes with the Director" program in which I scheduled two hours each month and invited randomly selected employees to come to my office and talk openly about strengths, opportunities, and suggestions from their perspectives.

Next, I scheduled two one-hour blocks each week to physically walk around the hospital and speak with various teams and employees about how we can help them do their jobs better. On yet another level, I cultivated organizational change by having each of the four senior leadership team members schedule two hours to work with business areas that performed well on certain metrics (similar to the "Undercover Boss" TV show, but not undercover). This strategy became extremely popular as employees could see leadership making an effort to better understand their unique roles. Some members of the senior leadership team claimed to have difficulty finding the time for my cultural improvement initiatives. To gain their commitment, I listened to their concerns, and then explained my overall vision for the employees and patients, and shared how I had been able to find the time in my schedule. I also committed to going on rounds with them, and to visit areas under their direct responsibility so they could celebrate the successes of their staff to the Acting Director. Throughout this period, I also represented and spoke about the hospital's programs and staff at various community and outreach events.

As a result, within one year, I made incredible strides in improving the culture across the 3,500-member workforce. On the next employee satisfaction survey, the participation rate of employees (69%) significantly surpassed the average across 7 hospitals (64%) and the national average (60%). Further, the hospital showed marked increases in all three focus areas compared to 2015. Namely, Workgroup Communication increased by 0.1 and Conflict Resolution increased 0.16 (highest in the region). The hospital's most favorable score was in Employee Engagement, which reached 4.30 out of 5, demonstrating that staff connected strongly to the mission. These scores reflected a major transformation from the toxic environment I had inherited months earlier.

LEADING PEOPLE

In 2018, I was serving as Executive Manager at the Clay Sheers VA Medical Center in Utah. In this role, I directed a 150-member staff, including a 15-member Patient Administration Service (PAS) team located in a separate building from the main hospital. I soon identified low performance and productivity, as the team was not processing enough medical claims to eliminate the large backlog of 3,200 claims. The PAS Supervisor was not supporting or motivating his team, but instead was acting very critical and punitive, such as raising his voice and allegedly making negative comments about women. I set out to form a cohesive team that could reduce the backlog and go on to meet and exceed organizational goals.

I first brought together the Chief Financial Officer (CFO) and PAS Chief to clearly outline the problem and impacts, such as veterans being sent to collection agencies, and angry calls from vendors who were not being paid. I also shared my vision of revamping the team's efforts and focusing on the backlog. I then established regular meetings with the PAS Chief and guided her in developing a plan to use over time and weekend work to reduce the backlog. To demonstrate my commitment and support to the team, I came in and helped without requesting pay or comp time. In addition, I encouraged casual dress, brought in donuts, and ordered pizza each day the staff came in on the weekend while frequently walking around thanking team members for their dedication and hard work. I also obtained support from another facility, which processed hundreds of claims outside of the hospital.

It did not take long for the conflict between the CFO and PAS Chief to reveal itself. The CFO was very critical of the PAS Chief for allowing the backlog to happen, as this problem made it nearly impossible for the CFO to do her job in providing me and the Medical Center Director with accurate budget projections. The conflict at their level was having a negative effect across their respective teams. I held several conversations with these two individuals both separately and together to help them understand each other's perspective. For instance, I coached the CFO about the impact her behavior and tone of voice had on the PAS Chief. I learned that she intended to increase the sense of urgency, and did not seem to realize the harsh nature of her tone. I talked with her about ways she could lighten her interpersonal style and educated her about the complexity of the PAS Chief position.

Meanwhile, I focused a great deal of time in developing the PAS Chief, who had been in her position for less than a year and needed support and guidance. I took her under my wing by meeting with her frequently and mentoring her in developing and working toward short- and long-term goals. For instance, I helped her to become comfortable in soliciting other departments and hospitals to gain needed resources, and in ways to more effectively communicate with the CFO. These and other related efforts improved overall diversity of thought by helping each person see and respect the other individual's perspective and area of expertise. Next, I helped the PAS Chief to work with Human Resources (HR) and place her underperforming subordinate supervisor on a Performance Improvement Plan (PIP) with specific deliverables and timelines to ensure success. In addition, I sat down with several high-potential staff members discussing their development and promotion goals and the behaviors and skills they would need to advance.

My inclusive leadership during this period led to outstanding results. Using the PIP, the PAS Chief was able to guide her subordinate supervisor in delivering quality daily reports and helping to drive productivity across the team. The claims inventory backlog was indeed reduced from 3,200 to zero within one month, and calls from angry veterans and vendors due to backlog issues all but vanished. Moving forward, the PAS team met and withheld the standard of processing 39 claims per day per person in the order received. Morale improved dramatically, and PAS team members expressed their pride in eliminating the backlog. The Director thanked me for this team-building success, and recognized me in front of the hospital's senior leadership team.

Another example took place in 2017 in my role as Program Director of at Maxwell Hospital. In this capacity, I directed an 11-member senior staff in managing a highly diverse 350-member workforce working throughout the hospital and several external facilities. The existing Operating Room (OR) space was terribly old, leading to numerous surgeries being canceled, interrupted, or delayed, creating quality concerns for patients and operational inefficiencies. With the arrival of the new Chief of Surgery, I learned that although the grand opening of the new OR was scheduled, it was far from ready. In fact, the OR was in an outdated room in the basement level of the hospital. Key opinion leaders and department heads were in conflict, even shouting at each other during meetings, and I stepped in to unify the team around a common cause.

I immediately coordinated a series of meetings with representatives from across the hospital's business areas, including Surgery, Quality, Logistics, Engineering, Information Technology, and Nursing. I shared my intent of moving the OR out of the basement and into a brand-new, state-of-the-art location for our veterans. I then asked for their expertise in defining the problems at hand, and fostered team commitment and trust by highlighting to the group each member's unique expertise that made them essential to the success of this project. With a sense of shared purpose emerging, I guided the senior staff in identifying the factors required to open the new OR, assigned ownership for each factor, and tasked each owner to develop an action plan with expected completion dates. While rallying the team around these efforts, I continued to drive progress through recurring meetings, and worked with my Public Affairs Officer to coordinate a ribbon-cutting ceremony and tour with key leaders and stakeholders, such as veterans and Congressional offices.

Equally focused on developing my team members, I sat down with them individually to discuss their career aspirations, create training plans, and provide developmental assignments. For instance, my Chief of Logistics expressed concern that his reputation with the team and me would suffer if the Contracting Department did not award equipment in time. I reassured him that he would be fine, and cited an example when we had overcome a similar obstacle together in the past. This solidified his support of my strategy, and I mentored him on how to elevate any problems appropriately so that there were no surprises. At one point, a sense of conflict arose when many hospital services became frustrated with the Contracting Department for delays, poor communication, and lack of follow-up. I invited the contracting staff to our staff meetings, and asked them to share how and why they prioritized certain contracting actions. With this new insight, the hospital services could better address their customers' needs. Moreover, now that the services understood the contracting office's barriers, they began to think outside of the box and identify ways to maximize their shared resources.

The team was very balanced in terms of backgrounds, ages, levels of education and experience, and personality types. However, some team members did not understand each other's disciplines, such as a staff member who criticized an Engineer's Indian accent (broken English) and perceived lack of follow-up. I coached this employee about the importance of diversity and all of our differences, and highlighted that this Engineer's fortitude to overcoming barriers is tremendous, as he had bravely left his family in India as a young adult to immigrate to the U.S. I talked about how that fortitude and tenacity to achieve success were exactly what we needed, and coached the employee on how to harness those values from the Engineer.

As a result of my leadership and conflict resolution, the team worked together effectively and the grand opening of the OR occurred, as expected. The hospital held a well-received ribbon-cutting ceremony that garnered positive media attention. Since then, the Chief of Surgery and other staff thanked me numerous times for getting the new OR open, and patients began to regularly compliment staff about the new space. The infrastructure challenges that were so common in the old OR became a thing of the past, and OR operations were consistent and reliable. The Chief of Logistics that I mentored was later selected as for a major promotion at another facility.

RESULTS DRIVEN

In 2017, I served as Health Systems Director in the Veterans Affairs (VA) Agency of Toronto. Our VA Ambulatory Care Center (VAACC) was the lowest-scoring facility across the region in scheduling patients for care within 30 days. Patient satisfaction was suffering, and I knew that in the long term, this could lead to patients seeking care elsewhere and the facility losing money. I was accountable to the Regional Director for improving performance and bringing the VAACC's access up to the regional average within 45 days. The veterans were my customers, and I was determined to provide them with the type of excellent support they deserved.

Snapping into action to address this growing strategic problem, I scheduled a site visit at the VAACC. After closely assessing the situation and meeting with the Associate Director's Health Systems Specialist, I engaged her to champion the initiative under my guidance. I further explained that we would employ a patient-centered approach found to be effective at other facilities. Still seeking even more detailed insight on the excessive wait times, I directed the specialist to generate a complete report. It revealed a total of 861 patients currently scheduled for appointments beyond 30 days. Next, I helped her to identify solutions and opportunities to streamline business processes.

For instance, there seemed to always be long wait times in conducting registry exams when patients first entered the hospital. I decided to change the Registry Exam appointment slot from 90 to 60 minutes, which aligned better with other facilities and drastically increased capacity for more exams. I also instructed the Health Systems Specialist to better utilize unused positions and strategically redeploy staff to focus on reducing the backlog. Since part of the strategy included a surge of evening and weekend work, I used overtime and awards to incentivize staff. I also mentored the specialist on several tools and methods she could use to detect possible problems early, such as the Access List that provided detailed, comparative data on patient wait times across the country, and a database that provided numerous tools and educational materials. To ensure the needed transparency and accountability, I then charged her with presenting a daily report to the Director and to me. Concurrently, I directed the Chief of the Patient Business Service to reduce scheduling errors, as a recent audit showed a 64% scheduling error rate.

As a result of my leadership, problem solving, and technical program knowledge, the Toronto VA and its 36,000 veteran customers each year were positioned for long-term success. In less than a month , I led the VAACC staff in reducing the number of patients scheduled beyond 30 days from 861 to only 81 (a 90% reduction). This success and related metrics elevated us to first place across the nation in patient access. The Regional Director overseeing five hospitals showcased my approach in multiple venues. Most importantly, veteran patients could now obtain high-quality services within 30 days in virtually any clinic at the facility.

Another example occurred in 2011, during my time as Quality Supervisor at Shaw Hospital in Texas. I was invited to an emergency meeting with my Engineering Service leaders, and officials from an Architectural Engineering firm explained that the condition of our 15-story hospital building was "imminently hazardous." They had observed cracks on the 2,000-pound overhanging concrete structures (called "fins") of the tower's exterior walls. In other words, large chunks of concrete were at risk of falling off the building on to pedestrians and buildings below. This was a critical situation not only because of the obvious safety concern, but because this building housed the majority of the facility's healthcare, including 194 inpatient beds and virtually 100% of its outpatient primary care and specialty-care services.

My customers included the 56,000+ veterans, employees, and visitors who used the facility each year, and the Service Chiefs who ran all of the operations in the facility. I was directly accountable to these customers and to the Hospital Director for resolving this major issue. I quickly decided that closing the building for repair was not a viable option, as there were no alternative medical facilities in the area to provide our customers with the services they relied upon. With this in mind, I instructed the Architectural Engineering firm to provide me with a written document within 24 hours detailing the issues and their recommendations for remediation. I shared the document with the Hospital Director and expressed my need for immediate funding to secure and then repair the fins. Meanwhile, I also shared the document with the Director of the Regional Acquisition Center and urged her to make this contract a top priority.

Now that I had mitigated the risk of an accident, I organized a series of meetings with executive leadership, Service Chiefs, and other key officials to develop the facility's first-ever strategic Emergency Management Plan. I charged the Emergency Preparedness Coordinator with spearheading this written plan and drove accountability by meeting with him and key department leaders each day to ensure hospital operations would remain safe if an evacuation became necessary. The Service Chiefs who oversaw areas in this building had marked concerns about the impact this issue would have on their ability to deliver care to our veterans, so I spent considerable time helping to resolve their unique issues. For instance, the Pharmacy Chief expressed concern that one of the fins might fall through the ceiling of their waiting area. I brought my Engineering experts in to analyze and discuss their concerns, and found that it was an extremely unlikely scenario. This thoughtful, expert-driven feedback reduced the Pharmacy's concerns, and renewed their efforts to outline a strong contingency plan in the event they did have to evacuate.

As a result, I successfully directed the development of a comprehensive Emergency Management Plan within only two weeks. This provided the hospital and its customers and stakeholders with peace of mind and demonstrated our commitment. Under my leadership, an $817K construction project was awarded within only one month to temporarily secure the fins—a step that normally took longer than six months. The construction repair was complete within two months, with no negative impacts to patient care or to the facility's public image. Internal customers expressed confidence in the actions taken, and appreciated being so involved in the emergency planning process. Over the next year, employee satisfaction rose to well above the national average, and the hospital went on to safely provide services to more than 56,000 veterans. On a broader scale, my efforts to mitigate risk and sustain hospital operations directly supported higher-level goals and objectives.

BUSINESS ACUMEN

In 2016, I was serving as Managing Director at Freemont Hospital in Wyoming. As Chair of the hospital's Resource Board, I played a key leadership role in managing and justifying the complex $600M annual budget. Among other things, this responsibility included oversight of procurement and monitoring expenditures to ensure efficient use of resources. Upon arriving in the position, I identified several problems with the hospital's overall financial management practices. First, the Resource Board spent most of its time and energy reviewing and approving day-to-day hiring decisions for thousands of positions in the hospital. While I, of course, needed Human Resources (HR) to address these issues, the Board needed to focus on the hospital's overall budget and financial strategy. In addition, supervisors were frustrated because they had to wait for the monthly Resource Board meetings in order to seek approval for any changes to their internal budgets. Considering these and other related issues, I decided to implement a decentralized budget and change the associated business practices.

In Fiscal Year (FY) 2016, I piloted the decentralized budget process with one large clinical service and one large operations service. To prepare for a hospital-wide implementation, I then directed my Chief of Finance to draft a Finance Business Rules document outlining the authorities and financial responsibilities managers possessed at various levels of the organization. I finalized this document, vetted it through the Resource Board, and then disseminated it across the hospital and in meetings to outline the new budget process. The new strategy modified several business practices. For instance, only requests for new programs or increases in a Service's decentralized budget would need to be presented to the Resource Board. All other changes to staffing could be made at the department level without Resource Board review. Moreover, in FY 2017, Service Chiefs would begin receiving specific dollar amounts for personnel services, such as salaries, benefits, and overtime.

My financial planning, management, and oversight led to strong, lasting results. Service Chiefs appreciated their new budget autonomy, and selecting officials could begin recruitment without delay. My Engineering Service Chief raised concerns about managing high workloads in his interior design program; for instance, he reallocated funds from an underutilized section of his department to the interior design section, which better funded the facility's construction program. The hospital observed a net increase of 54 positions while staying within budget.

Under the previous financial model, this growth in full-time employees would have cost an additional $5M. The Resource Board also benefited from this initiative, as its agendas now address strategic priorities and initiatives instead of day-to-day issues.

Another example also took place during my role as Managing Director, where I directly supervised the Chief of Human Resources (HR) in managing personnel administration activities for a 3,500-member workforce. The Dependent Credentialing program ensured all appropriate background checks, references, and licenses were updated for our clinical staff, such as social workers and technicians. I learned from our higher headquarters (HQ) organization that the credentialing program was performing poorly. In addressing this issue with my HR Chief, I found that he did not have a system to properly track and update the credentials of our clinicians. At that time, 179 of the 1,500 clinicians had incomplete documentation in their files. This was a critical issue, because he could not assure me that all the staff treating my patients were in good standing with active licenses. Further, I found that my Chief of HR had not responded to a formal notification letter from the Central office a full year earlier— nor had he followed their direction to alert me and the Hospital Director of the issue.

I soon realized that the HR Chief lacked the leadership or resources to develop an action plan and remedy the situation. However, I recognized that the Credentialing and Privileging (C&P) Program Manager oversaw very similar credentialing requirements for independent medical providers. She had actually led training sessions across the seven hospitals in the region on the credentialing program. I decided to realign the dependent credentialing program from HR to C&P, then consulted with the C&P Program Manager (PM) to share my reasoning and expectations. I then notified the rest of the hospital leadership, and met regularly with the PM. I oversaw her efforts to develop a tracking database and to oversee the process. In my meetings with the PM, I oversaw the tracking spreadsheet she created to complete the documentation of all 179 clinicians. In this process, we discovered that two employees allowed their licenses to lapse while treating patients, a problem that would not have occurred if the program were working properly. I also oversaw efforts to rewrite the Position Descriptions (PDs) of the C&P staff to align with the needs of the PM's existing staff, then recruited to permanently fill those positions.

As a result of my human capital management, the higher-level organization and the Central Office expressed renewed confidence in the hospital, given the strength of my action plan. Within six months, 100% of clinicians were brought into compliance, which has been maintained since then. The two clinicians with expired licenses were quickly taken out of patient care, mitigating any impact on patients. In addition, the C&P Program Manager's Independent C&P program is stronger overall because it now has more depth in covering the program with additional employees that are all on the same PD. Consequently, high operational tempo in the dependent credentialing program can be better resourced with staff typically working in the independent credentialing program, and vice versa. Finally, my changes improved the succession planning for the Program Manager (PM) position, as the PM intends to retire within the next year.

A final example took place in 2017, also during my role as Managing Director. In 2017, the nationwide community was using an outdated and time-intensive software program to track employees' time and leave. It was clumsy; it was time-intensive for employees, timekeepers, and supervisors to use; and it created non-value-added work. More specifically, it created separate records for the employee requests for leave and supervisor approvals on timecards, which required a tremendous amount of work to reconcile hundreds of differences in these records after each pay period ended.

A new, web-based timekeeping software program was being released nationally, and I led implementation as its executive sponsor at my hospital. I researched and learned more about the strengths and weaknesses of the system from the Director of another hospital in which the new system was piloted. I instructed my Chief of Finance to develop tools and educate all 3,500 employees on the new software, and helped to promote the importance of this initiative at various hospital-wide staff meetings. As the go-live date approached, I provided resources for the Chief of Finance to make needed adjustments, such as increased availability of training rooms. Due to unexpected idiosyncrasies in the software, closing the books for the first pay period required me to approve considerable overtime from timekeepers and Finance staff. I also assigned staff members from other areas to assist.

As a result of my efforts in managing this technology upgrade initiative, all necessary employees were trained on time, and the new timekeeping system was fully implemented within nine months. Employees have embraced the new user-friendly system, which is more efficient than ever in ensuring employees are being properly compensated. Finance staff, employees, timekeepers, and supervisors are no longer spending countless hours reconciling payroll exceptions. In fact, the number of payroll exceptions dropped from several hundred per pay period to zero within one month of full implementation. Finally, this initiative demonstrated my hospital's ongoing commitment to higher-level modernization and process improvements.

BUILDING COALITIONS

In 2016, I served as the Acting Director (an SES position) at Blanchfield Hospital in Kentucky, where I interacted with a broad array of internal and external stakeholder agencies at the local, regional, and national levels. For example, the Office of Research Oversight (ORO) is a very powerful entity that has the authority to close research activities at regional hospitals. I soon discovered that the ORO staff had a contentious relationship and lack of trust with my hospital's research program. Senior ORO leadership questioned the judgment of my Associate Chief of Staff for Research about numerous issues. By the time I became involved, ORO leadership was routinely attending our Internal Review Board (IRB) meetings via video conference. This level of oversight was very rare and the ORO Director called me personally to outline the severity of his concerns for our research program. He also mentioned the distinct possibility of sending an assessment team to my hospital for a for-cause site review.

I was determined to overcome these issues and build a strong coalition of stakeholders that could work toward the greater good of both the hospital and the region's priorities. To accomplish this, I conducted meetings with the IRB Chair, my Associate Chief of Staff for Research, and my Research Compliance Officer and briefed them about ORO's concerns. I then initiated regular calls with the ORO Director, thanking him for his concern and committing to attend the monthly IRB meetings. During the meetings, I gained even more clarity on the specific issues and personalities at play. To foster lines of open communication and partnering at other levels of my staff, I sometimes had the Research Compliance Officer brief the ORO staff about hot-button issues and my related action plans.

In one particular research effort, ORO disagreed with our IRB's interpretation of guidelines regarding use of participants outside the U.S. There was intense pressure from ORO that the study be closed or moved to a non-VA facility for completion because it did not comply with the VA's regulations. However, the IRB insisted that the study be restarted immediately. Taking a diplomatic and tactful approach, I negotiated for a "win-win" solution between all parties. Upon closely analyzing the issue, I realized that regulations had allowed this study to be performed when it was initially approved, but regulations had been slightly modified halfway through the study, thus causing the compliance problem. I then devised an alternative option to submit a waiver to the Central Office to restart the study. If they approved it, this would support our case that the study adhered to regulations, and the issue would be closed. Understanding the sensitive relationships involved, I played a direct role in editing the language of the waiver request to ensure a balanced approach was presented.

Being in his position for many years, the Associate Chief of Staff was especially resistant to what he perceived as "heavy-handed" oversight by ORO. He specifically criticized ORO staffs' expertise in research, and pointed out that the ORO Director was not a Medical Doctor. As I was working with the Associate Chief of Staff for Research to minimize personal agendas and counterproductive politics, I learned that he had been accused of not allocating funding appropriately within his department. When this came to light, he quickly decided to step down from his position. Although this was an unfortunate situation, it helped to build considerable trust with ORO because it showed that I was holding this Manager accountable, and that I was keeping him informed about a key vacancy in his area of oversight responsibility.

As a result, the Central Office approved the waiver and the study was restarted. With the tension around the policy interpretation resolved, the relationship between ORO, the IRB, and my hospital in general became much more collaborative. Over time, ORO decreased its oversight of the IRB. Due to my strengthened relationship with the ORO Director, he provided significant support in ongoing recruiting efforts to find a new Associate Chief of Staff for Research. He also offered and I accepted a consultative site visit from his office to help my interim Associate Chief of Staff to manage the transition. Similarly, when I had a critical vacancy in an Administrative Officer position, the ORO Director offered to send one of his staff members on a detail to help.

A final example began in 2017, while I was serving as Chief of Staff at the local VA Hospital. A local reporter from a prominent newspaper wrote a negative article about the facility's largest outpatient clinic. The article stated that this clinic's wait times in mental health had more than doubled from 6 days to 15 days in October 2015, more than twice the 7-day average wait time for the regional system as a whole. The article implied that poor, untimely care was being provided to veterans, and criticized two members of my Public Affairs (PA) staff for not responding. These claims were inaccurate. Considering the negative media attention across the community, I knew that if this story was not corrected, my hospital would be further criticized by larger media outlets and veterans might choose not to seek mental healthcare when they truly need it. I also saw this as an opportunity to highlight the fact that my mental health program had been frequently recognized for providing top-notch and timely care for veterans.

First, I sought input from the two staff members named in the article and learned that they were acting in their roles and were uncertain about how to respond to reporters. They admitted that they could have responded in a timelier manner. I then coached them about the importance of keeping reporters informed and of forming partnerships through in-person or at least telephone contact to build rapport, instead of relying on impersonal and easily misinterpreted emails. I then called the reporter personally and apologized for the lack of timeliness in our response. Next, I explained the actions I had taken already, committed to answering her question about wait times as soon as possible, and invited her to meet me and the Mental Health department head at the clinic for a tour.

As a result, I was able to form a clear and concise response to the pressing question in the media. I explained that we did see a temporary increase in wait times due to unforeseen departures in psychiatry staff at the clinic, and highlighted the progress we had made since filling those positions. Approximately one week later, she and her photographer interviewed me, the Mental Health department head, and a patient at the clinic. The reporter then wrote a very positive follow-up article that discussed the unforeseen departures of health providers, and stated, "wait times have tapered off." The article went on to commend us for increasing the use of telehealth technology by 32% to increase access for veterans. Perhaps most significantly, we now have a strong and productive relationship with this newspaper, which will help with my continual efforts to build a local coalition of support.

SAMPLE ECQs: U.S. MILITARY TO SES

LEADING CHANGE

In December 2016, I became the Director of Staff at the Air Force's 577th Air Logistics Wing. In this role, I direct a 45-member staff and play a key role in leading a 15K-member organization comprised of 250 subordinate units with varying sizes and missions. The staff's primary goal and role is to provide executive leadership and subject-matter expertise to help subordinates units effectively achieve their complex mission readiness requirements. In other words, the staff was expected to provide combat-ready forces in support of worldwide operations.

Making my own strategic assessment of the internal and external environment, I knew that major change was needed. I also identified a number of challenges and obstacles. Throughout the previous two years, the senior staff had endured a 75% reduction in force as part of higher-level force realignment. This reduction had shifted the expertise and knowledge on the staff, but no one had taken the time to re-envision how we supported subordinate units during and after the high-level staff changes. Consequently, the internal organizational climate had become one of simply maintaining the status quo, with subpar performance, morale, and readiness becoming a chronic problem. Externally, subordinate Commanders and organizations had lost confidence and faith in the ability of the staff to advocate their positions and affect the desired outcomes. Similarly, many functional experts at headquarters (HQ) had learned to expect little from the existing 577th staff. In the midst of internal challenges and external scrutiny, I remained optimistic and believed that I could influence positive organizational change.

Within weeks of becoming Director of Staff, and assimilating my own assessment and feedback from mentors and peers, I outlined and presented a new strategic vision and outline of a plan to senior leadership (two-star General level). My presentation clearly identified and validated senior leaders' existing concerns of performance and production among their staff. My vision was to focus and reenergize the staff while ensuring efforts and activities added true value to the organization. With high-level support in place for my vision, I began to develop a new strategic approach for the staff. Among other things, my plan and mission were geared toward supporting subordinate units, and providing combat-ready forces that were optimally aligned with the organization's overarching mission. I then led my staff in identifying five key areas that required major process improvements and change among the various leaders and directorates: 1) Providing subject-matter expertise; 2) Audit compliance; 3) Influencing readiness reports; 4) Facilitating equipment needs; and 5) Effective workforce resource allocation. Using these critical areas as a framework, I then led efforts to develop a comprehensive implementation plan.

Next, I commenced the staff and organizational revitalization effort that was considered highly innovative since it was unprecedented within the organization. During implementation, I encountered strong negative feedback and resistance based on earlier attempts before my tenure at a somewhat similar initiative that had failed miserably. Although the Commander and myself were driven for faster results, we knew that hardline tactics too early would have alienated late adopters. Instead, we worked together patiently to shift the staff members from dissenters to believers in our long-term vision and goals. I pushed through these obstacles and built support through a collaborative and multifaceted approach. I began conducting weekly strategic planning meetings to grow and enhance the importance of our vision and mission, and I demonstrated flexibility with certain deadlines and milestones. Further, I began one-on-one interactions with staff, addressing concerns and past failures as well as explaining the strategic roadmap I authored. This type of individually calibrated communications was important, since the entire team was not ready for all the details, but needed to come along at a different pace.

As a result, I am currently in the final phase of my one-year plan to establish a relevant strategic planning model for running an effective staff during a time of reduced staffing and resources. With vision, mission, and goals aligned and themed between subordinates and higher HQ, and with clearly defined staff roles in supporting subordinate units, the culture has already shifted dramatically. The staff is now much more empowered and focused, which has increased and improved the overall sense of purpose, pride, and performance in helping subordinates units effectively achieve mission readiness requirements. I interact daily with subordinate leaders, and consistently received positive comments about the staff's timely and effective support. On another level, the staff's reputation with HQ is also increasing. Finally, I have received personal acknowledgment of our progress and effectiveness from several senior executives.

Another example began in 2012, when I became the Commander of the U.S. Air Force's 484th Airlift Wing at Fort Polk, LA. In this role, I led a 70-member senior staff and oversaw the training, operation, and administration of a 2.8K-member workforce dispersed among 21 subordinate units. I soon discovered that the previous Commander had led the staff in developing meaningful strategic plans to optimize fundamental issues, such as overall planning and resource management. However, while implementing those plans, the Commander deployed for many months and did not return to the position. Consequently, while the organization certainly had many strengths, the cultural changes had not taken hold and the staff had not continued to implement the strategies and techniques. Instead, the staff focused almost solely on immediate and operational planning and resource management in response to deployments or disaster responses. To address these issues and drive the needed changes, I set out on a two-year journey to broaden the staff's planning perspective and abilities, and therefore improve the entire culture at virtually all levels.

I planned and carried out numerous actions to accomplish my goals, such as directing the completion of 19 different unit-level program analyses. In doing so, I clearly identified 500 daily business processes that needed to be managed and coordinated across the organization. I then implemented several improvement techniques, organizing each process into one of a dozen key categories. Next, I prioritized the categories and showed the staff how to use the prioritization to strategically plan and allocate resources. During weekly strategic planning meetings and one-on-one meetings with staff members, I further developed the culture and refined the strategic plan by increasing understanding of proven business success formulas. In a creative move, I also coordinated for my staff to regularly visiting a local Toyota production facility. Since the business processes involved with aircraft production/maintenance are somewhat similar to the automobile industry, the staff learned a great deal about effective internal control measures and techniques from a corporate perspective. I also implemented and trained personnel in how to use Human Capital Assessment models, including strategic mapping techniques.

Within two years, I successfully revitalized the staff's mindset and energy, which created positive ripple effects at all levels. Using the new strategic plans and tools, and with new insights from corporate industry, the staff was better able to plan and allocate resources. The following selected results will serve to illustrate the scope and impact of my successful change leadership efforts: The organization achieved the highest rate of individual medical readiness in the entire Command, an extremely difficult undertaking for an organization of its size. The staff embraced and now uses internal control measures to gauge effectiveness toward meeting goals and objectives. As the organizational culture changed, I led efforts to form key partnerships with other mission partners within the community. Using the strategic framework and thinking I put in place, the culture continued to mature and evolve to one based on proactive and highly effective planning and resource allocation.

LEADING PEOPLE

In May 2017, I became the Commanding Officer of the U.S. Air Force's 599th Aviation Regiment. The organization was comprised of more than 1,500 diverse personnel, including a 1,222-member senior staff, more than 17 subordinate Commanders, and 15 senior civilian employees. When I became Commander, I inherited a range of leadership challenges. A lack of accountability from my predecessor had allowed program/process owners to lose

interest in performing at high levels, but instead performing well below average and even ignoring new strategic policies. Morale varied among subordinate organizations, but was mostly low. Several new key leaders lacked a sense of vision and direction. Underpinning all of these challenges was the fact that the organization was scheduled for a demanding and comprehensive compliance inspection to be conducted by the Inspector General in the coming months. The critical and high-visibility inspection would include a thorough examination of approximately 200 programs and processes. I was determined to strengthen my team, improve the working environment, and lead the organization to pass the inspection.

A reflection of the society from which they came, my staff and workforce were incredibly diverse. I had employees in their teens and others in their 60s, some with high school diplomas and some with advanced degrees, and a wide range of cultural and technical backgrounds. I decided to galvanize this diverse team by focusing strongly on the pending inspection, which represented the health of virtually every functional and business area in the organization. I established an inspection preparation team and hand-selected several key leaders. Fully aware that an interconnected, diverse team will generate innovative ideas through their differing viewpoints, I included a mid-level female Manager on the inspection team, and another leader with specific experience that could assist our financial management program. Though none of the these individuals had a history of managing this scale of initiative in such a short period of time, I was able to share my vision, articulate the details of what was needed, and lead in developing an inspection readiness tracking matrix. I continued to strengthen the overall staff and inspection team through weekly staff meetings. Through these meetings and many one-on-one interactions, I articulated my vision for success and fostered open and honest feedback and collaborative communications. To further strengthen the team's rapport and mutual appreciation, I also scheduled offsite team-building activities and social events such as holiday potlucks.

As people began to notice the positive energy, the importance of strong performance and desire for achieving excellence permeated throughout many groups. Building on this momentum, I mentored my staff members on their personal and professional goals, and directed them to do the same among their subordinates. I also provided training opportunities and developmental assignments, whenever possible. Since the inspection team members would not have time to become experts in each different program and process, they would need to learn accurate, deep, and thorough investigative skills to help determine the program status. To accelerate this process, from my previous assignment, I called upon subordinates whom I had mentored through this process over the previous three years, and who had recently "aced" a similar inspection. Under my guidance, these individuals spent five days coaching the inspection team. Additionally, the rapid acceleration from status quo to high performance was jarring for many. To minimize what I perceived as a growing sense of tension and conflict, I found those individuals naturally prone to be driven, and empowered them to lead. I also identified the quieter or reserved personnel with untapped talent and gave them specific roles and strong recognition.

My ability to build and lead my staff and the overall workforce improved the organization on many levels. The organization passed the major inspection with only a few programs not meeting standard, a result that seemed virtually impossible when I arrived. The inspection team recognized multiple top performers. In addition, the inspection team leader lauded my inspection readiness tracking matrix and stated that it "should be the benchmark for the Command!" I was able to develop the staff's skills and mindset from "tactical workers" to strategic-minded leaders. In the supportive mentoring environment I created, four of my Lieutenant Colonels (O-5) transformed from "just getting by" to enrolling in Master's degree programs, competing and being selected for their own commands. Further, two of them were later promoted to Colonels (O-6). The base earned recognition as having the highest position staffing rating (117%) among 30+ similar organizations. Finally, one of my previously struggling subordinate units was recognized as #1 in the entire Command.

In another example, from 2010 until 2012, I served as the Commander of the 222nd Aviation Group. The organization consisted of more than 500 Reserve personnel, whom I led through a leadership cadre of 40 Lieutenant Colonels and 50 GS-12s, -13s, and -14s. Our complex mission was founded on operating several types of aircraft in support of critical national emergencies and the ongoing wars in the Middle East. Immediately after taking command, significant challenges became readily apparent. Due to internal personnel conflicts, a lack of leadership and oversight from my predecessor, and a lack of focus on professional development, morale was low, conflict was high, and there was no vision for the future. Since there was no formal organizational structure of diagrams, work activities were haphazard and everyone seemed stuck in the "daily grind." I wanted to develop a more engaged organization with a clear vision and strategy.

To formalize the structure and importance of teams, I created an organizational chart for the senior staff and all subordinate units. I then established weekly staff meetings to share current requirements, solicit feedback, and address any program or performance issues. I worked to rapidly address those issues, which included establishing focused working groups. When forming these groups, and when assigning new leadership throughout the organization, I often brought in new talent with diverse and specialized experience that I knew would fit well into the organization. I also hired a female into a key leadership role, and went to great lengths to get out of the office and spend time with employees in each work area. Not only did this build trust and rapport, but it also helped me to assess leadership strengths and weaknesses. For instance, three members of my staff had simply maintained their role as pilots, with no effort toward leading the team or growing themselves professionally. I initiated offsite mentorship and leadership conferences for the staff, and brought in a professor and author on team leadership from the University of Southern California's Marshall School of Business. When people moved or retired, I began cycling members of my staff through the open positions on 120-day rotations. This approach encouraged cross-training until I found a suitable replacement. I also worked closely with subordinate Commanders to implement key training programs in various areas. During this period, I resolved several interpersonal conflicts by working closely with the individuals and leaders involved, and getting them focused on shared goals.

My leadership in this position paved the way for a new level of excellence and a new standard for organizational pride and achievements. By implementing the civilian annual appraisal system, I was able to personally recognize individual performance with increased pay, Time-Off awards, and Notable Achievement awards. Eight of the officers I mentored were promoted to Colonels, and one to Brigadier General (one-star). Once considered "just going through the motions," my organization was recognized with an Air Force Outstanding Unit Award. Organizational pride and morale reached new heights, and enrollment in developmental education skyrocketed. Further, my organization was a key contributor to the larger command winning a coveted "Raincross Trophy" awarded to the top of 14 organizations in the higher HQ organization. External respect grew across the entire Command and the larger Air Force community. Based on my performance in this role, I was later promoted to Wing Commander and then entrusted to lead a 2,800-member workforce.

RESULTS DRIVEN

In 2016, I became the Commander of the U.S. Air Force's 404th Aviation Group on Fort Bragg, North Carolina. As part of my broad duties and scope of responsibility, I directed the full spectrum of program activities for a 2.8K-member workforce spread across almost 2 dozen organizations in 18 different buildings. I also oversaw a complex aviation program consisting of 15 aircraft, 3.8K annual flying hours, and an $85M civilian and military payroll budget. I was directly accountable to my two-star General leadership for ensuring the organization maintained a high rate of mission readiness (our ability to provide trained and capable employees to support worldwide missions).

One of the most important indicators of organizational readiness was medical care and readiness. I was frus-

trated by the slow, long-drawn-out times for completing medical care for wounded personnel. Regardless of the nature of injury or illness, the administration involved with working through the medical care process was unacceptably long. On my own initiative, and while maintaining a strategic awareness of the larger organization, I spent significant time assessing the business processes associated with caring for wounded personnel. I quickly identified a lack of any kind of documented business processes. This created a great deal of uncertainly and made decision making for leaders much less informed and effective. Leveraging my technical knowledge of business improvement processes, and of the organization's wartime and peacetime missions, I immediately set out to solve this growing organizational problem. My customers in this initiative included the wounded personnel themselves, along with the higher headquarters (HQ) organization that relied on us for having a capable and ready workforce.

Initially, I brought together more than 20 subordinate Commanders, explained my findings and intent, and then engaged them all to help me resolve the problem. I then instilled a sense of accountability by reminding them of their own responsibilities to their personnel and to the overall mission of ensuring mission readiness. Next, I led the entire leadership staff through a Rapid Improvement Event (RIE) that allowed us to discuss, explore, and formalize the entire process of providing medical care from beginning to end. As a group, we created an intricate "value stream map" that visually illustrated nearly 200 different administrative actions, decision points, reviews, boards, and evaluations. This comprehensive resource ensured complete transparency and took the mystery out of what was required to meet customer needs. With a renewed and objective sense of clarity about our operations, I then led the staff in identifying bottlenecks and areas for improvement. Then, I guided efforts and made numerous decisions in order to streamline the overall policies and procedures. For instance, I created a resource utilization system that incorporated the input of all participating organizations. I also led the staff in devising an eight-step process for setting performance standards and evaluating program success. Next, I implemented new strategies to improve efficiency, which led me to establish partnerships with various external agencies involved in medical care.

The strategies, steps, and strategic process I put in place have greatly improved critical business processes, which, in turn, improved the quality of customer care and support. I decreased the organization's overall medical processing time by nearly 80%, accelerating important medical care for my customers. Additionally, since medical case managers now knew that their performance had the appropriate oversight, the application of policy standards became more compliant and case administration improved by approximately 20%. As an added benefit, more efficient operations reduced wasteful spending by 40%, saving an estimated $3-4M annually. I was asked to brief multiple senior officials and peers regarding the comprehensive value stream map. In fact, the product became one the most requested, utilized, and effective tools at improving medical care processes across the entire higher HQ. This initiative also caught the attention of the higher HQ Commanding Officer (three-star) and Vice Commander (two-star), who both lauded my organization as the best in the entire Command at mastering these difficult medical processes.

Another example began in 2014, when I became the Commanding Officer (Colonel, O-6) of the U.S. Air Force's Aviation Security Force. The organization was comprised of 200 civilian employees and 1,200 Air Force personnel. Within weeks of arriving, I identified a critical deficiency in various programs. More specifically, there was a complete failure across the organization to comply with U.S. Air Force physical fitness standards. With no formal fitness program in place, more than 700 personnel were either non-compliant or had never been tested under the recently implemented Air Force Fitness standard. Additionally, the Individual Medical Readiness rating was well below the Commander standard of 80%, a lowly 68%. This meant that the medical unit was not meeting standards, and nearly 400 personnel in the organization were not medically eligible to deploy in a timely manner. My predecessor gave no emphasis to compliance and subsequently, no subordinate Commanders within the organization did, either. I was accountable to senior leadership for complying with strategic guidelines, as well as for providing a physically fit and medically eligible workforce. I intended to solve these two related organizational problems and change the prevailing mindset about physical fitness.

Digging deeper into the situation, I realized that part of the challenge was the cold weather in our part of the country (northern Pittsburgh, PA). Since we had no indoor physical testing facility, historically, the unit had simply ignored the requirement during inclement weather. I led my staff through evaluating three indoor testing facilities, and then identified funding and secured use of the facility. To drive momentum and gain support, I established a weekly fitness education and active exercise program. I also created an informal "Beat the Boss" contest, challenging team members to surpass my own fitness score. My personal example of scoring higher than 95/100 inspired a positive culture and friendly competition among peer groups. I also hired a Fitness Program Manager, and leveraged his knowledge to develop a customer service-oriented approach to reduce apprehension among personnel taking the test. I ensured compliance and accountability by following through with required actions, as needed, such as formal counseling for those who failed the test, demotions, and even discharge from the Air Force. I had several difficult conversations with personnel who were in tears when they realized that their failure to meet fitness standards could delay or negate promotion opportunities, or end in a discharge from the service. Fortunately, these few cases sent a clear message that our organization would comply with the Air Force standard. During this period, I also created a new Individual Medical Readiness Program, which included setting clear performance measures, quickly resolving any simple processes, and putting plans in place for more complex, long-term medical care issues.

By applying my problem-solving skills to these programmatic and organizational challenges, within eight months, I improved the on-time testing goal to 94%, which was the highest compliance rating among 40 similar units in the larger organization. Individual scores also improved, and I instituted a more efficient testing process that reduced testing time by 30%. These efficiencies led to an increase in hundreds of hours of training time per year that would have been inefficiently used on administering and retaking physical fitness tests. Concurrently, I improved my organization's medical readiness from 68% to 84%. This level of performance significantly contributed to my medical unit being named #1 in the Command for that year, an award never before earned by this unit! As per my plan and vision, these improvements on multiple levels of the organization resulted in a healthier, more compliant, and more confident workforce.

BUSINESS ACUMEN

From 2015-2017, I served as the Chief of Staff at the Air Force Logistics Group. In this capacity, I played a key role in the strategic planning and budgeting process for the organization's 250 subordinate units with annual budgets ranging from $5M to more than $200M. While analyzing program operations, I realized that most of the leadership staff did not understand or appreciate how the new Air Force Inspection System (AFIS) would affect budget creation, justification, and execution. In the past, subordinate units would use inspection preparation to justify multimillion-dollar requests to bring on part-time personnel. The AFIS represented a new paradigm, and leaders would have to establish their own Inspector General's Office and internal inspection team. In other words, a last-minute push to prepare would no longer be the norm. Instead, organizational leaders would need to be much more involved in self-inspections and maintaining readiness as the norm. This operational shift affected overall personnel readiness and related financial requests and management decisions and processes. In an environment of shrinking budgets, I was determined to improve the organization's overall ability to manage its complex budgets in full compliance with the new AFIS requirements.

I assessed the financial management tools and techniques being used at different levels of the organization, and then brought all subordinate leaders for a summit focused on the new budget realities. I led discussions of best practices from across the organization in terms of budgeting tools and forecasting models. I also introduced a new financial planning model that I had learned from one of my mentors, and that I knew would help leaders prioritize their program activities through a fiscal lens. Called the "formula for success," this idea was built from a basic business model of maximizing profits by reducing non-ready financial, human capital, and other resources while minimizing inefficiencies to maximize throughput. Though the military does not work for profit, this approach brought fiscal context to our operations.

My efforts in assessing the effects of the AFIS, and then changing the way the organization approached budget planning at the strategic level, led to excellent results. Although the culture is still adapting, many of the 250 subordinate units now use the new model to produce detailed justification for all fiscal expenditures throughout the year. In addition, due to my emphasis on sound financial management, the overall organization closed out the $400M Fiscal Year (FY) 2014 budget with 99.3% accuracy.

Another example occurred while I was serving as Director of Operations for the U.S. Air Force's 88th Air Group. I led a diverse 2.8K-member workforce comprised of civilian, government, and Air Force Reserve employees. During my tenure, I had to maintain ongoing global operations and support during major staffing and budget constraints. Many members of the civilian workforce were furloughed during FY 2013, and there was a coming reduction of 140 civilian positions within the organization. Moreover, we had more than 80 vacancies in the Maintenance Group alone, which totaled more than 150K annual lost production hours. These challenges placed a great strain on the organization as a whole, and I needed to retain the best workforce possible through this difficult time.

I took immediate action to address the sense of uncertainty caused by these human capital challenges. For instance, I quickly identified the most talented leaders and made some key personnel realignments. Working closely with these leaders, I then reprioritized and reallocated critical resources. I also spent significant time working with staff members to help them meet their personal and professional goals. Next, I coordinated multiple town hall meetings for the civilian employees in order to share all information available about the furlough. I worked with the local labor union representative to ensure we complied with all Collective Bargaining Agreements in a proper and timely manner. In addition, I coordinated with our local Civilian Personnel Office to hold recurring meetings to address potential downsizing actions, such as Priority Placement, Voluntary Early Retirement Authority, and Voluntary Separation Incentive Payments. My own Human Resources Office handled development of vacancy announcements, selection, and in-processing. Meanwhile, by educating personnel on the pending downsizing, I identified those who wanted to retrain into other career fields or move to another organization. Other individuals found contract civilian work in their same career field for a full-time employment, and remained as part-time Reserve personnel. As the workforce shifted, I ensured my staff focused on diversity. I wanted to keep our pipeline of young talent coming in, while retaining as many experienced personnel as possible to the transfer of skills and knowledge.

As a result of my effective human capital management, I was able to confidently shepherd the organization through this transitional period. By leading my team through a detailed study of the new organizational staffing plan and then cross training and realigning personnel effectively, we lost a minimum of employees due solely to the furlough, and successfully retained many talented and driven employees. In addition, I achieved virtually no reduction in operational capability during this significant workforce reduction, and maintained the same rate of aircraft availability for worldwide missions by partnering with other organizations.

As a seasoned Officer in the modern U.S. Air Force, I have witnessed and embraced the proliferation of cutting-edge technology in the 21st-century workplace. Further, as a Pilot with more than 5,500 flying hours, I have an extremely high technical aptitude. For example, from 2014–2015, I was deployed to Kuwait as the Chief of the Programs Oversight Division within U.S. Pacific Command. Working at the strategic level, I was involved in planning massive logistical processes to perfectly synchronize all personnel, cargo, and equipment movement in and out of the Command's area of responsibility (AOR). As one can imagine, there are numerous complex Information Technology (IT) systems in place to accomplish these strategic tasks, such as the Joint Operation Planning and Execution System (JOPES). In addition, the Global Decision Support System is intended to deliver robust Command and Control (C2), enabling information sharing across classified and unclassified networks and with other military and joint systems.

Though I had used portions of these complex systems throughout my career, my new position required a more in-depth study of their purpose, capabilities, and implementation. I pored over joint publications and spent countless hours with action officer-level system users to gain a thorough understanding of the capabilities. My own staff members, and my liaison officers located in Afghanistan, each knew their "own" systems. To increase overall effectiveness, I trained them on how the various systems interacted. I also visited cargo collection and staging areas in multiple locations in Afghanistan to teach the logistics team about technical system requirements for cargo planning and the importance of inputting logistics requirements into the JOPES. This critical step allowed cargo planners to properly prioritize movement of key assets with higher-level requirements.

By leveraging and expanding my knowledge of many IT platforms/systems, I was able to streamline and integrate complex global movement of cargo and personnel. In collaboration with program analysis teams, I pinpointed a wasteful legacy system and made changes that saved approximately $10M a month. Additionally, by properly leveraging the systems, my team achieved a 100% on-time delivery of life-saving armored personnel carriers. Finally, the organization increased on-time movement of tens of thousands of personnel to an amazing 99%.

BUILDING COALITIONS

On three occasions during 2016 and 2017, I was deployed to Korea as the Director of The Joint Program Coordination Team. This high-level team was comprised of approximately 40 personnel, and played a key role in facilitating several recurring multinational training exercises by mentoring and educating all U.S. and Korean agencies on the best ways to utilize their aviation assets. For decades, these exercises demonstrated to the world and Republic of Korea leadership the U.S. commitment to our bilateral agreement for the defense of Korea.

Performance during these events is highly stressful for everyone and senior leaders move cautiously with little room for error. Further, these exercises are critical to the careers and evaluations for the Korean officers, and mistakes are not allowed. Building successful partnerships and relationships in such an environment is especially challenging, especially since one must work through interpreters and be very clear and thoughtful in all written and verbal communications. Fully aware of the political sensitivities at play, I set out to build a strong coalition of stakeholders to strengthen international ties and ensure the most possible benefit from the training exercises.

To begin forming productive partnerships, I studied the organizational structure of the Korean military and government, learning about the key leaders and influencers. I then sought, established, and nurtured many partnerships with U.S. and Korean military personnel and senior leaders, along with the Korean International Humanitarian Assistance Center and other participating organizations. Being sensitive to Korean military culture, I recognized the high-visibility responsibilities of the Korean senior leadership, and successfully communicated these dynamics to U.S. General Officers. Leveraging this support, I was able to secure a meeting with one of the most senior Korean leaders and provide him with the information, tools, and processes needed to confidently brief his own leadership.

The purpose of all this relationship building and the content of most conversations centered on military aviation operations. Calling upon my vast expertise in global aviation operations, I studied the strategic operation plan for the exercise and identified potential areas of concern. Essentially, there was a disconnect between two key systems, so I identified the responsible officers on both sides and taught them how to work the systems and communicate priorities. I also developed a visual depiction (called value steam mapping) showing the entire planning and business process from beginning to end. Next, I built relationships with senior Korean logistics leaders and convinced them that my process was both accurate and effective.

One particular U.S. Army Colonel in charge of the Civilian Affairs branch was the linchpin of connecting U.S. capabilities with Korean requirements. Unfortunately, he refused to address the problems I found with the systems, stating that they were not his responsibility. Since he was working directly with his Korean counterpart, the Korean Officer was listening to his input and not mine. I had to tactfully work around this barrier, knowing that the issues would come full circle and fall directly on these two officers. Rather than step aside and watch the negative and potentially harsh consequence on these individuals for failing to understand or address the issues, I sat down with them and patiently explained the situation again, and that I had already secured full commitment from both of their most senior leadership. After several conversations and tactful negotiations, they finally agreed. When the General Officers came asking questions about the process, the Colonel and his Korean counterpart were able to answer appropriately.

The international coalition I helped build worked synergistically during the exercise, and both the U.S. and Korean militaries optimized their use of aviation assets. In addition, the four-star General overseeing the entire region briefed my collaborative process to the entire U.S. military staff in Korea. I was then tasked to spend time one-on-one sharing and interacting with the Korean Generals on the importance of the interagency coordination process. Since I had established myself as the trusted "go-to" expert and formed so many strong relationships, I was requested to return for each subsequent exercise.

A final example occurred in 2018 in the aftermath of a devastating earthquake in Peru. I served as the Crisis Action Team (CAT) Director for U.S. Department of Defense (DOD). In this role, I supported humanitarian/disaster relief efforts by leading a 14-member team through 24/7 coordination and sequencing of aircraft arrivals and departures from 63 different nations. The overwhelming international outpour of support created significant logistical challenges for the flow of aircraft. I would need to use my interpersonal skills and experience in global aviation and airfield operations to manage this "crisis of goodwill."

I built relationships with several external organizations and coalition partners, then formed a Joint Disaster Assistance Group. This international group included Pakistan liaison personnel, Pakistan Air Force and Army officials, U.S. Embassy officials, and other stakeholders. Working together, we devised an effective flight approval and coordination process to bring order to the initial chaos. Throughout this high-visibility mission, I briefed a two-star General twice daily and the DOD four-star once each week.

With aviation assets under better control, I also wanted to help position Pakistan for success in future emergencies. I spent time with the Pakistan Colonel in charge of the airfield where the U.S. Air Force's newly formed Contingency Response Group (CRG) operated, which would handle this type of operation. I learned that since the entire CRG concept was new to the U.S. Air Force, and many of the Commanders were very uncomfortable with relinquishing control of some of their personnel for 45-day success. Acting as a diplomatic problem solver, I listened attentively to all sides of the issue. I then negotiated and mediated between key stakeholders to gain consensus on a way ahead for the CRG with which everyone could agree.

By the time I completed my deployment 45 days later, I had ensured 100% delivery of humanitarian assistance from 63 countries. Aircraft brought in more than 9,000 tons of relief supplies, saving many thousands of lives. During this operation, I was also able to validate and build support for a new U.S. Air Force approach to contingency response. In addition, I greatly improved relationships between the military, the U.S. Embassy staff, and other key stakeholders. I was personally recognized by a two-star General for my efforts, and was awarded the Joint Meritorious Service Medal.

SAMPLE ECQs: CORPORATE TO SES

LEADING CHANGE

I served as a senior-level corporate executive from 2014 to 2018 with Smart Technologies, Inc., providing end-to-end solutions to federal, military, and U.S. governmental agencies, ranging from security assessment and systems engineering to installation, construction, and support. Taking a strategic view of our operations, success, and relationships with external agencies, I determined we needed to improve the overall approach to customer service. At the time, Total Quality Management (TQM) was a national initiative and global trend for changing quality management practices. A program of this scope would require a great deal of change across all functional and organizational levels, but would position us for long-term success. TQM was a new and difficult concept to grasp, especially for senior personnel, management, internal and external customers, and suppliers. These groups had been trained to believe "quality" was more a manufacturing issue related to parts being rejected during the manufacturing process than a "corporate-wide culture." Despite internal and external resistance and scrutiny, I remained steadfast and optimistic that we could implement such a program. My objective was to tear down the traditional barriers, while leading a corporate-wide cultural shift. I set out to gain support and systematically implement the TQM initiative directed at increasing customer satisfaction, revenue, and profits.

To support and promote the vision, I embraced and implemented the role of a Corporate Quality Chairman; attended a graduate course in Quality, Performance, and Productivity at Xavier University to acquire a mastery of the required concepts and tools; and developed a comprehensive strategic plan. Within this plan, all functional departments were required to change their business operations in a major way and demonstrate quality was no longer "only" a manufacturing issue, but a way of corporate life. I fostered relationships with senior management and internal stakeholders, and engaged with early adopters. In addition, I presented numerous briefings and educated the staff on a host of new and effective concepts, including Pareto Analysis, and statistical process controls, and began cultivating relationships with external suppliers and customers, soliciting their feedback and clearly identifying our goals their requirements. Throughout this period, I advocated for this innovative, transparent, and collaborative approach to quality. TQM gave employees, supervisors, and departments at various levels the opportunity to engage and take personal accountability and reject the work of a prior individual or department, not allowing a command and control or dictatorial type environment and management role. As Chairman, I was able to mitigate arguments, finger-pointing, and indecision and set the foundation for success. Once employees, management, and even the Board of Directors realized the program could be used more as an empowering tool than as a negative "report card" against them, they began embracing the TQM corporate culture concept.

As a result of leading this cross-functional corporate change initiative, the company instituted a new corporate vision, operational philosophy, and business paradigm driven the customer. Under my leadership, the company thrived and I continued detailing out a five-year strategic plan. These efforts included the development and establishment of new policies, procedures, specifications, and guidelines that are still in place today (to include providing the industry's best warranty program). The TQM initiative was integral in the company's highly effective market strategy, which helped increased revenue by over 300%. From a more long-term perspective, our new vision and focus positioned the company as a "global leader" in the protection of critical resources. Eventually, we became the "first and only" commercial company to achieve the Department of Defense (DOD) nuclear certification for integrated access control solutions.

Another example of my ability to lead organizational change occurred in 2016, while serving as President and CEO of Carrier Technologies. Internally, resources were very tight and the company had almost no ability to hire outside support. In fact, our very survival hinged on increasing profits and revenue. Assessing the external landscape, I realized that we had gained a reputation as one of many basic product providers and that we had no competitive advantage within a large industry. Taking a strategic view and leveraging the TQM concepts we had already developed, I conceived an innovative and revolutionary idea for the organization. Specifically, I realized that we were better suited to install and service our products than any other organization. We were the experts and could do it better, faster, and less expensively. This was a completely new concept in the industry. Historically, companies in the industry were either considered solely a "products" or "services" company. I was determined to implement a new vision and paradigm shift that would essentially transform us into a "hybrid company" that provided both products and associated services and support, potentially doubling our revenues.

This was a major undertaking that would require the entire company evolve and change. To accomplish this, I led a series of "white board" collaborative sessions with senior staff and Board of Director members. Additionally, I actively encouraged all employees to propose ideas for expanding the business. I then used a process of elimination to identify those with the highest probabilities of success and led in development of action plans and milestones. This approach led to a collaborative strategic plan with employee engagement and buy-in at all levels. After gaining the right level of support and energizing the organization around the changes, I led development of the necessary policies, procedures, and controls and in selling the concept to customers. Since we would be offering our services to government customers, I worked closely with executive-level General Services Administration (G) personnel to establish and gain approval for a new federal pricing model as well as a distribution approach.

As a result, customers quickly embraced our new approach, and we selectively and incrementally chose projects that would include those new additional services and that we felt we were prepared and staged to handle. Sales activity grew rapidly, increasing our pool of project opportunities from the $20M range to more than $120M. Over time, customers began to rely on us to identify third-party product solutions that would seamlessly integrate with the solutions we were providing. This often required us to develop additional software/hardware interfaces, further expanding growth and contributing to a consistent 30% annual growth for nine consecutive years. Ultimately, this was sustained, and steady growth was a key metric that attracted multiple acquisition offers from billion-dollar corporations.

LEADING PEOPLE

As the Vice-President and General Manager of Creative Solutions in 2018, I guided a staff of approximately 45 people though numerous initiatives, including the sale and realignment of several business divisions, and a major acquisition. During some of these changes, morale dropped and conflict arose, creating many leadership challenges as the organization struggled to maintain its identity.

I always approached a new problem by first removing emotion, then defining the issue, outlining the basic opportunities, risks, and rewards to all parties. Next, I established clear lines of responsibility and clarified my expectations. I then led the staff in identifying common goals and aligning our plans with overarching objectives. Using frequent meetings and briefings, I fostered open and honest communications and shared problem solving. Further, I explained how important each individual's experience and ideas were to our overall success and encouraged cross-training and collaboration. As I hired new employees into the team, I ensured the team was diverse in terms of education levels, experience levels, technical specialties, cultural backgrounds, and personalities. I often matched senior employees with junior employees to help integrate them into the team culture while quietly building a mentoring relationship.

I also discussed their career development goals and led staff members to new heights of professionalism by fostering an environment of continual learning and development. As a trusted advisor and mentor, I provided training and developmental opportunities, whenever possible. For example, I established policies to support upward mobility, such as helping to pay for job-related education. In several cases, these policies helped employees achieve advanced degrees and industry certifications.

During this period, a rift arose between a senior executive and his own team regarding a response to a particular agency on a large-scale contract proposal. The situation was causing negative tension and conflict across the entire team, and core parts of the solicitation had to be rewritten at the very last minute. When I questioned the executive (in private), he could not explain or justify his actions, although his team confirmed that they suggested an alternative approach. Given the importance of this proposal and lack of time available, I stepped in and led the effort, and placed the executive who had been in charge in a supporting role to me only. After completing the rewrite in time to meet the submittal deadline, I sat down with the executive to discuss his thoughts and decision-making process and requested a written summary. Meanwhile, I notified my Human Resources (HR) department of the situation, since the individual had previously been verbally counseled about a similar issue. I also felt that this recent issue warranted elevating the situation in the form of a written warning. My written and verbal communications and counseling resolved the conflict.

As a result, the company became the leader in the protection of critical resources for the U.S. government and a globally recognized entity in that industry. In the entire decade with the organization, I was never involved in any employee Equal Employment Opportunity (EEO) concerns or other HR issues. As an enduring mark of my team's success, we obtained a nearly 75% market penetration and in certain markets we were the only commercial company to ever meet Department of the Interior standards.

RESULTS DRIVEN

As Chief Executive Officer (CEO) and Corporate Quality Chairman of Champion Technologies in 2015, I saw a market opportunity for us to submit for and obtain the Department of Labor (DOL) certification for our Electronic Security Platform. By doing so, we could greatly improve our already-strong customer service and support. This was the most rigorous testing in the industry, and simply obtaining approval for this testing was an extremely difficult task. Further, the approval process and combined testing could take three to five years and cost millions of dollars in technical software, hardware, and product development. Since our customers would be agencies and facilities that supported or had nuclear missions that mandated this type of certification toolbox for their electronic security platforms, I felt we should be accountable for providing the best possible support, as well. I was determined to become the first and only commercial entity to meet the test requirements and obtain certification.

Expectations were high, since we had invested over $12M in developing the platform and staging for this prestigious certification, and the government would have to spend considerable time, money, and effort during the testing and approval process. Taking decisive action to solve the inherent issues with this massive undertaking, I first set out to obtain approval for testing. After numerous high-level agency meetings, reviews, and presentations, we gained approval to move forward. I immediately took the lead, established goals, objectives, and responsibilities and empowered the team members. I encouraged functional managers to surface issues or concerns early, come to meetings prepared, and offer meaningful suggestions and solutions that linked to our end goal. I then established functional weekly staff meetings with a focus on key issues and problem solving. Internally, I utilized numerous reporting and tracking tools to ensure transparency and accountability, such as milestone/Gantt charts, as well as Microsoft (MS) Excel, PowerPoint, and Access documents. We also utilized specific industry software to track software development, revision control, product costing, suppliers, and overall logistics.

From a technical standpoint, we encountered numerous issues ranging from specific product capabilities in software, data communications modes, redundancy, encryption standards, and military standards. In each case, I utilized a systematic approach to break down the issue, identify the required resources, instituted management oversight and reporting and developed action plans. In addition, the testing and certification process required us to comply with numerous agency specifications by implanting new policies and procedures. Similarly, we obtained and maintained a federal secure classified facility, established a number of personnel security clearances, and established a formal Facility Security Officer position. I integrated all of these overlapping efforts and activities into an aggressive implementation phase that lasted approximately two years.

As a result, we passed the test and obtained the Nuclear Certification—a first—and to this day, we are the only company to have ever passed the full set of agency requirements. After we passed, the government actually relaxed certain testing parameters because our competitors claimed unfair competitive advantage due to our certification. Most importantly, gaining this certification enabled us to expand and improve our service and support to agency customers. Additionally, this certification positioned the organization for long-term success, providing marketing opportunities, highly visible status, and an increase in sales and sustained growth. Finally, the certification and capability poised the company for a major acquisition.

Another example began in 2014, in my role as President and CEO of Wondermark, Inc. The company was suffering from a lack of senior corporate leadership, vision, strategy, and even execution. Sales were down, product intellectual property was old, and competition was very strong. From an operational standpoint, the company was struggling with logistics and supplier management. Overall quality was lacking, there was no new product development pending, and employee morale was very low. Based on my broad success of building and improving programs and organizations, I was hired and held accountable for turning the organization around. My customers in this endeavor included the Board of Directors, employees, and the market. I was determined to provide them with world-class leadership and support, while "righting the ship" in 18 months.

For the first six months, I focused on gaining the trust of employees and stakeholders and avoiding the looming short-term financial disaster. I accomplished this through ongoing communications and through sound operational management with a focus on logistics, planning, and inventory control. I implemented a state-of-the-art

enterprise resources planning (ERP) technology platform to provide end-to-end integrated operational and financial corporate management. With the right tools in place, I then engaged employees in resolving complex logistical issues to remedy longstanding inefficiencies and poor internal as well as external supplier based understanding of quality and customer service.

While driving and overseeing progress at the operational level, I also developed a comprehensive five-year strategic plan that included a business summary, charts, tables, and spreadsheets that reflected the path ahead. The plan was founded on a new customer-centric culture that rallied employees around organizational pride and excellence in service. To instill the needed accountability, I instituted employee empowerment; I developed and implemented metrics for assessing quality/customer satisfaction; and I am now expanding our global supplier base.

My leadership and executive perspective during this period led to strong results. Within the first six months, we shifted millions of dollars of inventory that had been sitting in warehouses to customers. Moreover, within 12 months, I had stabilized the overall company revenues and shifted the tide toward rapid operational organization growth and improvement. I reduced the company's product line while increasing sales, and developed detailed financials and analysis. Created a very successful and systematic five-year business plan, performed a company-sponsored buyback of stock from a major shareholder, and instituted a complete new corporate culture leveraging a proven operational philosophy. Over the past couple of years, I led the organization (double digit year over year growth) and sustainable results in improving productivity by 21% and overall revenues by 23%. The Board of Directors, customers, and stakeholders lauded my efforts in effectively avoiding a "cash call" from investors and stabilizing the company while simultaneously positioning it for long-term growth.

BUSINESS ACUMEN

The most significant financial issue in my career occurred in 2017, while I was serving as Chief Executive Officer (CEO) of Verbatim Technologies, Inc. In this role, I closely monitored all financials, income statements, balance sheets, and cash flows and created a series of 11 Microsoft Excel spreadsheets focused on tracking specific data points (metrics), such as financial and operational ratios, sales forecasts, backlog product and services mix, revenue figures, profits, and cash flows. Through my analysis and monitoring, I determined early on that our steady 30% year-over-year growth actually put the company at risk. In other words, we were growing too fast, and if I did not modify the corporate financing structure, we could quickly use our draining cash reserves and face serious cash shortages. To accomplish this, I began to proactively and aggressively monitor and manage all revenues. The approach allowed us to avoid turning away business, from either a business or a customer-service perspective, and I was able to focus on approaches to manage our delicate financial predicament. First, working with financial partners, I extended bank lines of credit and product lead times to increase our purchase order backlog and overall stability while slowing annual growth to less than 30%. I then reevaluated pricing and increased where appropriate to increase margins.

While these steps increased profitability and helped to stabilize cash flows and reserves, they did not resolve the problem completely. With several large-scale Department of Defense (DOD) and agency program opportunities, we were well positioned to win ($100M+), again we risked draining cash reserves. Realizing we needed to share some of the financial risk, I began to aggressively partner with several large Government Prime Contractors (worth billions of dollars each). As a direct result of my effective financial planning, management, analyses, negotiating skill, and oversight, we generated more than $75M in sales, with a pipeline of projects and opportunities that exceeded an additional $120M.

In mid-2014, I cofounded Sharpedge Corporation, which licensed a unique laser-based Intellectual Property

(IP) from the University of Utah for use as a nonlethal weapon. After funding the company and negotiating the agreement with the university's Office of Technology Commercialization and began to build the highly specialized team required to be successful. In this particular situation, it was imperative that to enlist professors with unique training and expertise. Their knowledge would help us to secure the technology, obtain the requisite patents to protect the IP, and create credibility within the industry. I approached two world-class professors, each with extensive background and knowledge on this specific IP, and used a negotiated equity strategy position to incentivize the professors as cofounders and Chief Technology Officers by offering them an equity stake in the business entity.

As a result of this human capital planning and management, the specialized team I assembled performed extremely well. We obtained independent verification of the technology via an outside governmental research lab valued at $5M worth of key research and development and were awarded a U.S. patent in 2015. When we presented our technology to the government agency responsible for this type of product solution, they were very impressed with our highly innovative IP and market approach.

A final example took place in 2017, while I served as Director of Program Improvements for Faultproof Technology Group. I was involved in our purchase of a 21-year-old sports publication. Assessing the current business and technology landscape, I set out to seamlessly integrate the recent explosion in social media applications with the Horns Illustrated website to increase website activity, traffic, and sales.

I took a lead role in developing the specifications for a major redesign of a full commerce-based website along with the associated social media platforms of Facebook and Twitter. Using an innovative approach, I developed a concept that would allow us to "live stream" our Facebook and Twitter feeds on the website's homepage (in multiple languages) and then proposed the addition of a digital edition of the publication. This would be an online publication and a subscription service model. Additionally, I developed a concept that would provide live audio streaming from local sports radio stations to users on the homepage. I wrote the specification, developed a general design, then subcontracted the actual website coding and activation.

As a result of my conceiving, developing, coordinating, and leading these Internet and web development initiatives, the new site was tested and went live within four months. With a little marketing, our website activity exploded from a few hundred users to well over 18K in just a few weeks. Further, with social media activity ("likes"), our reach mushroomed to over 150K followers. All areas of the business have been positively affected by this initiative. Finally, our online growth has attracted new advertisers who are interested in how we leveraged social media to become more visible in the community.

BUILDING COALITIONS

In 2017, I was one of nine local executives selected to serve as an Entrepreneur in Residence at the University of Montana, which maintains an impressive list of Intellectual Property (IP), which they desired to commercialize. Meanwhile, the university was spending millions of dollars each year to maintain ongoing patent and Research and Development (R&D) costs. In this paid, temporary position, I would help to identify the most promising technologies and then market them to potential investors. Stakeholders in this initiative included leadership staff, professors, government officials, and several investors. I built a strong coalition with a shared vision and goal of commercializing the university's IP for the benefit of all parties.

First, I helped forge productive partnerships with the professors and reviewed approximately 80 different technologies. The professors understood the technology but often lacked real-world exposure regarding the complex planning, processes, personnel, and funding required to achieve successful commercialization. Conversely, inves-

tors were more focused on how fast the IP could be taken from R&D to commercialization. These two approaches (academia versus capitalism) represented totally different and opposing viewpoints.

While working to bridge the gap between these two viewpoints, it quickly became apparent the existing systems and approach being used was not conducive to developing a rapid, clear, concise, and independent analysis of the true stage of the IP development. Visiting with the Commercialization Program Director (a Ph.D.), I proposed an approach that could inform and empower all stakeholders. Specifically, I proposed we merge and modify two government concepts I was familiar with called Technology Readiness Levels (TRL) and Quad Charts and combine them as common tool for defining a realistic IP development stage.

As with most new concepts in any business, there was a community of resistance. The university had a process they had always used, professors did not like the idea of being forced to commit to a certain structure (basically flushing out how far along the path to commercialization the technology actually was), and a number of the other executives had their own ideas and agendas. Still, I saw this as a collaborative process opportunity and a way to optimize our effectiveness and strengthen the overall group. To unite stakeholders around my vision, I first developed the concept, and then presented it to the Program Director and used examples from two recent meetings to clearly demonstrate the need for a more formal system for defining IP stages. After gaining the Program Director's support, I began to engage with other stakeholders to expand the alliance and support, explaining that these were generally accepted governmental programs.

As a result, I successfully united this group of stakeholders. We achieved consensus on a standard format for utilizing both tools as I had envisioned. We used this collaborative method on the remaining IP reviews, and although the program ended a few months later, our combined review efforts led to the licensing of six university technologies.

Another example occurred approximately a year later, while I was still serving at the University of Montana. At the time, there was a major initiative taking place that pertained to licensing agreements for solar technology. Stakeholders consisted of a large, publicly traded multinational solar corporation, a large European power utility, and the university. Business relationships had deteriorated into a complex and technical series of ownership positioning and legal battles. Tensions were running high, key personnel were no longer on speaking terms, companies were delinquent on licensing payments, and ongoing commercialization of the technology was at risk. Additionally, legal costs alone were already in the tens of millions of dollars and the outcome could be in the hundreds of millions of dollars and have major negative global impact. Finally, all parties had their own agendas, as this highly visible and political issue crossed multiple borders. Because of my reputation as an effective negotiator and my previous experience with individuals in the battery technology industry, I was asked to help. The objective was to bring stakeholders together, mend professional relationships, and resolve the complex licensing issues. I was provided the authority and autonomy to approach stakeholders to resolve this issue.

My primary goal was to avoid a legal battle and bring all parties back to the table for negotiations. First, I gathered all of the details, reviewed the history, and began to develop multiple action plans. The most effective strategy was to persuade the two largest partners to agree on a particular course of action and then try to convince the third partner that this was the best way forward. To accomplish this, I began to build strong relationships with all stakeholders and within a few weeks, I had attended numerous meetings, seminars, and a tradeshow regarding advanced battery technologies and sought the advice of renowned industry experts.

Although new to the industry and situation, this played to my advantage as stakeholders quickly saw my role and approach as an independent party acting in an unbiased role for the common good. Through a series of introduction phone calls and emails, I was able to persuade certain parties to meet without attorneys present in an attempt to reach a mutually beneficial solution without legal action. I met with these individual on a one-on-one basis. During these meetings, I presented a number of viable scenarios that we could implement, outlined the pros/cons of each, and openly discussed the group's individual and shared issues, concerns, and objectives. Additionally, I stressed the concept of a common goal and solicited feedback from the group and as I went along gaining support. I continued to build and maintain rapport through in-person as well as virtual meetings. I narrowed the options and negotiated the finer aspects, then summarized them with the University Director.

Ultimately, my efforts resulted in a much more open and friendly dialog among all parties. Negotiations and conversations became friendlier and even the opposing legal teams came to mutual understanding and a new agreement was reached. All stakeholders benefited from this initiative and I played an integral, critical role in obtaining settlement and ending a lengthy and very costly ongoing legal battle.

CAREERPRO GLOBAL'S EXCLUSIVE ECQ BUILDERS

This ECQ builder is specifically designed to help you select and then share your top career stories for each ECQ.

Step 1: Brainstorm

Use the space below to write out potential topics for each ECQ based on the best practices. For example, you might write something like, "Operations Division Turnaround, 2009 to 2011." You may also want to print out the first three pages if you'd rather write than type during Step 1.

Leading Change 1	
Leading Change 2	
Leading People 1	
Leading People 2	
Results Driven 1	
Results Driven 2	
Business Acumen/Financial Management	
Business Acumen/Human Capital Management	
Business Acumen/Technology Management	
Building Coalitions 1	
Building Coalitions 2	

Step 2: Outline/Compare

Next, compare your potential topics/stories to the competency questions for the respective ECQ in the builder below (see the actions sections) and ask yourself, "Will I be able to provide a few sentences or a paragraph on most—if not all—of these important competency questions?"

If the answer is **No**, then try to find another ECQ where the story might be a better fit. If the answer is **Yes**, then the story is probably a good fit, so you can move on to Step 3!

Remember, there are many ways to talk about how you led change, led people, created results, etc. However, the competencies tell you what skills OPM (Office of Personnel Management) thinks are most important among members of the SES, so it's critical to tell your stories through the "lens" of those competencies.

Step 3: Develop
Fill out the builder, and when you're done, copy/paste everything over to a Microsoft (MS) Word document with Times New Roman size 12 font and 1" margins all around.

ECQ AND COMPETENCY OVERVIEW

Leading Change	Leading People	Results Driven	Business Acumen	Building Coalitions
• Creativity/ Innovation • External Awareness • Flexibility • Resilience • Strategic Thinking • Vision	• Conflict Management • Levering Diversity • Developing Others • Team Building	• Accountability • Customer Service • Decisiveness • Entrepreneurship • Problem Solving • Technical Credibility	• Financial Mgmt • Human Capital Mgmt • Technology Mgmt	• Partnering • Political Savvy • Influencing/ Negotiating

Fundamental Competencies:

Fundamental competencies do not need to be addressed directly but should be integrated over the course of the complete ECQ narrative.

Interpersonal Skills	Written Communication	Oral Communication	Continual Learning	Integrity/ Honesty	Public Service Motivation

ECQ 1: LEADING CHANGE

Overview: The following builder will walk you through the process of developing your narrative for Leading Change in the Challenge-Context-Action-Result (CCAR) format, as well as help you address all of the competencies.

Think about, select, and list situations (achievements or accomplishments) in which your efforts brought about strategic change, both within and outside the organization, to meet an organizational goal. Start with an external vision of the program—describe how it was perceived by outsiders or government entities, or if it encountered any resistance that you had to deal with.

Demonstrate how you struck the phrase "That's how we've always done it" from your vocabulary, as well as that of your team. Discuss how you abandoned familiar or comfortable ways of doing business to embrace changing times, economy, and political environments.

Inherent to this ECQ is the ability to establish an organizational vision and to implement it in a continually changing environment (**Vision/Creativity and Innovation**). Included are such factors as balancing change and continuity while creating a healthy work environment and focusing on long-term goals (**Strategic Thinking**); identifying and keeping up-to-date on key national and international policies and economic, political, and social trends that affect the organization (**External Awareness**); and dealing effectively with pressure and maintaining focus and intensity while remaining optimistic and persistent, even under adversity (**Flexibility and Resilience**).

IDEAS FOR SELECTING YOUR EXAMPLES

√ Developing a new vision for an organization in disorder or shifting the organizational culture while overcoming resistance and obtaining buy-in
√ Standing up a new organization; garnering support, resources, and manpower from scratch
√ Designing/implementing new, streamlined policies or business processes to improve operations, cost reductions, and overall performance
√ Introducing automated programs, tools, and technologies to optimize business performance
√ Leading a merger, acquisition, joint venture, and business-building initiative
√ Challenging others to go beyond their limits to bring the organization to new heights by daring to change, despite resistance and scrutiny

The following questions are meant to serve as a guide in prompting you to fully explain the situation of your example. If a question does not apply, simply indicate with "N/A" and move on to the next question.

TOPIC OF THIS EXAMPLE: _____

=== CHALLENGE/CONTEXT ===

What was the title of your job or the role you were playing in this example? What was the year the story took place or began?

Your Response: _____

_____

_____

_____

Describe the situation that drove the organization to seek change, by addressing some or all of the following questions. Your response should be one challenge/context paragraph of perhaps 10-12 lines, tops. This way, you save most of the space on the page for the most important things—your actions and results:

✓ Was there a set timeline or due date for this project? What type of pressure were you under?

✓ What was the organizational climate at the time? (e.g., was it stuck in the "we've always done it that way" mentality in terms of complacency and unwillingness to try anything new?) Was there a local, national, or international policy or trend driving this change?

✓ What was the external climate at the time? (e.g., how was your organization viewed from external parties? Was it high visibility? Were you being watched by other organizations? Were expectations high?)

✓ Who was going to be most affected by this change? (e.g., whose work would become easier, and who would be given extra responsibility? Who was for, and who was against, the change?)

✓ What were the challenges associated with this change? What needed to happen to make the change(s)? Did you have to seek permission/approval, deal with resistant people, meet a tight time deadline, develop a program from inception through production, write new policy, etc.?

Your Response: _____

_____

_____

_____

=== ACTION ===

THIS IS THE MOST IMPORTANT PART OF THE ENTIRE BUILDER! Remember, the competency questions below reflect what is most important to OPM!

In the space below, please describe exactly what you did—your actions, decisions, communications, etc.—that moved the problem/challenge to resolution or outcome. The best way to do this is by providing a few thoughts/sentences, or a paragraph for each question below.

- ✓ What was your plan of action? (**Strategic Thinking**) Was the vision of this project established by mandate, or did you create the vision to improve a process or result? (**Vision**)
- ✓ Did it involve introducing any cutting-edge programs or processes that challenged conventional approaches? (**Creativity and Innovation**)
- ✓ Did you encounter any unexpected obstacles or problems? [e.g., how did you adapt to new information, changing conditions, or unexpected obstacles? What did you do to overcome any setbacks and achieve buy-in from those resistant to change? (**Flexibility**)]

Your Response: _____

_____

_____

_____

_____

_____

=== RESULT ===

Describe results, outcomes, or long-term impacts of your efforts. At a senior level, there should be more than one identifiable, measurable result from your efforts. (Quantify with numbers whenever possible.)

- ✓ Did the result have an immediate impact?
- ✓ Address here the problems or resistance you described in the Challenge/Context section, if possible.
- ✓ Include quantified evidence of your successful change leadership, if possible.
- ✓ Was your performance recognized, either formally or informally?

Your Response: _____

_____

_____

_____

_____

_____

_____

Specialized Training:
What training have you undergone that supports this accomplishment?

Your Response: _____

_____

_____

The following questions are meant to serve as a guide in prompting you to fully explain the situation of your example. If a question does not apply, simply indicate with "N/A" and move on to the next question.

TOPIC OF THIS EXAMPLE: _____

=== CHALLENGE/CONTEXT ===

What was the title of your job or the role you were playing in this example? What was the year the story took place or began?

Your Response: _____

_____

_____

_____

Describe the situation that drove the organization to seek change, by addressing some or all of the following questions. Your response should be one challenge/context paragraph of perhaps 10-12 lines, tops. This way, you save most of the space on the page for the most important things—your actions and results:

✓ Was there a set timeline or due date for this project? What type of pressure were you under?
✓ What was the organizational climate at the time? (e.g., was it stuck in the "we've always done it that way" mentality in terms of complacency and unwillingness to try anything new?) Was there a local, national, or international policy or trend driving this change?
✓ What was the external climate at the time? (e.g., how was your organization viewed from external parties? Was it high visibility? Were you being watched by other organizations? Were expectations high?)
✓ Who was going to be most affected by this change? (e.g., whose work would become easier, and who would be given extra responsibility? Who was for, and who was against, the change?)
✓ What were the challenges associated with this change? What needed to happen to make the change(s)? Did you have to seek permission/approval, deal with resistant people, meet a tight time deadline, develop a program from inception through production, write new policy, etc.?

Your Response: _____

_____

_____

_____

=== ACTION ===

THIS IS THE MOST IMPORTANT PART OF THE ENTIRE BUILDER! Remember, the competency questions below reflect what is most important to OPM!

In the space below, please describe exactly what you did—your actions, decisions, communications, etc.—that moved the problem/challenge to resolution or outcome. The best way to do this is by providing a few thoughts/sentences, or a paragraph for each question below.

- ✓ What was your plan of action? (**Strategic Thinking**) Was the vision of this project established by mandate, or did you create the vision to improve a process or result? (**Vision**)
- ✓ Did it involve introducing any cutting-edge programs or processes that challenged conventional approaches? (**Creativity and Innovation**)
- ✓ Did you encounter any unexpected obstacles or problems? [e.g., how did you adapt to new information, changing conditions, or unexpected obstacles? What did you do to overcome any setbacks and achieve buy-in from those resistant to change? (**Flexibility**)]

Your Response: _____

_____

_____

_____

_____

_____

_____

=== RESULT ===

Describe results, outcomes, or long-term impacts of your efforts. At a senior level, there should be more than one identifiable, measurable result from your efforts. (Quantify with numbers whenever possible.)

- ✓ Did the result have an immediate impact?
- ✓ Address here the problems or resistance you described in the Challenge/Context section, if possible.
- ✓ Include quantified evidence of your successful change leadership, if possible.
- ✓ Was your performance recognized, either formally or informally?

Your Response: _____

_____

_____

_____

_____

_____

_____

Specialized Training:
What training have you undergone that supports this accomplishment?

Your Response: _____

_____

_____

ECQ 2: LEADING PEOPLE

Overview: This ECQ involves the ability to lead people toward meeting the organization's vision, mission, and goals. Inherent to this ECQ is the ability to provide an inclusive workplace that fosters the development of others, facilitates cooperation and teamwork, and supports constructive resolution of conflicts. Think about examples of you leading people in either meeting or turning around organizational and/or individual performance.

Once you explain the situation and leadership challenges you faced, you want to address the competencies in the Action section. Describe exactly what you did to build a stronger team and how individual efforts helped the overall team (**Team Building**). Give examples of team-building exercises you have implemented to get a fractured workforce to become a team. Talk about office incentives, awards, and/or social events you've sponsored to create bonds of camaraderie and team spirit.

You should also discuss how you mentored and encouraged employees to continue their education or training with either technical or leadership opportunities (**Developing Others**). Discuss workforce development. This factor should affirm a solid commitment to the professional development of your employees and/or subordinate managers. Describe affirmative employment achievements and challenges, your recruitment and retention of highly qualified people, and your dedication to ensuring your staff takes advantage of all opportunities for growth presented to them.

The manner in which you resolve conflict (**Conflict Management**) is of utmost importance to the Office of Personnel Management (OPM), since a perfect, conflict-free environment does not exist. What is important is *how* you address that conflict between two employees or, on a larger scale, between management and labor. OPM is interested in your process of de-escalating workplace unpleasantness, employee rivalry, or any other disturbance that distracts from the work at hand and has a negative impact on productivity.

Finally, one of the top evaluation criteria for the ECQs overall is **Leveraging Diversity**, which you can address in a number of ways. Think of any time in your career when race/gender/age/physically challenged status or other diversity elements played a positive and important role in setting up a workgroup, networking outside your agency, or building coalitions. You could also discuss how you recruited from diverse educational institutions and/or started internship programs to encourage interest in a particular area and mentored your interns through to successful completion of the program.

IDEAS FOR SELECTING YOUR EXAMPLES

√ Taking a dysfunctional staff and motivating them by determining skills gaps, addressing gaps through hiring and training and development, emphasizing team as well as individual performance, and making the group more professional and productive.

√ Rallying your team around a specific challenge or problem while demonstrating your ability to build the team, develop subordinates, manage conflict, and leverage diversity.

LEADING PEOPLE: EXAMPLE 1

TOPIC OF THIS EXAMPLE: _____

=== CHALLENGE/CONTEXT ===

What is the topic of this example? What was the title of your job or the role you were playing in this example? In what year did this story take place or begin?

Your Response: _____

_____

_____

_____

What were the challenges associated with this position or situation? (e.g., what needed to happen to strengthen the team, develop the individuals and the workforce as a whole, overcome conflict, and leverage diversity? Did you have to seek permission/approval, deal with resistant people, meet a tight time deadline, develop a program from inception through production, write new policy, etc.?)

✓ Was there a set timeline or due date for this project? What type of pressure were you under?
✓ What were the leadership challenges you had to overcome? Low morale? Lack of previous leadership? Low productivity? Internal conflict?

Your Response: _____

_____

_____

=== ACTION ===

THIS IS THE MOST IMPORTANT PART OF THE ENTIRE BUILDER! Remember, the competency questions below reflect what is most important to OPM!

In the space below, please describe exactly what you did—your actions, decisions, communications, etc.—that moved the problem/challenge to resolution or outcome. The best way to do this is by providing a few thoughts/sentences, or a paragraph, for each question below.

✓ Describe how you brought the team together and built a stronger sense of pride and teamwork. Maybe you held weekly meetings, social gatherings, incentives, awards, time off, etc. (**Team Building**)
✓ Did you have to handle conflicts between two or more employees/groups? What did you do to resolve the tension in a constructive manner? (**Conflict Management**)

- ✓ Did you provide opportunities for, or encourage employees and staff to enroll in, professional development opportunities or extend anyone's responsibilities to a higher level of job description or expectation? Did you utilize intern programs, fellowships, or other professional development programs to recruit young talent? Did you then arrange for them to be mentored into the mainstream? (**Developing Others**)
- ✓ Did you encourage female candidates in a traditionally male-dominated field or recruit minorities, etc.? Did you select teams for projects that included a diverse mix of individuals— professionally, educationally, culturally, racially, etc.? (**Leveraging Diversity**)

Your Response: _____

_____

_____

_____

_____

_____

_____

=== RESULT ===

Describe results, outcomes, or long-term impacts of your efforts. At a senior level, there should be more than one identifiable, measurable result from your efforts. (Quantify with numbers whenever possible.)

- ✓ Did the result have an immediate impact?
- ✓ Address here the problems or resistance you described in the Challenge/Context section, if possible.
- ✓ Include quantified evidence of your efforts, if possible.
- ✓ Was your performance recognized, either formally or informally?

Your Response: _____

_____

_____

_____

_____

_____

Specialized Training:
What training have you undergone that supports this accomplishment?

Your Response: _____

_____

_____

TOPIC OF THIS EXAMPLE: _____

=== CHALLENGE/CONTEXT ===

What is the topic of this example? What was the title of your job or the role you were playing in this example? In what year did this story take place or begin?

Your Response: _____

_____

_____

_____

What were the challenges associated with this position or situation? (e.g., what needed to happen to strengthen the team, develop the individuals and the workforce as a whole, overcome conflict, and leverage diversity? Did you have to seek permission/approval, deal with resistant people, meet a tight time deadline, develop a program from inception through production, write new policy, etc.?)

✓ Was there a set timeline or due date for this project? What type of pressure were you under?
✓ What were the leadership challenges you had to overcome? Low morale? Lack of previous leadership? Low productivity? Internal conflict?

Your Response: _____

_____

_____

=== ACTION ===

THIS IS THE MOST IMPORTANT PART OF THE ENTIRE BUILDER! Remember, the competency questions below reflect what is most important to OPM!

In the space below, please describe exactly what you did—your actions, decisions, communications, etc.—that moved the problem/challenge to resolution or outcome. The best way to do this is by providing a few thoughts/sentences, or a paragraph, for each question below.

✓ Describe how you brought the team together and built a stronger sense of pride and teamwork. Maybe you held weekly meetings, social gatherings, incentives, awards, time off, etc. (**Team Building**)
✓ Did you have to handle conflicts between two or more employees/groups? What did you do to resolve the tension in a constructive manner? (**Conflict Management**)

✓ Did you provide opportunities for, or encourage employees and staff to enroll in, professional development opportunities or extend anyone's responsibilities to a higher level of job description or expectation? Did you utilize intern programs, fellowships, or other professional development programs to recruit young talent? Did you then arrange for them to be mentored into the mainstream? (**Developing Others**)

✓ Did you encourage female candidates in a traditionally male-dominated field or recruit minorities, etc.? Did you select teams for projects that included a diverse mix of individuals—professionally, educationally, culturally, racially, etc.? (**Leveraging Diversity**)

Your Response: _____

_____

_____

_____

_____

_____

_____

=== RESULT ===

Describe results, outcomes, or long-term impacts of your efforts. At a senior level, there should be more than one identifiable, measurable result from your efforts. (Quantify with numbers whenever possible.)

✓ Did the result have an immediate impact?
✓ Address here the problems or resistance you described in the Challenge/Context section, if possible.
✓ Include quantified evidence of your efforts, if possible.
✓ Was your performance recognized, either formally or informally?

Your Response: _____

_____

_____

_____

_____

_____

_____

Specialized Training:
What training have you undergone that supports this accomplishment?

Your Response: _____

_____

_____

ECQ 3: RESULTS DRIVEN

This ECQ involves the ability to meet organizational goals and customer expectations, even in the midst of major challenges. Inherent to the ECQ is the ability to own and manage responsibilities and make decisions that produce high-quality results by applying technical knowledge (note: **technical credibility** doesn't need to be about technology; it means technical credibility in your own field of expertise) to solve problems and improve customer service.

Accountability is prime here; you must provide before-and-after data, percentages, growth figures, etc. Describe how you maintained your personal accountability through metrics, spreadsheets, or reports, but perhaps even more importantly, describe how you kept others accountable through budget adherence, milestone reporting, or other specific program oversight/management tools.

Don't forget **customer service**. Whom was this initiative going to benefit? How? How did your actions improve the business or bottom line, save money, or streamline the company's processes?

Other factors include: identifying and resolving organizational problems, distinguishing between relevant and irrelevant information to make logical decisions (**Problem Solving**); exercising good judgment by making sound, well-informed, and timely decisions; exercising the ability to be proactive and achievement-oriented (**Decisiveness**); and positioning your customers and the organization for future success (**Entrepreneurship**).

IDEAS FOR SELECTING YOUR EXAMPLES

√   Major-scale projects/programs you directed that solved a strategic/organizational problem and positively affected your organization, either by improving business practices or through monetary savings or profit (e.g., describe how you established objectives, developed milestones, assigned responsibilities, held people accountable through reports and/or meetings, made tough decisions to avoid project delays, and completed the project on time and within budget, despite obstacles).
√   Problems you solved that increased productivity or resulted in other benefits to the organization.
√   Ideas you turned into reality that had financial or operational impact on the organization.
√   Recognition for noteworthy or exceptional service and attention to customers.
√   Incorporating work improvement methods that were successfully implemented.
√   Taking a major work unit/program problem and turning things around.
√   Improving customer service.

TOPIC OF THIS EXAMPLE: _____

=== CHALLENGE/CONTEXT ===

✓ What was the title of your job or the role you were playing in this example?
✓ In what year did this story take place or begin?
✓ What was the problem or challenge you had to overcome? Perhaps there was some growing problem that you were tasked to deal with. Or, maybe you took action when no one else knew what to do.
✓ What was the pressure to complete this project?
✓ Was this an opportunity to improve the organization's production, products, or customer service?
✓ Who were your customers in this example?

Your Response: _____

_____

_____

_____

=== ACTION ===

Describe exactly what you did—your actions, decisions, communications, etc.—that moved the problem/challenge to resolution or outcome. The best way to do this is by providing a few thoughts/sentences, or a paragraph for each question below. These questions are *very important*, because they represent the required competencies (in **bold**) for this ECQ, or the "lens" through which OPM wants you to tell the story.

✓ To whom were you accountable? How did you improve accountability through internal controls, policies, governance, etc.? (**Accountability**)
✓ Who exactly were your customers, and how did you plan to improve service and support? (**Customer Service**)
✓ Describe exactly what you did (your actions, decisions, communications, etc.) that moved the project, task, or problem to resolution or outcome (**Problem Solving**).
✓ Were you responsible for any make-or-break decision(s) that could have affected the project? (**Decisiveness**)
✓ How did you position your customer and/or the organization for future/continued success and growth? (**Entrepreneurship**)

Your Response: _____

_____

_____

_____

_____

_____

=== RESULT ===

Describe results, outcomes, or long-term impacts of your efforts. At a senior level, there should be more than one identifiable, measurable result from your efforts. (Quantify with numbers whenever possible.)

✓ What happened? Did the result have an immediate impact?

✓ Address here the problems or resistance you described in the Challenge/Context section, if possible.

✓ Was your performance recognized, either formally or informally?

✓ Could results be measured as a business return? (e.g., did the project contribute to substantial changes in employee job function/process, monetary/time savings, streamlined procedures or improved business practices, or improved customer service?)

Your Response: _____

_____

_____

_____

_____

_____

_____

Specialized Training:
What training have you undergone that supports this accomplishment?

Your Response: _____

_____

_____

TOPIC OF THIS EXAMPLE: _____

=== CHALLENGE/CONTEXT ===

✓ What was the title of your job or the role you were playing in this example?
✓ In what year did this story take place or begin?
✓ What was the problem or challenge you had to overcome? Perhaps there was some growing problem that you were tasked to deal with. Or, maybe you took action when no one else knew what to do.
✓ What was the pressure to complete this project?
✓ Was this an opportunity to improve the organization's production, products, or customer service?
✓ Who were your customers in this example?

Your Response: _____

_____

_____

_____

=== ACTION ===

Describe exactly what you did—your actions, decisions, communications, etc.—that moved the problem/challenge to resolution or outcome. The best way to do this is by providing a few thoughts/sentences, or a paragraph for each question below. These questions are *very important*, because they represent the required competencies (in **bold**) for this ECQ, or the "lens" through which OPM wants you to tell the story.

✓ To whom were you accountable? How did you improve accountability through internal controls, policies, governance, etc.? (**Accountability**)
✓ Who exactly were your customers, and how did you plan to improve service and support? (**Customer Service**)
✓ Describe exactly what you did (your actions, decisions, communications, etc.) that moved the project, task, or problem to resolution or outcome (**Problem Solving**).
✓ Were you responsible for any make-or-break decision(s) that could have affected the project? (**Decisiveness**)
✓ How did you position your customer and/or the organization for future/continued success and growth? (**Entrepreneurship**)

Your Response: _____

_____

_____

_____

_____

_____

=== RESULT ===

Describe results, outcomes, or long-term impacts of your efforts. At a senior level, there should be more than one identifiable, measurable result from your efforts. (Quantify with numbers whenever possible.)

✓ What happened? Did the result have an immediate impact?
✓ Address here the problems or resistance you described in the Challenge/Context section, if possible.
✓ Was your performance recognized, either formally or informally?
✓ Could results be measured as a business return? (e.g., did the project contribute to substantial changes in employee job function/process, monetary/time savings, streamlined procedures or improved business practices, or improved customer service?)

Your Response: _____

_____

_____

_____

_____

_____

Specialized Training:
What training have you undergone that supports this accomplishment?

Your Response: _____

_____

_____

ECQ 4: BUSINESS ACUMEN

OPM defines Business Acumen as the composite of three main business functions: Financial Management, Human Capital Management, and Technology Management. This ECQ involves the ability to manage human, financial, and information resources strategically. It is as if you are writing three "mini" ECQs under the Business Acumen umbrella.

Financial Management: Financial Management refers to experience gained with procedures for establishing and justifying budgets, securing resources, and managing finances. If you have been particularly successful in establishing, restructuring, or improving financial management and accounting procedures and/or reducing costs/increasing efficiency, you should select a high-profile example of the project, your process, obstacles encountered, and the results or impact of your work.

Human Capital Management: Human Capital Management is similar to Leading People in that it refers to your ability to manage Human Resources (HR). The difference is that Leading People is more focused on your hands-on work with your staff, including interpersonal skills necessary to mediate conflict, to personally mentor and encourage performance, to build teams, and to encourage an inclusive workplace. The content for the Human Capital Management element of Business Acumen, however, should be targeted at a more global view that the workforce is the company's fundamental asset and requires serious time and effort to see results in areas like productivity, long-term employment, and a constantly rising level of profit or performance.

Technology Management: Technology Management is the effective initiation, implementation, and use of Information Technology (IT), technological developments, technology systems, and information resources to achieve results and streamline business processes in the modern workplace. These could be other resources, depending on your field (video, satellite, wireless resources, etc.).

IDEAS FOR SELECTING YOUR EXAMPLES

Financial Management:
- ✓ Leading the development of a creative budget strategy to get something funded that otherwise wouldn't have been funded.
- ✓ Managing a program or project that experienced funding problems, which involved examining priorities, adjusting work scope, implementing cost-saving techniques, and securing additional funding, to solve the budget crisis and to enable the program/project to meet milestones.
- ✓ Have you prepared, justified, and administered program budgets? In what amount?
- ✓ Have you made creative use of a procurement system, leading a source evaluation board under difficult circumstances, streamlining the use of contracts by a program, or managing the development of an important solicitation?

Human Capital Management:
- ✓ Leading a staffing analysis or recruiting drive to hire and train new staff and better align work with overarching strategic goals.

- ✓ Have you assessed current and future staffing needs based on organizational goals and budget realities? Did you develop staffing plans and/or realign human capital to optimize business practices?
- ✓ Have you acquired and developed staffs whose size, skills, and deployment met organizational needs? If so, how?
- ✓ Have you successfully recruited personnel and/or improved their performance within the organization?
- ✓ Have you been involved in improving traditional employee benefits?
- ✓ Have you introduced any innovative employee benefits and incentives (e.g., flex time, onsite daycare, etc.)?

Technology Management:
- ✓ Playing a lead role in developing and/or implementing some new technology or automated process in the workplace that leverages technology to improve business processes and increase efficiency.
- ✓ Have you expanded any information systems and technologies?
- ✓ Have you connected technology to critical functional business areas of accounting, finance, marketing, HR, and operations? (In other words, how have you expanded electronic government?)
- ✓ Have you integrated technology's vital role in helping your organization gain a competitive advantage?
- ✓ Have you led any technology projects to transform business operations or practices?
- ✓ Have you designed aggressive solutions to standardize business practices through leading-edge technologies?

FINANCIAL MANAGEMENT

TOPIC OF THIS EXAMPLE: _____

=== CHALLENGE/CONTEXT ===

What is the title of your job or the role you were playing in this example? Include the approximate dates of the example you are relating.

- ✓ What was the financial problem or situation you were dealing with?
- ✓ What would happen if you didn't manage the budget/funds effectively? What type of pressure were you under to complete this project?
- ✓ Describe your most significant career responsibility for funds, allocations, procurement, or acquisition and any projects you led or actions you have taken to reduce costs, save money, or increase income.

Your Response: _____

_____

_____

- -

=== ACTION ===

Describe exactly what you did—your actions, decisions, communications, etc.—that moved the financial problem/challenge to resolution or outcome.

Your Response: _____

_____

_____

_____

_____

_____

=== RESULT ===

Describe results, outcomes, or long-term impacts of your efforts. At a senior level, there should be more than one identifiable, measurable result from your efforts. (Quantify with numbers whenever possible.)

✓ What happened? Did the result have an immediate impact?
✓ Address here the problems or resistance you described in the Challenge/Context section, if possible.
✓ Was your performance recognized, either formally or informally?
✓ Could results be measured as a business return? (e.g., did the project contribute to substantial changes in employee job function/process, monetary/time savings, streamlined procedures or improved business practices, or improved customer service?)

Your Response: _____

_____

_____

_____

Specialized Training:

What training have you undergone that supports this accomplishment?

Your Response: _____

_____

_____

HUMAN CAPITAL MANAGEMENT

TOPIC OF THIS EXAMPLE: _____

=== CHALLENGE/CONTEXT ===

What is the title of your job or the role you were playing in this example? Include the approximate dates of the example you are relating.

✓ What was your role in the human capital function?
✓ What was the human capital challenge/situation you had to overcome?

Your Response: _____

_____

_____

_____

=== ACTION ===

Describe exactly what you did—your actions, decisions, communications, etc.—that moved the human capital problem/challenge to resolution or outcome.

✓ Did you make any targeted investments in your talent? Who? Why?
✓ What type of research did you conduct? Describe any data analysis you performed.

- ✓ Did you have to make any data-driven (money, funding, etc.) human capital decisions? What were they?
- ✓ Did you consolidate management functions and streamline administrative operations?

Your Response: _____

_____

_____

_____

_____

_____

=== RESULT ===

Describe results, outcomes, or long-term impacts of your efforts. At a senior level, there should be more than one identifiable, measurable result from your efforts. (Quantify with numbers whenever possible.)

- ✓ What happened? Did the result have an immediate impact?
- ✓ Address here the problems or resistance you described in the Challenge/Context section, if possible.
- ✓ Was your performance recognized, either formally or informally?
- ✓ Could results be measured as a business return? (e.g., did the project contribute to substantial changes in employee job function/process, monetary/time savings, streamlined procedures or improved business practices, or improved customer service?)

Your Response: _____

_____

_____

_____

Specialized Training:
What training have you undergone that supports this accomplishment?

Your Response: _____

_____

_____

TECHNOLOGY MANAGEMENT

TOPIC OF THIS EXAMPLE: _____

=== CHALLENGE/CONTEXT ===
What is the title of your job or the role you were playing in this example? Include the approximate dates of the example you are relating.

Your Response: _____

_____

_____

_____

=== ACTION ===

Describe exactly what you did—your actions, decisions, communications, etc.—that moved the technology problem/challenge to resolution or outcome.

✓ Have you led technological conversions (systems, computers, etc.)? What was the dollar amount of the project?
✓ Have you implemented automated programs, tools, and technologies to optimize business performance?
✓ Have you introduced the latest technology advances into business/program operations?

Your Response: _____

_____

_____

_____

=== RESULT ===

Describe results, outcomes, or long-term impacts of your efforts. At a senior level, there should be more than one identifiable, measurable result from your efforts. (Quantify with numbers whenever possible.)

- ✓ What happened? Did the result have an immediate impact?
- ✓ Address here the problems or resistance you described in the Challenge/Context section, if possible.
- ✓ Was your performance recognized, either formally or informally?
- ✓ Could results be measured as a business return? (e.g., did the project contribute to substantial changes in employee job function/process, monetary/time savings, streamlined procedures or improved business practices, or improved customer service?)

Your Response: _____

_____

_____

_____

Specialized Training:
What training have you undergone that supports this accomplishment?

Your Response: _____

_____

_____

_____

ECQ 5: Building Coalitions

This ECQ involves the ability to build coalitions to achieve common goals. It addresses how you convince others, build consensus through give-and-take, gain cooperation from others to obtain information and accomplish goals, and facilitate win-win situations (**Influencing/Negotiating**). You will want to demonstrate how you develop networks and build alliances, using contacts to build and strengthen internal support bases (**Partnering**), as well as how you express facts and ideas in a clear, convincing, and organized manner (**Written Communication**).

The key factor to think about when drafting this ECQ is a time within the last five to seven years when you served as a uniting force, building alliances and **overcoming politics** to forge a group that was focused on a shared set of goals. What we're looking for here are engaging stories about how, for the good of the organization or project, you brought adversarial parties together to work together in a positive manner. We need to see it from the inside; we need to understand each party's side and the methods of negotiation and mediation you employed to accomplish your goal.

IDEAS FOR SELECTING YOUR EXAMPLES

√ A coalition you built to form a partnership of mutual benefit between two entities.

√ A situation in which you mastered organizational politics using political savvy to both influence positive change and achieve career success at the same time, even when negative organizational politics were evident.

√ A situation in which you had to use strong persuasive/negotiation skills to achieve an organizational goal or forge an interagency or multinational agreement or Memorandum of Understanding.

√ Describe how you've established partnerships to get things done that organizations working on their own could not have achieved, overcoming resistance to cooperate, perhaps as a member of a taskforce or working group, and playing the lead role in bringing members who previously could not agree to consensus.

BUILDING COALITIONS: EXAMPLE 1

TOPIC OF THIS EXAMPLE: _____

=== CHALLENGE/CONTEXT ===

State the title of your job or the role you were playing in this example and the year the story took place or began.

Your Response: _____

_____

_____

_____

===SITUATION ===

Describe the situation that drove the organization to seek your actions or solutions. What was the problem, situation, or partnership/coalition that needed to be built/salvaged?

✓ Who were the customers, stakeholders, or partners involved? Why did you need to bring them together? How would the organizations, workforce, country, community, enterprise, etc., benefit from this coalition?
✓ What were the problems associated with bringing these stakeholders together? Were there competing priorities, politics, etc.?

Your Response: _____

_____

_____

_____

=== ACTION ===

Describe exactly what you did—your actions, decisions, communications, etc.—that moved the problem/challenge to resolution or outcome. The best way to do this is by providing a few thoughts/sentences, or a paragraph for each question below. These questions are *very important*, because they represent the required competencies (in **bold**) for this ECQ, or the "lens" through which OPM wants you to tell the story.

✓ Describe exactly what you did to form partnerships with key stakeholders, and why. With whom did you conduct briefings and other meetings? (**Partnering**)
✓ Were negotiations a part of this example? Did you participate in the negotiations? Who were willing partners and who had to be convinced? How did you achieve buy-in from those resistant to partnership or compromise? (**Influencing/Negotiating**)
✓ Did any of the partners have hidden agendas? (**Political Savvy**)
✓ Were there any behind-the-scenes activities or backdoor politics of which you had to be aware? How did you overcome those? (**Political Savvy**)

Your Response: _____

_____

_____

_____

_____

_____

_____

=== RESULT ===

Describe results, outcomes, or long-term impacts of your efforts. At a senior level, there should be more than one identifiable, measurable result from your efforts. (Quantify with numbers whenever possible.)

✓ What happened? Did the result have an immediate impact?
✓ Address here the problems or resistance you described in the Challenge/Context section, if possible.
✓ Was your performance recognized, either formally or informally?
✓ How did your efforts strengthen interagency relations? How did the coalition or group perform?

Your Response: _____

_____

_____

_____

Specialized Training:
What training have you undergone that supports this accomplishment?

Your Response: _____

_____

_____

BUILDING COALITIONS: EXAMPLE 2

TOPIC OF THIS EXAMPLE: _____

=== CHALLENGE/CONTEXT ===

State the title of your job or the role you were playing in this example and the year the story took place or began.

Your Response: _____

_____

_____

_____

===SITUATION ===

Describe the situation that drove the organization to seek your actions or solutions. What was the problem, situation, or partnership/coalition that needed to be built/salvaged?

✓ Who were the customers, stakeholders, or partners involved? Why did you need to bring them together? How would the organizations, workforce, country, community, enterprise, etc., benefit from this coalition?

✓ What were the problems associated with bringing these stakeholders together? Were there competing priorities, politics, etc.?

Your Response: _____

_____

_____

_____

=== ACTION ===

Describe exactly what you did—your actions, decisions, communications, etc.—that moved the problem/challenge to resolution or outcome. The best way to do this is by providing a few thoughts/sentences, or a paragraph for each question below. These questions are *very important*, because they represent the required competencies (in **bold**) for this ECQ, or the "lens" through which OPM wants you to tell the story.

- ✓ Describe exactly what you did to form partnerships with key stakeholders, and why. With whom did you conduct briefings and other meetings? (**Partnering**)
- ✓ Were negotiations a part of this example? Did you participate in the negotiations? Who were willing partners and who had to be convinced? How did you achieve buy-in from those resistant to partnership or compromise? (**Influencing/Negotiating**)
- ✓ Did any of the partners have hidden agendas? (**Political Savvy**)
- ✓ Were there any behind-the-scenes activities or backdoor politics of which you had to be aware? How did you overcome those? (**Political Savvy**)

Your Response: _____

_____

_____

_____

_____

_____

_____

_____

=== RESULT ===

Describe results, outcomes, or long-term impacts of your efforts. At a senior level, there should be more than one identifiable, measurable result from your efforts. (Quantify with numbers whenever possible.)

- ✓ What happened? Did the result have an immediate impact?
- ✓ Address here the problems or resistance you described in the Challenge/Context section, if possible.
- ✓ Was your performance recognized, either formally or informally?
- ✓ How did your efforts strengthen interagency relations? How did the coalition or group perform?

Your Response: _____

_____

_____

_____

Specialized Training:
What training have you undergone that supports this accomplishment?

Your Response: _____

_____

_____

FUNDAMENTAL ECQ COMPETENCIES:

Finally, although the "fundamental competencies" are not required to be addressed directly in the narratives, we do recommend integrating each of them once somewhere in the overall ECQs.
FUNDAMENTAL ECQ COMPETENCIES:

Finally, although the "fundamental competencies" are not required to be addressed directly in the narratives, we do recommend integrating each of them once somewhere in the overall ECQs.

ACCOMPLISHMENTS WORKSHEET

JOB INFORMATION:

(You might want to write in your job title, start and end dates, and any other information to help you be organized for when you develop your resume.)

_____

_____

_____

TOP DUTIES:

1. _____

2. _____

3. _____

4. _____

5. _____

6. _____

7. _____

8. _____

TOP RESULTS/ACCOMPLSHMENTS:

1. _____

_____

2. _____

_____

3. _____

_____

4. _____

_____

5. _____

_____

6. _____

_____

7. _____

_____

8. _____

_____

To learn more about the Senior Executive Service (SES), please use the following resources:

OPM Guide to Senior Executive Service Qualifications
www.opm.gov/ses/references/GuidetoSESQuals_2010.pdf

SES Frequently Asked Questions
www.opm.gov/ses/about_ses/faqs.asp

The Plum Book
www.govinfo.gov/collection/plum-book?path=/GPO/United%20States%20Government%20Policy%20and%20Supporting%20Positions%20%2528Plum%20Book%2529

The Fact Book
www.opm.gov/feddata/factbook/index.asp

The Presidential Transition Guide
www.chcoc.gov/Transmittals/TransmittalDetails.aspx?TransmittalID=1300

SES Career Path
www.usajobs.gov

- SES Federal Resume Template (with instructions)
- Accomplishments Worksheet
- Blank SES Federal Resume Template
- Five-Page All-Inclusive Template
- Five-Page All-Inclusive Resume Sample 1: GS-15 to SES
- Five-Page All-Inclusive Resume Sample 2: Corporate to SES
- Sample SES Resume 3: Corporate to SES
- Sample SES Resume 4: GS-14 and Navy Reserve Officer to SES
- Five-Page All-Inclusive Resume with integrated TQs
- Five-Page All-Inclusive Resume without TQs
- Cover Letter/Letter of Interest Sample
- Blank Cover Letter/Letter of Interest Template (with instructions)
- Blank Cover Letter/Letter of Interest Template
- Technical Qualifications: GS-15 to SES (with CCAR highlighted)
- Technical Qualifications: GS-15 to SES (with CCAR highlighted)
- Technical Qualifications: Corporate to SES
- Sample ECQs: GS-15 to SES (with annotations)
- Sample ECQs: GS-15 to SES
- Sample ECQs: U.S. Military to SES
- Sample ECQs: Corporate to SES
- ECQ Builders
- Blank ECQ Brainstorming worksheet
- Blank ECQ and TQ Outline worksheets
- ECQ Best Practices Guide

Thanks for your services. I was one of four personnel invited to interview for the SES position you helped get my ECQs in shape for. If all works out, I'll write a more thorough review and recommendation for you guys. —
M. T.

My writer assigned to me was a godsend. She took her time to find out more information about me and not just the documents I gave her. She was polite and most of all a total professional! 4/5 stars for now but if I get the job and pass all the wickets, CareerPro Global will get a 5/5 from me. — Dr. Michels

I submitted my application for my first SES position! You wouldn't believe how difficult it has been to get to this moment but I couldn't have done it without your help. Rest easy knowing that what you do is very valuable for the rank and file "wannabes" who want to move up in career status. While I'm always the one who tells others how to "package" themselves, I could/would have never guessed how to write the ECQs, MTQs, and DQs to promote myself. — Anna

I strongly endorse CareerPro's SES writing services. Bottom line: although not accepted for the first position I applied for with the ECQs and TQs CareerPro drafted, I was interviewed and accepted for the second position—and the ECQs and TQs sailed through OPM with no edits/questions at all (something the hiring director for my office said she had not seen in her 10 years there). I have now started my new position. While I consider myself a reasonably good writer, the ECQs and TQs I produced were simply not good enough. I was not fully comfortable with hiring a writing service like CareerPro, but after some reflection, I decided that it was worth the investment.

My writer worked with me intensively over the next three weeks, asking detailed questions and kicking several drafts back and forth with me to make sure he captured my career in a way that ensured all of the "bases" that both the hiring office and OPM wanted to see were covered. — Mike Condray

My writer did an outstanding job providing the feedback I needed in order to ultimately write good draft ECQs. He demonstrated the utmost of professionalism, tact, and knowledge. I am grateful that I had him helping me. — V. M.

CareerPro was wonderful to work with. They worked with me to elicit the aspects of my experience that would shine on the ECQs. This was not a cookie-cutter process, but very personalized to my experience and expertise. And it resulted in a positive outcome—I was appointed to the SES! — S. Arnold

I think the hardest thing for most people to do is market themselves. At least I know it is for me. This process allowed me to feed him raw data about me and then he was able to turn it into a product I could never have done on my own. I thought everything was explained well upfront. My obligations, your obligations, timelines, etc. Very efficient process. — A. Fountain

I was so amazed and blessed to have the team that I had to assist me with this resume process. My writer was truly amazing and professional. I felt like I was in great hands and that I had an encourager and good friend that was walking me through every step of the process. This could not have been more perfect for me and it was worth every penny! Thank you for being the best!! — J. Grounds

careerproplus.com – seswriters.com
militaryresumewriters.com
1-800-471-9201

After serving more than 60,000 clients over the past three decades, we can assist you with:
Resume Development for:

- Private Sector to Federal
- Federal to Federal
- Federal to Private Sector
- Military to Federal
- Military to Private Sector
- Private Sector to Private Sector

SES Application Coaching & Development: Resume, ECQs, and TQs

Interview Preparation

Expert Training, Consulting, and Coaching:

- Onsite USAJOBS resume workshops (or webinars)
- Tailored presentations, workshops, webinars, etc., to meet agency needs
- Online ECQ Writing Courses (seswriters.com)
- SES Application and ECQ Editing/Coaching
- Award Justifications
- Writing Effective CCAR Accomplishments and Narratives

Notes

Notes

Notes

Notes

Notes

Notes

Notes

Notes